THE AU[THOR]

Jackie Hewitt-Main was a happy child ... until she went to school. Always full of bright ideas and keen to learn about the world, she couldn't understand why she had so much difficulty learning to read and write.

At forty she was diagnosed with severe dyslexia. This was both a revelation and a turning point. With appropriate support, she went on to study for a degree in special educational needs, followed by her PGCE teaching qualification.

After periods of research in prisons and working with at risk youngsters, Jackie introduced her own unique approach to teaching and mentoring prisoners with learning difficulties.

The huge success of Jackie's project is the subject of this book, told through the astonishing and often heartrending stories of some of the prisoners themselves, their progress in learning and the lasting impact it had on their lives.

Mainspring Publishing

Visit www.mainspring.com to see our books and resources and to find out more about the 'Dyslexia Behind Bars' project which is the subject of this book. You will also be able to find news of our continuing story as we roll out this programme across prisons and other places of learning in the UK and abroad.

The Cascade Foundation

Visit www.thecascadefoundation.org to learn about the The Cascade Foundation, the charity that promotes and supports Jackie Hewitt-Main's unique approach to teaching and mentoring prisoners with dyslexia and other learning difficulties, ex-offenders and their families, and dyslexic adults and children in schools, colleges and other settings.

TRANSFORMING PRISONERS' LIVES

Helping Dyslexic and other Prisoners to Make a New Start

TOLD THROUGH THE PRISONERS' OWN STORIES

JACKIE HEWITT-MAIN
with Jacquie Buttriss

Published by
Mainspring Publishing

First published 2013 by Mainspring Publishing
40 Kents Hill Road, Benfleet, Essex, SS7 5PL

ISBN 978-0-9572901-1-2

Printed and bound by ICG, 93 Hangleton Road, Hove,
East Sussex, BN3 7GH

This book is dedicated to:

- the 3,000 prisoners, learners and NEETs I interviewed, who told me what challenged them and gave me the inspiration to move forward,

- Sue Blackburn for changing my life,

- Dr Liam Chapman for giving me back my life,

- my mother and sister for the years they played with me,

- Jacquie Buttriss for understanding and,

- most importantly, my boys for being my Musketeers.

All the events in this book actually happened, and are described by the author, Jackie Hewitt-Main as they appeared to her at the time. They are her own impressions and, as such, present her personal perspective of some of the situations that occurred in the prison.

CONTENTS

The names of all the prisoners, ex-offenders, many officers and some of the places featured in this book have been changed to protect their identities, but the author and publisher hold evidence that each was a bona fide participant in this project.

PROLOGUE

'Will you listen to that!' a prison officer stopped me on the induction wing.

'It sounds like he's kicking off.' I said.

'Yes, he's smashing his cell up all right. Not a good start to his life inside.'

'Who's in there?'

'Can't remember his name. He's new. The poor beggar seemed all right when he arrived. I put him in there and shut the door only a few minutes ago. Now listen to him!' He paused and tilted his head to one side, puzzled. 'I've seen it with new inmates before. What makes a man turn like that, do you think?'

I'd only been in the prison a short while, but to me the cause seemed obvious.

'Did you give him any paperwork to look at?'

'Yes,' nodded the officer. 'I gave him a letter when we were walking down to the cell.'

'Do you know if he can read?'

'How do you mean?'

'Well, do you know if he has any problems with reading?'

'No?' he said, as if it were a question.

'Well, that could have been an important letter from his solicitor, about his case maybe. Or it could have been bad news from his family, or even a "Dear John" letter. Sitting in a cell, alone, with a letter in his hand, addressed to him, that he can't read ... Just think how that would make him feel. How would you feel if it was you holding that letter and you couldn't read?'

'I never thought of that.'

CHAPTER 1

FRED

Late for my first day at the prison, I was shaking with anxiety by the time I found a parking space and confused by the signs on the lamp-posts. Normally I would be able to look at them quietly and work them out, but now I was in a panic and they crowded in on me like a taunting mob.

I turned off the engine and shut my eyes: 'Please God, help me to do things right and keep me safe.' As I opened them again, a small white feather wafted in through the open window, circled round my shoulder and landed in my lap. Astonished at first, I smiled and relaxed a little. It seemed like a good omen.

As I rushed round to the front entrance, a tall white van turned into the yard, its two tiny windows high on the side, like lopsided eyes, winking in the sunlight. It pulled into a caged security area at one end of the building, where the steel mesh gates clanged shut behind. I wondered how many men were in the van, and what they felt when they heard that sound. A shiver ran down my spine.

I spoke into the box on the wall. 'Hello. I'm Jackie Hewitt-Main.'

After a pause, the doors slid open and I walked into the dark reception area, surrounded by high banks of steel lockers and handleless doors. Faint echoes of shouts and clanking metal resounded from somewhere far beyond.

I quaked at the harsh scrutiny of the two officers behind the toughened glass. I could hardly believe I had chosen to do this. 'Please God, keep me safe,' I repeated silently.

'Passport and driving licence,' barked the female officer.

As she took them off to be copied and checked, I convinced myself there would be some mistake and they would find out I was a train robber or a serial killer. But after a long wait, she gave me the all clear.

'Put all your things in a locker, your phone, your keys, everything, then post the locker key in there.' She pointed at a slot in the counter. 'And I'll look after it.'

Could I trust her? I had no option. 'What about my folder?' I asked. 'I need to take that in with me.'

She looked down at a ledger. 'Well you can't I'm afraid. There's nothing here about you taking in a folder. You'll have to ask permission next time.'

'Several steel doors and gates later, I was in a small room with another woman officer. She handed me some paper.

'What's this?' I said, dreading her answer.

'You have to fill in this form.'

The old anxiety welled up inside me. As a dyslexic, this was my worst nightmare, having to fill in a form on the spot, with no preparation.

'But I need help,' I reluctantly admitted to this stranger. I never used to tell people, but now I was getting braver. 'I'm dyslexic. Can I take it home and fill it in tonight?'

'No, you have to do it now or you can't do your induction.'

Flustered and frustrated, I tried to make the print stand still so that I could read it and after a few minutes, I began to decipher the instructions. My reading had improved a lot since I'd had help to do my degree and my teaching qualification, but I couldn't take it all in without going through it a few times I made a start, writing my name and address in the first boxes, hoping I could get the spelling right under pressure.

'Here,' she said with a loud sigh as she snatched the form from me. 'If it's that difficult, you can tell me what to put and I'll write it.'

Next I was introduced to the Head of Learning and Skills.

'You'll be having your induction later, but first the Deputy Governor has asked to see you. Goodness knows why. She doesn't usually bother with us.'

She walked me across the barren yard towards the Victorian management block, with its sombre, brick-built facade. I felt a deep sense of dread as my companion unlocked the outer door and we made our way down a dark, musty corridor. We came to another door with a posh copper name-plate, knocked and went in. This was a frightening moment for me. Would this very important person understand my work? Would she even be interested? And if

13

she was, would she be willing to give me the freedom I needed to work the way I do?

The woman behind the desk was on the phone and pointed at two chairs facing her, so we sat down. As we waited for her to finish the call, I couldn't help but notice her long lacquered nails, her thick blond hair and the fluffy, pink pen on her desk, giving a very different impression from what I had expected.

As she put down the receiver, she made her first eye-contact with me and smiled.

'Hello Jackie,' she said. 'I've been looking forward to meeting you. I've heard so much about you.'

The Head of Learning and Skills shifted in her chair, but I took no notice. I was so pleased that the Deputy Governor, who was the king pin of the prison, managing all its day to day functions and responsible for everything that happened, was interested in my project, which must have seemed like a big risk to her.

'Thank you for allowing me to come and start my project here.'

'Don't thank me.' She swept back a stray blond wisp with her hand. I should be the one thanking you for bringing your project to us and letting us benefit from your work. Anyway, let me tell you a bit about me and then you'll realise why I'm so pleased you are joining us,' she continued. 'Before I came into the prison service, I had my own PR business, and I started out by studying education, so I am really excited about your work.'

Wow, I thought. What a relief to know she's on my side. But of course, it's still her prison, so I'll have to watch my step.

Finally, I was in a small classroom with two young prison officers. It was induction day for us all. The officer leading this session wrote a long list of rules up on the whiteboard. But his handwriting was terrible and it looked like there were spelling mistakes too, so I couldn't read any of it. I panicked.

'Could you please read the rules out for us?' I asked. The other two looked relieved.

Some of the rules seemed sensible enough, but every one had to be strictly obeyed. I was petrified that I might accidentally touch one of the prisoners while working with them, which would expel me forever. I wouldn't mind being expelled, but I so much wanted to help these men that I knew I had to be very careful.

'Here are your keys,' said the officer. 'You must make doubly sure that you lock and check every door or gate you go through.' He paused. 'We don't want you aiding and abetting an escape.' He smiled, but it was no laughing matter to me. I'd always been clumsy with locks, like the time I broke our front door key in the lock when I was a child and my mother had been so cross with me. I'd never forgotten that. Now I dreaded repeating that crime inside the prison.

'And you must make sure that no prisoner can ever see your key,' he said, showing us how to attach the key to a long chain on the leather belt that we had to wear at all times. 'So you have to put it away in this purse.' He slipped a latched leather pocket onto the belt and tucked the key inside it, with its chain dangling. 'If any prisoner catches sight of your key, he can memorise it and draw it for a visitor to have it copied for him. They might be a bunch of losers, but they're crafty gits, this lot. You'd be surprised how devious they can be,' he smirked. 'But not clever enough to fool us.'

I think my mouth dropped open and he probably thought I was impressed, but I was wondering how he got away with being so arrogant, and so demeaning.

Putting on the leather belt and chain, I was surprised by its weight, how clumsy it felt, and the sound of the chain clanking as I moved around. Would I ever get used to it?

"Right, it's time for our quick tour. I'll take you round all the wings of the prison, but don't worry. The men are all locked up while we do our tour. It should only take twenty minutes, but if you have any questions, do ask as we go round.'

He obviously hadn't bargained for me – chatty Jackie. I asked loads of questions and kept talking all the time, so they got quite fed up with me. But this was my chance to learn about everything, so every time our guy stopped and introduced us to officers, I would shake their hands and tell them why I was there. I told them about my project, asked them what their jobs were like and did they know anything about dyslexia ... so our tour took an hour and a half.

I spent the rest of that day and the next looking around, observing in different parts of the prison and talking to officers and inmates, to see how everything worked and get my bearings. I was appalled at some of the things I learned and what seemed like failures in the system, but all the more determined to make improvements happen as quickly as I could.

As I entered the prison's computer unit to see what they did, I found a group of men with a female teacher. She was the one who had been so negative towards me when I first introduced myself to the education team earlier that second day. The one who had turned away when I went to shake her hand. When I entered the computer room that afternoon, she looked at me with distaste.

I walked over in my usual cheery way. 'Hello. I'm Jackie,' I began with a smile. 'I hope you don't mind if I just sit in on a bit of your lesson as I was asked to have a look round before I start my project.'

'If you must,' she shrugged. 'But you might as well know that I'm pissed off,' she paused, then launched into a tirade. 'Why the bloody hell are you coming in here to help these men for nothing and you've bloody well got funding for it? I've got a dyslexic son and I've paid my taxes, but his school won't help him at all.'

'Well, I'm sorry you feel that way,' I said. 'Maybe we could have a chat about that sometime. I have a dyslexic son too, and a brain-damaged son, but I was the only one who helped them, so I understand how you feel.'

'We were all doing fine.' She continued. 'Then they told us you were coming. I'm sorry to be so negative, but we've had do-gooders like you before, swanning in, interfering with everything and then going away again, when they've had enough. Then we're left to pick up the pieces.'

'Well, I intend to be here a long time,' I said. 'And I want to work with you, not against you. I'm not here to interfere. My project is about helping everyone, including the staff, to do our best for these prisoners.'

'Huh,' she sneered and turned towards the dozen or so men who sat waiting at their computers, all of whom had heard the conversation and gave me sympathetic smiles or winks as I walked round. They were all different ages and most of them looked rough with their earrings, stubble and tattoos, but I didn't let that worry me just then.

The teacher explained quickly how to change the fonts and sizes on the word-processor toolbar. 'Now I'd like you to change this text to a courier font and size 16,' she told them.

Whilst most got on with it, I noticed that the oldest man in the room was staring at his computer screen, his hands making fists and his face reddening with anger, a muscle throbbing at the corner of his jaw. I went over to him.

'Have you done much work with the computer?' I asked him.

'No. I ain't never used one before,' he said in a gravelly cockney accent. 'I wanted to learn, but she's going too bloody fast for me. I've forgotten what she said and I don't know how to do this.'

I could sense his frustration, just like I had often felt in the past. Now he was holding one fist up, like a boxer, ready to do some damage. I had to act fast.

'Hold on a minute. Just wait while I see if we can sit in the glass room next door and have a chat about this. Would that be OK with you?'

He nodded.

Like most rooms used for teaching in prison, the classrooms and group rooms were glass-sided so that officers could stand nearby and keep watch, ready for action if one of the prisoners kicked off. They always seemed to expect any class would end in a riot.

'Who is that older man?' I asked the tutor, pointing him out to her.

'Oh, that's Fred,' she sneered. 'I don't know why he joined this class. He'll never learn anything.'

'I think he's getting a bit fed up with himself. Is it all right with you if we sit in the glass room next door and have a chat to calm him down?'

'If you want,' she shrugged. 'He'll be no loss to the class. We'll get on quicker without him.'

I beckoned Fred to follow me through the open doorway.

He sat down with a sullen scowl. I chose the chair facing him.

'I'm Jackie,' I began. 'When I left school I could hardly read or write.' As I spoke, I was watching him closely, especially his body language and what was behind his eyes. There was a tiny spark there when I started to tell him my story.

'I was always a failure at school,' I continued. 'I got bullied a lot. They'd say "are you thick or something" and call me stupid. I used to self-harm when I was in the classroom, under the desk so no-one could see me. I felt I was no use to anybody. I even tried to commit suicide.'

I paused to let my words sink in, as I suspected that he might be dyslexic too and would need time to process what I said. His shoulders dropped, his whole body began to relax gradually as the tension fell away and I could see from his expression that he was interested. Something I said had obviously engaged him.

'I was finally diagnosed in my forties as severely dyslexic,' I continued, and waited again.

He opened his mouth as if he was about to say something, but first he studied my face as if he wasn't sure whether he dared. Then, suddenly he blurted it out.

'I ain't never been able to read or write either. I'm 67 and I don't even know my ABC. I ain't never told anybody before, not even my wife. She thinks I just don't like reading. And she fills in any forms we get. But she's always getting on at me to write her a letter – every visiting time she asks me. "Just one letter, Fred." But I can't tell her.' A tear came to his eye as he said it – this big, tough man, a lifelong criminal. I felt a bit emotional myself. Then he brightened slightly. 'But I ain't never met anybody like you, that's told me they had the same problems as me.'

'Well, I have, and I know exactly how you feel. I know how awful it is. I went through it all, just like you. Did you get bullied at school like I was, for not being able to read and write?'

'I bloody well did,' he nodded, and launched into his own experiences, as if finally released after all those years of secret suffering. 'The teachers called me a dunce and put me at the back of the class so I wouldn't stop the others learning. I always used to go to school – never missed one day. I even got a certificate for it once. They made me milk monitor, it was the only thing I was good at, but I never passed any tests and I left school at fifteen, without any qualifications. The teachers at my school were useless. They thought I didn't have no brain, because I couldn't learn. Now I know I'm just dopey.'

'The first thing is that you definitely do have a brain and you're not dopey at all. It's just that the way you were taught at school wasn't the right learning style for you,'

He was more alert now. 'What's a learning style?'

'Well, when you learn how to do something, do you learn best by listening to the instructions, by reading what to do, or by trying it out with your hands?'

'With my hands, definitely,' he said, with a quizzical look.

'So that means your best learning style is practical. Do you like making things? Or doing physical activities like sports?'

'Yeah. I used to be a champion boxer when I was a lad. I worked hard at that, trained every day. I won the Festival of Britain title when I was twelve.'

'Wow! That sounds amazing. It just shows what a great practical learner you are.'

'Yeah,' he smiled. 'I suppose it does. I never thought of that.'

'And when you were at school, teachers used to think that intelligence was just about reading, writing, maths and being good at tests,' I said. 'My teachers were the same. Now we know there is something called multiple intelligences. I wish I'd known about that when I was young, but a few years ago I went to America to meet the professor who discovered multi-intelligences. He told me all about it.'

'What d'you mean? I always thought I didn't have no intelligence.' He looked confused. 'Intelligence is using your brain, ain't it?'

'Yes, but there are different ways the brain can work. And there are all different ways people can be intelligent, not just with reading or maths. For example, you can have interpersonal intelligence. That would be when someone is good at getting on with other people and understanding some of the things about how people are with each other.'

'So I could have found all this out when I was younger?'

'Maybe a little younger, but people haven't known about it for very long.'

'If I'd known I wasn't dopey, I wouldn't have got into so much trouble.'

'What brought you into prison in the first place?'

'Well, when I left school, I worked on the markets, down the East End, and carried on with my boxing. I got to know all the gangs – a lot of them came to our club. Like Ronnie and Reggie Kray. They were older than me, but they often came in and we got friendly. They were ruthless in crime, but good fun when they came to the club. I tried not to get too involved with them outside. Then I got my call-up papers. Well, I didn't want to go in the army, so I ran away to Scotland and worked on different building sites up there, so the Bill couldn't find me. Then my Dad asked me to come back and help him run his snooker hall. There were a lot of duckers and divers in there. He got beaten up a few times, so I thought I'd better go back and help him. That was the worst mistake I made. I got in with the gangs again and got done for doing an armed robbery. It was a bullion robbery, so I got twenty-two years for that one. Then I got done again soon after, and that was another twenty years.'

'So what are you in for now?'

'Drugs. They said I was a drugs baron. But all I did was to pay for their premises, to grow the plants and all that. And I just did a bit of other stuff on the side. I got seventeen years this time, so I'll probably go out in my box.'

'I hope not.'

I looked at my watch and realised the time was going and Fred would soon have to return to his cell. 'I'm going to do some learning workshops where I can teach some of the men about learning styles and multiple intelligences. Would you like to come do you think?'

The shutters came down again in his eyes and he dropped his head down.

I knew the signs. 'Or maybe you wouldn't want to be learning in a classroom? I used to be frightened of classrooms ...'

He lifted his head. 'Yeah, that's me too,' he smiled ruefully. 'Classrooms give me the heebie-jeebies.'

'OK. Well how about we have a one-to-one session, just you and me? I'll be in again tomorrow morning. I'll find somewhere we can go. What shall we start with?'

'Maybe the ABC, but I ain't learnt it in 67 years,' he said, in an Eeyore voice, 'so I ain't got a lot of hope.'

'But you've never done it my way!'

'Ok,' he grinned. 'I'll give it a go.'

On my way back to the education office, I was walking down a corridor when I heard a shrill alarm go off and the steel doors each end of the corridor closed. I didn't know what to do. I was stuck there and there were no other doors out of the corridor, so I just had to wait till the panic was over. I hoped it wasn't a fire.

Eventually, I began to hear distant noises round about, but still the doors were closed. I called out, but nobody heard me. So I tried it louder. Still nothing. I shouted and shouted, getting myself in a state. It had been more than an hour now. Suddenly, there was a swish, the doors slid open again and an officer walked through.

'Sorry,' he said. 'When they opened the doors again they somehow missed out this section. It wasn't till a cleaner heard you shouting that we realised.'

The next morning, a Friday, I came in early with some alphabet sheets that the security officers allowed me to bring in. I went to the deputy governor and asked her if I could work with Fred in a small room and explained why – his fear of classrooms.

She thought about it for a moment. 'What are you going to do with him?'

'I'm just going to start him off on learning his alphabet.'

She looked dubious. 'Mmm. Well, I could ask the senior officer on that wing to let you use the library,' she said. 'There should be a table and some chairs in there. Would that do?'

'Yes thanks. That will be fine.'

'You've got your whistle to blow if anything goes wrong?'

I checked that it was on my belt chain, along with my prison keys. 'Yes, but I don't think I'll need it.'

'Don't raise your hopes,' she added as I got up to leave. 'He's an old dog ...'

'But I'm going to teach him a new way of learning.'

'We'll see,' she shrugged.

As I walked off to Fred's wing, I stewed over this scepticism I kept meeting from everybody. I hadn't been there long, only a few days, so they didn't know what I could do yet. But I would show them. I'd make them all see – these men who couldn't read were not stupid. They were just dyslexic. They could be very bright and full of ideas, like I had always been, but our brains are wired differently from most people's.

I put my key in the lock to E wing, turned it carefully and breathed a sigh of relief as the door clanged open, then I quickly turned to push it closed and pushed it two or three more times to check that it was locked. I went through the security space and unlocked the door to the common area at the bottom of the wing.

The first thing that hit me was the stench – the heavy odour of a hundred men's dirty laundry – their unwashed pants, socks, everything, all being piled up on a sheet at the bottom of the open staircase that went through the middle of the building. I gagged at the foul smell and swallowed like mad to prevent the nausea taking me over.

The next thing that struck me was the echoing clamour of prisoners coming out of their cells, shouting to one another, jeering, throwing toilet rolls over the railings around each landing so they unravelled down to the ground floor. And the clinking of keys in locks, the jangling of chains on officers' belts and the clanking of metal doors

It was only then that I noticed the greyness of the walls and the contrast of the bright blue banisters and railings. This was the old Victorian wing of the prison and no amount of paint could have altered its austerity.

Fred had told some of his mates about me and that I was going to help him. Now a few of them called out to me.

'Hello Miss, have you come to help old Freddie?'
'Can you help me too?'

'What about me?'

At this rate, I'd soon be teaching the whole prison! But, not yet. My first job was to speak to the prisoners and listen to their stories. That was what the first part of the funding was for, interviewing them, assessing any that might need learning support and setting up some mentoring for them. I'd only agreed to come and work with Fred because he seemed so convinced he couldn't learn, and I knew I could help him.

I went over to the nearest officer. 'Can you tell me where the library is? I'm going to work in there with one of your prisoners this morning.'

'Yes, we were told you would be coming. I'll take you there,' he said.

'Which prisoner is it?' he asked when we got to the library.

'Fred. I'm afraid I don't know his last name.'

'There's only one Fred on this wing. Everyone knows Freddie. He was friends with the Kray brothers, you know.' He unlocked the door.

'Really?' Of course, I did know, but I thought I'd better not let on.

'Yes, he knew all the old East End gangs when he was a lad. Got in with all the wrong sorts did our Freddie. You want to watch him - he's on a very long sentence. I'll go and get him for you and then I'll sit outside the open door, just in case you have any trouble with him.'

'Hi Fred. How are you today?'
'OK. What are we doing in here?'

'It was the only room they could find me that wasn't a classroom.'

He grinned.

'Let's sit down first,' I said. 'I've brought some things in for you.' I showed him the alphabet sheets. 'This one is the alphabet in capital letters, and this is one with pictures, so you can see what words start with those sounds. Then I've also got some sheets for you to practise the shapes of the letters.'

He looked at them all with me as I read them out to him, but he was glazing over already.

'OK,' I said. 'Let's leave those there for a minute. It's your turn to do some work.'

I got him to stand up next to me. 'Let's start with the letter F, because that's the beginning of your name.'

'I can write that one,' he said.

'But can you write it in the air?' I showed him how.

'I dunno, I never tried.'

'Well let's do it, and say F as you're doing it. Now can you trace it with your finger on your other hand. Do it again and say F. That's great. Now let's try it with the letter A.'

We went on doing this through the beginning letters of the alphabet, till we got to F again. 'How does that feel?'

'Funny,' he made a face, but he had a spark in his eyes. 'But what's it for?'

'Well, when we were at school, the teachers just taught us to write the letters with pencils on paper, didn't they?'

'Yeah.'

'But you really need to use some of your other senses if you're going to properly learn a letter or a word. So making the shape of a letter physically, seeing it and saying the letter at the same time, helps your hand, your eyes, your mouth, your ears and your brain to work together to recognise the shape of it. Later you can try having the picture of something in your mind that starts with that letter, so that you know what sound it makes, and we'll also try some other things.'

'I like doing it this way,' he said. 'I think I could learn it a bit better now.'

'Great.' We spent the rest of that session doing practical activities to learn the letters. Then I gave him the alphabet sheets to take back to his cell.

'I'm afraid I won't be in again till next Wednesday,' I said. 'And we'll have another session then.'

'OK. But, what am I supposed to do with these?'

'You don't have to do any writing or anything, unless you want to. There are plenty of other ways of learning.'

'What, in my cell?'

'Yes, you could do some more of what we were doing this morning. That will help you get used to the letters. And let's think what else you could do.' I paused. 'What have you got in your cell? You could use the things around you. Do you have a tube of toothpaste?'

'Yeah.' He looked puzzled.

'Well, you could try squeezing it out to draw the letters in your basin. And you could draw the letters in the air with your toothbrush, or you could wet your fingers and draw them on the floor. Every time you do a letter, say it as well. You could try making the shapes of letters with other things too. Like pens or torn up bits of paper, or anything else you've got. Look at the pictures that go with the letters too. And if you've got a mirror, you could breathe on it, then make the shape of a letter on that.'

'You're a rum 'un. I ain't never learnt nothing like this before.'

'But when you were boxing, didn't you learn by acting it out?'

'Yeah, I suppose so.'

'So that's what you're going to do to learn your alphabet. Do it slowly at first. Just concentrate on one letter the first day.'

'OK. I'll give it a try, but don't hold out too much hope. I'm just a dopey old dog, so I'm not good at learning.'

The following Wednesday, I turned up at the prison and found everyone waiting for me. The security officer in reception smiled as she handed me a note that read 'Freddie wants to see you. Can you please go to see him straight away.' As I folded it up again and put it in my pocket I asked the officer 'Do you know what this is about?'

'Yes,' she said. 'Everybody's talking about it. Go and see for yourself.' I was intrigued, not least by the change in this woman's attitude towards me.

The Deputy Governor was there when I walked across the yard. 'Fred's been waiting for you since Monday,' she said with a smile.

The Governor popped out too when he saw me. 'It's all round the prison,' he said. 'Fred Suggs wants to see you.'

I was astonished. What could this be about?'

When I went into the wing, everyone seemed to know. 'Fred's already asked me three times this morning what time you would come,' said the officer I'd spoken to the last time.

'Freddie's told me about you,' said one of the inmates. 'Can I have a lesson too?'

'Can you teach me to write?' asked another.

I couldn't believe the change in attitude from the staff and it was great to see the prisoners wanting to learn. Hopefully I'd soon be able to help a lot of them.

Then I spotted Fred himself. He walked towards me with the widest grin I could imagine. 'I've done it!' He said.

'Great,' I said, thinking he could perhaps do the first three or four letters.

We went up to the library. He was walking like an excited child – keen to show me what he'd learnt.

'I know my alphabet, the whole alphabet. It only took me two days,' he said, his face shining with pride. 'I did the things you showed me. I did them every minute I could. I ran out of toothpaste, but I still carried on writing the letters with my fingers everywhere, and my toothbrush, like you said. It never made no sense to me before, but now I get it. I really get it. I couldn't wait for you to come so I could show you! I've waited 67 years for this.'

He stood up and recited his whole alphabet in the right order, making the shapes on the table as he said the letters. Then at the end he stood back. 'What do you think of that?'

'Fantastic. Amazing!' I was genuinely astonished at how well he'd done. 'I think you've done brilliantly.'

'You didn't expect that, did you?'

'Well, not all of it and not so quickly, but I'm so happy that you've done it.'

'Look,' he handed me the alphabet handwriting practice sheets. 'I've done all those too. Every time I did what you told me and said the letters when I wrote them. Now I can do it.'

'This is really great, Fred. I'm so proud of you.' I could have hugged him, but I knew that was forbidden.

'I couldn't wait till you came, so I told my mates I couldn't read and I'd done all this. I've never told anybody before, but they were glad for me. Even some of the officers were pleased when I told them.'

'I'm not surprised.'

'You're a saint,' he said. 'I know it's not allowed, but if it was I would give you a kiss. I can't wait now to learn some more, so that I can write a letter to my wife.'

'Well, let's get on with it then!

Two weeks later, Freddie did just that, and he told me about it the following Wednesday.

'It was just a short letter,' he said. 'Just three or four lines, and I had to keep starting again whenever I made a mistake. But it was the first letter I've ever written in my life.' He puffed out his chest with pride and I felt almost as excited as he did.

'That's brilliant, I said. 'Was she surprised? Do you know how she felt about it?'

'Yes. I rang her the next day and she burst into tears, crying on the phone. *"All these years we've been married, Fred,"* she said. *"And this is your first ever letter to me. I'm so happy, I can't stop crying."* That made me feel good.'

'You've worked so hard at this, Fred. It's a great achievement.'

31

'And I couldn't have done it without you. Like I said, you've done miracles with me. I'm like a different man. I never thought this would happen to me, and now I know I'm not dopey after all.'

CHAPTER 2

ROCKY

Newly arrived prisoners often stay on the induction wing for two or three nights so they can be settled in and be briefed about the prison rules. An officer will give them a form to fill in to find out what work or education they've done in the past and what they want to do while they're inside. Far from putting new prisoners at their ease, many of them can't read the form, let alone fill it in.

When I arrived at the induction wing to start interviewing prisoners, I was met with the same sort of negative attitude that the IT teacher showed me when I walked into her computer room. At least nobody in the induction wing was quite so rude, but I could feel their resentment like a vice around the whole wing. Nobody wanted me to see new prisoners, let alone speak to them. It was excuse after excuse, so I changed tack.

.   'Do you have any trusty prisoners who can talk with the new entrants?' I asked an officer.

'What about?'

'Well, to be a friendly face and answer any of their questions,' I replied. 'Like whether they would like any help with filling in their form, or with any reading or writing any letters, and the prison rules.'

'No. We've never been asked to do that. I'm not sure it would be allowed anyway.'

33

I paused to think about this. It was certainly an idea I could mention to the prison management. Meanwhile, I was a bit concerned for any of the new inmates who might have learning difficulties of any kind. So I asked a female officer on the desk to refer any dyslexic prisoners to me so that I could come and help them.

'Oh, dyslexia – that's for schools isn't it? You won't find any of them here,' she said with a sneer. 'We don't have much dyslexia in this prison.'

'You do have some. I'm already working with one dyslexic man, and I am finding several more as I interview them.'

'Well, they must be an exceptions.'

'How do you find out if new prisoners have any reading or writing problems?' I asked. I don't know what I expected her answer to be, or even if she would have an answer. But it came back quickly.

'This,' she said, holding up the induction form. 'They just have to tick this box.'

I looked at where she was pointing, and the small print question next to it, which was so complex that many dyslexic adults would have difficulty reading it. I opened my mouth to say so, then thought better of it. After all, it probably wasn't her who designed the form.

'And what if they do tick this box?' I asked. 'Or if they tell you they have problems?'

'Well, if they tell me, I tick the box for them.'

'And then what happens?'

'Nothing. It is just put in this box. That's all.'

I couldn't resist the obvious question. 'So, what's the point?'

'So that we know,' she shrugged.

'OK. So if you or other officers know someone has literacy problems, you don't do anything about it?'

'No. That's not what it's for. It's just so we know.'

'And what if the men don't realise themselves that they have a learning difficulty, or they daren't admit it?'

'Well, that's up to them, isn't it? I can't be a mind-reader!'

I went away from this conversation fuming, thinking of all the poor guys who had come in through those forbidding gates, into a place that had no care for their needs, nor anyone to help them. This was definitely something I had to follow through. So I went to see the Deputy Governor straight away. I knew she had a firm manner, but sensed her heart was definitely in her job and she cared about the prisoners.

'So what do we need to do about this?' she asked, after I'd explained the officer's words to her, without revealing the woman's name or gender. I had no wish to get anyone into trouble when I'd only just arrived. I needed to get people to respect and support me, or if not me, then at least to support what I was doing.

'Well, as you know, my role from the beginning of this project was to interview all the prisoners, including those in the induction wing, so I could use some of this time to assess any of those who I suspect might have learning difficulties and suss out their problems. I could then start working with them. At the same time I could act as a kind of mentor to them when they first arrive.'

'Mmm. That sounds quite a good idea.'

'I'd need time to gather some assessment materials and put together a simple dyslexia checklist that the officers could use themselves when I can't be there. Would that be allowed?'

'Yes, as long as it's not a lot of extra work for them to do.'

'I'll make it as simple as I can.'

'OK. How much time do you need to get it in place?'

'Just a couple of days to do the checklist,' I said.

'Great.'

'I could do a briefing session for them as well if you like, about how to recognise hidden learning difficulties like dyslexia, how it affects people, how to help them cope with it better and the best ways to cater for their needs. Some of the officers themselves are probably dyslexic too.'

'Yes, I think that could be very useful.'

If you'll allow me to, I could do a briefing sometime later this month, once I've prepared it. We'd need a room to do it in and a time when as many of them as possible could be free.'

'Leave it with me. I'll sort all that out. I can get cover for some of the staff as long as it's not for too long.'

'OK. I'll do the checklist first and try it out with some of the prisoners when I interview them, to make sure it works.'

'Is everything else going all right so far?'

'Well, there is one other thing. Some of the officers in the induction wing seem reluctant to let me anywhere near the new inmates, but that's where I think I can be most use, to help them understand what they need while they're in prison and to make sure we put on the right provision for them.'

'Don't worry. You go off to do some interviews in one of the other wings this morning and I'll speak to the induction staff. Then you can go back on the induction wing and get things going there as soon as you like after that. Come back next week and let me know how it's going.'

I went to E wing and spent the next hour with Fred. He was really getting the hang of things now, especially on the Lexion dyslexia software. Only a few days ago he was afraid of computers, and now he loved them.

'I like it when the computer reads out the words to me at the same time as it highlights them in colours on the screen. It makes it so much easier to learn to read them.' Fred was definitely on a roll.

My next call was the VP wing, where they kept the vulnerable prisoners who might be violent or psychotic, self-harmers or paedophiles. Some of them were on suicide watch, whilst others were badly bullied and in need of emotional support. The officers on this wing really earned their money, and many of them were the more caring types, thank goodness. I spotted a friendly face – one of the few who had smiled and welcomed me when I was first introduced to her on my induction tour. This was senior officer Miss Amey. I went over and asked her if there was any particular prisoner she would like me to interview first.

'Yes, there's one we need some help with – Rocky – he's twenty-two and a lifer, in for murder. He's a bit of an enigma. Maybe you can get through to him, get him to talk to you about his problems. We really want to support him, but he does all he can to make enemies of us all. He assaulted one of my colleagues a couple of days ago.'

'Why was that? There must have been a reason.'

'He said it was because the officer laughed at the way he spoke.'

'OK, I'll see what I can do. Is there somewhere quiet for us to sit and talk? It's much more difficult to chat properly in a glass room, with noisy music on the loudspeakers and people all around looking in. It makes it hard to concentrate without getting tense, even for people without problems.'

Miss Amey sent a couple of her staff to get Rocky out of his cell. 'I'll get them to bring him to the office for you,' she said. 'It will take them a while as his cell is on the second landing.'

She took me along to the office and showed me in. It was cluttered and rather cramped, filled with the stale smell of cigarettes, but I moved a couple of chairs so that they were facing each other and wedged the door open to air it until he arrived. Dawn found another two chairs for the officers who were guarding him to sit on.

'Perhaps I could have a chat with you myself sometime,' she said as we waited. 'I always had difficulties with reading and writing when I was at school. Do you think I could be dyslexic.'

'I'll bring an assessment to do with you tomorrow if you like. Will you be on duty then?'

'Yes, that would be good.' She seemed pleased. 'I wonder where they've got to with Rocky. The officers will have to stay with him, I'm afraid. He's very strong and, like most gangsters, he can be extremely violent.'

I felt a momentary shudder at the thought, then steeled myself. Miss Amey said he needed help, and that was what I was here for. We stepped out of the office to see if he was coming.

That was the moment my fears dropped away as a big, well-toned, hunk of a man walked towards me, flanked by two burly officers, with their hands on their belts, in case of trouble. I was transfixed. He looked terrific – all muscles and really cool. I could almost see through his shirt at the sculptured chest beneath, like the famous Italian statue. In that first glance I understood him, the way his mind worked, and the reasons why. Body building was always a sign.

'I don't expect he'll last more than ten minutes with you,' she whispered. 'I've never known him to co-operate with anyone longer than five. He has a very short fuse, so ten minutes max.'

I ushered him into the room and over to the chair facing mine. His two officers settled themselves, one in front of the door, behind Rocky, picking up a newspaper to read, and the other just outside. Nobody could have escaped if they tried. There just wasn't space.

It was daunting, with the officers there, but I tried to ignore them and hoped Rocky would forget about them too.

I always look at a man's eyes before I begin to talk – his were cloudy and sullen.

'I can see you're a body-builder,' I began, with genuine admiration. 'It looks as if you're really good at it.'

He gave a half-smile. 'Yes, I wish I could spend more time in the gym, but they don't let me, so I do a lot of exercises in my cell to keep fit.'

'I've never done any body-building,' I said. 'But when I was at school, I used to do the same as you in a way, choosing something I knew I was good at, something I could control, so as not to feel such a failure.'

He looked surprised.

'When I was in secondary school, and I still couldn't read or write properly,' I continued. 'I used to roll my skirts over to make them as short as possible, and dyed my hair blonder so that I could flirt with all the older boys. The boys in my class knew I was useless in lessons, but the older ones took me at face value, so I made sure I looked as cool as I could. I went without food a lot of the time as well. I needed something I could have control of and I could do that with my eating, so I got very thin. I thought the boys would like that.'

I paused and noticed his eyes had cleared, with a definite look of interest, so I carried on.

'I was so useless at everything at school, everything except talking. I could always talk and I had lots of ideas, but nobody wanted to listen to them if I couldn't write them down.'

The atmosphere was very calm now and Rocky's fidgeting had stopped. He just looked at me and seemed about to say something, but it didn't come out.

'So do you have a reason why you do your body-building?' I prompted him.

He opened his mouth and tried to shape a word, and again nothing happened. For several seconds, he struggled to speak. Then I realised – he must have a stutter or something. Sure enough, when the words eventually came they were very staccato, like a malfunctioning machine-gun. I felt so sorry for him but I made sure I didn't show it in my face, as I sat and waited patiently for him to say what he wanted. But after the first sentence or two, seeing that I wasn't going to rush him, he began to take his time more patiently, speaking slowly and a little more easily now.

'I c-c-can't read and write either,' he said. 'I was always b-bullied at school because I was such a f-f-f-failure at everything.'

'Just like me,' nodded Jackie. 'I dreaded going to school because of all the bullying and not being able to learn.'

Rocky's eyes were alight and he spoke much more calmly. 'I p-probably wouldn't have got into so much t-t-trouble if I'd been able to learn like the others, or if someone had helped me.'

'What kind of trouble did you get into?'

'I got in with some older b-boys in a gang, on the estate where I lived. They didn't c-c-care that I c-couldn't read or write. They p-p-probably didn't even know.'

'Was that when you were still at school?'

'Yes.'

'What kind of trouble were you in then?'

'Drugs mostly, at f-first. T-t-taking them, then d-dealing them as well.'

'So how did you get into prison?'

'Well, they were all d-dealers, and because of my size and the f-fact I was already doing the b-b-body-building, they made me their debt-c-collector.'

'What did that involve?'

'I had to go round to see all the p-p-people who hadn't p-paid what they owed and rough them up, threaten them, take their stuff, that sort of thing. Anything to f-frighten them into p-p-paying.'

'And what if they couldn't get the money?'

'That wasn't my p-problem. I just got some of the others to join me and f-frighten them some more.'

'How did you feel about that?'

'I didn't feel anything. I was stoned most of the t-time, and I was just doing my job.'

'So is that how you got caught?'

'Yes, I shot a man who owed us a lot of money and refused to p-p-pay up. I legged it, but the c-cops came after me. They knew where I lived, so somebody must have grassed.' He had become very calm, but now he tensed up, as if bitter about that.

'Do you still have trouble with reading and writing?' I asked, to change the subject. It worked and he relaxed again. He looked interested in the draft checklist I had in my hand, so I showed it to him.

'I c-can't read any of that,' he said, straining his whole face. 'Only *t-to* and *the*.'

'I think you are probably dyslexic, like me,' I said, gently. 'Our brains don't work the same way as most people's and that makes it difficult for us to learn to read and write. Sometimes we need to find different ways to learn. Would you like me to help you improve your reading?'

The officer in front of the door leant forward. 'No, you can't do that.'

'Oh,' I sighed. I was disappointed. 'Really?'

'Yes, Governor's rules.' Then he sat back and carried on reading his paper.

'Right, well I'll show you some things you can do to help you learn to read. Would that be OK?'

'Yes, please.'

42

'Lets start with your name,' I said. 'Rocky – can you read that?'

'Yes, as long as the writing isn't too swirly.'

'Can you write it?'

'Yes, but sometimes I get the letters the wrong way round.'

'OK, let's say it as we write it in the air: Rock-y.' I stood next to him and we both wrote Rocky in the air.

'That's great,' I said. 'You did it better than me.'

'I don't know why, b-but it seems easier that way.'

'What about your surname?' asked. 'What's that?'

'Mitchell.'

'OK. Let's try writing that in the air now.'

We started it together, but then Rocky stopped.

'I c-can't remember which letter comes next,' he said.

' Let's cut it into two chunks to make it easier to spell.' I wrote Mitchell on a piece of paper and tore it into two between the two syllables. 'Now, say the sounds as you make the shapes. Mit ... chell.' I showed him how by writing the two parts in the air myself, then got him to do it.

'That was much easier,' he smiled. 'I d-didn't get in a muddle that time.'

'You can do that with any letters and words you want to learn. You have to say them as you write them, in the air, on the floor, anywhere. Take one letter – let's start with a.' We both wrote 'a' in the air. 'Now can you think of a short word starting with a?'

'And,' he suggested, his whole demeanour so calm now and engaged in what we were doing. He really seemed to be taking it onboard.

'That has three letters,' I said. So we'll do one at a time. Let's try writing on our hands this time.'

'Now let's look at your surname again,' I said, as I wrote it in large letters well apart on a sheet of paper. 'Mitchell. Now can you see if there are any other words in there?' I tore the paper into strips, one with each letter on it and arranged them in the right order on the table nearby as we stood up to look at them. 'What about this?' I separated out the first three letters. 'This is the first part of your name. Can you say that for me?'

He looked at it, then looked at me anxiously.

'It's OK,' I said. 'Just have a go.'

He looked hard at it again. For a terrible moment I thought he was going to sweep the whole lot aside and get into a strop, but he lowered his shoulders and tried to say the word.

'Mit?'

'Yes, that's it. Mit. Can you add on the next two letters?' I moved the 'c' and' h' across to join the end of 'Mit'. 'You saw how those first three letters make the word *Mit*? Now, with these next two letters on the end, what does that make?'

He looked at the five letters intently and he tried to sound them out, in two parts. 'Mit-ch.' Then he tried joining them together into one sound. 'Mitch.'

'That's it!' Next I assembled the last three letters of his surname. 'What do these letters together say?'

Again, he took a good look first: 'ell,' he said.

Can you see anything else there in the order of the letters?' I asked, as I put them all together to make his surname as a whole.

44

He stood and looked along the letters once, and then again. He opened his mouth, but said nothing. I wasn't sure whether he just couldn't say it, or wasn't sure enough to give it a try. Perhaps he needed a prompt.

'What about if you take the last letter of Mitch and put it in front of the last part of your name,' I said, covering up the first five letters, then revealing the h. 'Try it and see what you get.'

He separated out the two parts himself and moved the 'h' across. At first he looked puzzled, but suddenly he got it: 'h-h-hell!' He didn't mind that he was stuttering now.

'That's it!'

At this point, the officer stood up. 'It's time now. You've had an hour and we have to take this man back to his cell.'

Had we really been there an hour? This was amazing. Rocky seemed as surprised as me that he had been able to talk and concentrate for so long.

'The time's gone by so quickly,' I said with a smile. 'I'm glad we were able to have a good chat.'

'Thank you,' he said as he turned to go. 'It's the first time that anybody has really understood me. I've never told anyone before.'

'I'll try and get permission to see you again soon,' I promised him as they took him away. I did try, but without any luck, and he was transferred to another prison two days later.

The next time I saw Miss Amey she came over to tell me he'd gone. 'I don't know what it is with you,' she said. 'But after you start talking with these men, they all become as calm and quiet as kittens.'

I asked everyone, but nobody knew which prison he'd gone to, so I couldn't even follow him up with a letter – just one of the many frustrating problems I encountered in those early days of learning to work the system.

Although most of the staff on the VP wing were now my fans, and also on E wing where I worked with Fred, many of the officers on the other wings, including the induction staff, were still quite negative, so I had to find ways to try and win them round. On the induction wing I would shortly be doing the briefing for them and hoped that would help. But it was a different story in some parts of the prison. However, my reputation for helping people with learning difficulties seemed to be spreading amongst the prisoners, so they at least were on my side.

One morning, I was sitting talking with a small group of inmates in the central area, near the stairs, so there were a lot of men around. We were trying to discuss ideas for making things more dyslexia-friendly in the prison, but there was so much noise and movement, not to mention the curious ear-wigging from passing inmates, that it was very distracting and we could hardly hear each other. This was always a problem, as the officers wanted to keep us in their sight, but it made my work much more difficult as it was almost impossible to concentrate.

We'd just got into the discussion, when a new officer came over and, not understanding what I was doing, tried to ingratiate himself to the prisoners by picking on me.

'Hello blondie, give us a cuddle.'

I cringed as he came right over to me and plonked himself down in my lap.

'Please get up,' I said. 'You're too heavy for me.'

'Yes, get off her. Jackie's helping us,' added one of the lads, bravely. He could have been put on a charge sheet for that.

The officer was on a roll and ignored our pleas. 'Let's have a butcher's then,' he sniggered as he deliberately looked down the front of my blouse. 'Hey lads. She's got a lovely pair of coconuts.'

I know I blushed with embarrassment and didn't dare look at any of the guys, but they were all incensed at this officer's appalling behaviour in front of them.

'Get off Jackie and leave her alone,' said one of them.

As this odious officer got up, he knocked my glasses down my nose and leered as he whispered in my ear: 'I'm going to touch your bum when you move.'

'No you're not,' I protested loudly, for everyone to hear. 'If you think you're ever going to touch me again, I'll make an official complaint.' I readjusted my glasses.

'Yes, you can't treat a teacher like that. We'll report you,' said another of the prisoners, and they all joined in with their protests, protecting me as best they could.

The officer suddenly realised he'd made a mistake in assuming the men would be on his side and would join the lewd banter – far from it, as other prisoners nearby joined the group in siding against him. Smelling the start of a good fight, several more inmates ran down the stairs towards us, just as all the surrounding officers rushed in, whistles blowing for reinforcements, as a potential riot brewed.

I stood back, scared. To start with I was scared for myself – my own safety, but although I was shielded by a member of staff I knew, I soon realised this wasn't necessary,

47

as it wasn't me they were attacking and everyone was on my side. But I was very scared for the project. What if the management thought all this happened because of the work I was doing, that maybe my project had started a riot? They might not let me come into the prison any more. Then what would happen to Fred, and all the other men I was working with?

I was asked to leave the wing while they dealt with the situation, but I later found out that the prisoners in my group had managed to diffuse the situation by calling for calm, much to all the officers' relief, and everyone complied. The officer at the centre of this was later given a heavy reprimand for his behaviour and moved to another wing. I steered well clear of him after that, but this was another spur to try and find quieter places to work in on each wing.

I finalised the dyslexia checklist and gave it out to the officers on the induction wing that afternoon for them to read out to new prisoners and note down their answers. I was relieved that the deputy governor had obviously talked with them about it, so everyone just seemed to accept it and I didn't need to explain, though I couldn't help but notice a few silent scowls.

CHAPTER 3

ALEX

"Please tick to show which you would prefer to do, work or education."

That was one of the questions on the induction form that all newly arrived prisoners were asked to fill in. Six out of every ten left it blank.

'What is the alternative?' I asked an officer the first time I saw this form.

'Well, if they don't tick one of the boxes, they have to stay banged up in their cells all day. They must be crazy to want to do that.'

'So that would be 60% of new prisoners – are they all crazy?'

I was sure I knew what was in these prisoners' minds when they refused to answer that question. I made it a topic to discuss in all my interviews with new prisoners. What they said confirmed my suspicions. Whilst several told me they hadn't ticked because they didn't know what the question said or didn't want to admit they couldn't read, the majority had been able to ask someone to read it to them if necessary and were clear that they had left the boxes blank on purpose.

'I can't go into a classroom to learn,' was what many of them said. Fred had told me about his fear of classrooms as the place where he had always failed for so many years. I felt exactly the same, so why would anyone want to repeat such a negative experience. And anyway, if they had failed to learn at school, why should it be any different now? It took me a lot of cajoling and individual demonstrations to show the men they could all learn if they were taught in the right way to suit their learning styles. For example, at school we were all taught to spell by learning lists of words, and it didn't work. The majority of prisoners had practical learning styles, which meant they learnt best by doing, so they needed to use their hands and their senses to help them learn.

'If I say I want to do a job,' explained another prisoner, 'I might have to fill in a form or read the instructions, or write things down. Then they'd see I can't do none of those things. They would think I'm stupid and I'd get bullied. That's what always happens. It's why I don't tell no one I can't read or write. No one except you, because you understand.'

It's an indictment on the traditional prison system that it tries to replicate the learning or working situations where men have already endured years of failure and ridicule. My project was going to be very different.

One morning on the VP wing, in a tiny office, I interviewed 24-year-old Alex, doing a four-year sentence for stabbing his sister's rapist. This was his ninth custodial sentence, and one of the officers had already told me a little of Alex's story, so I had time to think how I would start off this interview.

As we sat down to face each other, at a slight angle so as not to seem confrontational, I did my usual thing of looking into Alex's eyes. He looked away, but I could see that his eyes were glazed and resentful, making it clear he'd rather not have to put up with this intervention in his life.

'I'm Jackie and I couldn't learn to read and write properly when I was at school, so I was a complete failure and it wasn't till I was forty that I was diagnosed with dyslexia.'

Now he made eye-contact with me, his head on one side with a look of bemusement as I set off on a path he obviously hadn't expected

I carried on, to engage his interest. 'I have two sons, Richard and Stuart, about your age. Richard is the older one and he's dyslexic like me. Stuart is two years younger and he did quite well at school because he didn't have dyslexia. But when he was fourteen, he was in a terrible car crash and suffered serious brain-damage, which meant he couldn't speak any more, let alone read and write. I started to teach him everything from the beginning again. It was just the three of us, Richard, Stuart and me. We used to call ourselves "The Three Musketeers", because we helped each other and stuck up for each other. Richard had always been close to his younger brother, taking him everywhere, so after the accident he became very protective of him, to make sure he didn't come to any more harm while he was recovering.' I stopped to allow Alex time to take all this in, and hoped he saw the link.

By now there was a clear spark of interest in his gaze and he nodded before speaking. 'That's like me. I've always been protective of my sister,' he said. 'We had a difficult time when we were children, especially me.'

'What were the difficult things?'

51

He hesitated for a moment, deciding what he felt able to tell me. 'My father was a fucking bastard. He bullied and threatened us all the time, especially me. He was a violent man and never a day went by without some fucking outburst or other, usually with a beating too. He called me fucking stupid and a lot of worse things.'

'Come on ...' I tried to make it sound light-hearted, so I gave a half-smile to show I wasn't shocked or angry, but just needed to make it clear. 'You're not going to talk to me like that, are you? I'm really interested in your story and I want to hear more about it, but I'd rather hear it without the swearing if you can manage it.' A lot of the prisoners were angry, especially when they first arrived, and most of them swore like mad. I never knew there were so many swear-words! But talking to them like this usually worked. I smiled again to confirm my expectation.

'OK, sorry Miss,' he said. 'I'll try.'

'Just call me Jackie,' I suggested. 'I don't like being formal.'

'OK Jackie.' He smiled.

'Did you have any difficulties with learning when you were at school?' I knew from the officer that he did.

'Mmm,' he murmured, and I waited to see if you would say anything more. 'They told me I was dyslexic at school.'

'So how did they help you?'

'They didn't. Not a thing. I still can't read and write.' Although his eyes were bright now, he remained a bit guarded. 'I always felt a failure at school, because I couldn't learn. The teachers thought I was stupid and the other kids bullied me all the time. Then I would come home and it would start all over again. I had nowhere to hide at home or at school. But then my father got into some serious trouble and landed up in jail, so it got a bit quieter at home. My brother went to prison soon after that too.'

'It sounds like you had a tough time,' I said.

'Yeah, they kicked me out of secondary school because I had my ear pierced and refused to take out the stud.'

'So what did you do then?'

'Well, my girlfriend had a baby when I was thirteen, a beautiful baby boy. I went to the hospital and everything. I held him just after he was born – he was the best thing that ever happened to me and it felt so good holding him and protecting him from the world. But then ...' Alex screwed up his face as the tears started to run down his cheeks. After about a minute or so, he managed to blurt out the rest of that sentence. 'A few days later he died of a hole in the heart. Just like that.' He paused again to try and control his tears. 'I was devastated. It was really bad, but I couldn't talk to anybody about it, not even my sister. She was the closest person in my family and I couldn't even talk to her about it. I shut it all up inside.'

'That must have been terrible for you.' I felt the tears coming and had to swallow hard and try to hold them back, but a few escaped and trickled down my face.

'Then the same year, my one friend at school, my best friend who always stuck up for me against the bullies ... he went and died – knocked down by a car and killed.' Alex went silent for several seconds as he thought back to those events.

I didn't want to disturb him.

Then he looked straight at me, with a piercing honesty. 'That was the worst year of my life. I wanted to kill myself.'

I returned his gaze and wished I could reach out to touch his arm and offer him some comfort, but of course it was not allowed. I waited again before I spoke. 'I wish I could have known you then,' I said. 'Maybe I could have helped you, because I've had a few times in my life too when I've wanted to commit suicide. I nearly did, but something always happened to stop me.'

'Really?' He looked surprised.

'Yes, I remember a lot of misery and feeling I had no value, no worth to anyone.'

'Yes, me too. Maybe I'd have been better off dead.'

'It sounds as if your sister probably wouldn't agree with that.'

'No, she's the one that kept me going. She even tried to help me learn to read, but I just couldn't do it.' His whole body tensed up and I recalled what the officer had said about his aggression and his violent crime. As Alex's pent-up emotion began to spill out in the set of his face and his taught muscles, I knew I needed to calm him down, but I wasn't afraid. I felt sure he wouldn't do me any harm.

'I did go back to school after that, but I walked out for good when another teacher called me stupid and thick.'

'Did they send you to another school?'

'No, I just kicked around and got in bits of trouble, nothing much, and I ended up in borstal. Then, when I was about sixteen, my sister was raped by a stranger who attacked her one night. Nobody knew who he was, but she saw him when we were out together a few months later and I beat him up for her – just punched him and kicked him. That was my first time inside. Then when I got out I beat him up again, a bit harder than before. That was the second time.'

'Was he tried in court for the rape?'

'Yeah, not long ago, but he got off. The bloody judge said she was asking for it, and I knew she wasn't.'

'That must have been awful.'

'Then he laughed at us when we got outside, so this time I was so angry, I got in a frenzy and beat him good and proper. I had a knife with me, just in case, so I used it. I stabbed him three times. That took the smile off his face. I felt good about that when I did it, but of course a lot of people were watching and the police arrested me again. I'd had a few burglaries in between, but nothing important. This time they threw the book at me and I got eight years, even though they said they weren't very deep wounds.'

I had been observing the way Alex spoke about everything, with a big chip on his shoulder. The officer had told me he wasn't popular and the other men always picked on him. That was one of the reasons he was in the VP wing, as he couldn't cope with the normal banter of prison life and always seemed to make himself the victim. Yes, I could see he was an angry young man and he had issues, but looking at him now, he seemed so meek and pitiful that I could hardly imagine him being really violent. Yet apparently he had been in a few fights already.

'I was raped a few days ago,' he said, in a wavering voice, with a sense of defeat.

I was shocked. 'Who by?'

'One of the men. I tell you, it's dangerous in here. The screws didn't even believe me at first – they thought I'd

55

made it up. But then another inmate said he'd been raped too, so that's when they knew it was real.'

We talked for a while longer about his issues with his family, drugs and alcohol. He'd had a spell of working as a roofer, but he had an aggressive boss who treated him badly, and he couldn't look for another job to get away because he couldn't fill in forms. But of course that job wouldn't be waiting for him after this longer sentence, so he'd have to think what else to do when he got out.

'I always wanted to work with animals,' he said. 'But I never got the chance.'

'Well maybe you will when you are released. We could look at what kinds of jobs there are.'

'Not many,' he murmured. 'And everybody wants a job like that, so I haven't got much of a chance.'

'I can help you to give yourself a better chance than before.'

'Maybe ... but I never got what I wanted, just a lot of grief.' Alex became very morose now and went over and over things in his childhood. It seemed to help him to talk, so I listened. I reckoned we could start on his learning another day. First he needed to talk and most of all he needed a good listener who understood.

Finally the officer came in to get him, so I arranged to come over the next morning with my dyslexia check-list and see which areas he most needed to work on.

'We could start on some things to help you improve your literacy skills if you like.'

'No, I can't go in a classroom.'

'Well, you won't have to. I'll find somewhere on the wing to teach you on your own, just you and me. Maybe we can use the library. Will you give it a go?'

'OK,' he shrugged, as if resigned to his fate. His head hung low as he left the room, but I knew it had helped him, being able to talk.

That afternoon I went to the induction wing to lead the briefing session for the staff. I walked into the room where it was going to be and was amazed to see so many people there. By now I had discovered that quite a few of the officers were dyslexic themselves, and several of them were there. But the room was full with staff from almost all the wings, including Senior Officer Miss Amey, who had told me she was dyslexic. She gave me a smile as I walked in. I found out that even some off-duty staff had come to see what it was all about.

'Hello everyone. I'm Jackie Hewitt-Main and I've had hidden learning difficulties all my life. I was a terrible failure at school and took to self-harming. I was suicidal too. I still can't read and write as well as most people, but I have taught myself to be a lot better than I used to be. The turning point for me was when a college tutor diagnosed me as severely dyslexic when I was about forty.' I paused to look around. Everyone was engaged and listening so I carried on.

'Now, I want to tell you some of the signs you can look out for that a prisoner might be dyslexic. Then we'll look at how dyslexia can affect people's lives and how to help them meet their learning needs, which are different from everyone else. For a start, dyslexic people's brains work differently, and people like me who are very dyslexic might be very good at other things to compensate. It might be art or music or sports, or with me it's talking – I'm very good at that! And I always come up with loads of wacky ideas.'

I told them about how most dyslexic people learn best and how to help them to cope with things like forms and tests. I shared with them some of what I'd found out from the interviews I'd done so far about the surprisingly large percentage of prisoners, 62%, who had not been able to pass their driving tests, because they couldn't read or write well enough to do the theory part. Straight away there were lots of jobs these men could not go for, and it affected their everyday lives too. I also told them about the six out of ten who didn't opt for either work or education and why that was.

The session went better than I had expected. I didn't go too far into it all that day, but several people said afterwards they enjoyed it.

'Thank you,' said one of the officers who had been really negative when I first arrived. 'I learnt a lot today. Now I will look out for some of the things you told us about.'

'Can we have another session sometime?' asked a guy from the IT workshop. 'I'm sure I've got some dyslexic people in with me. It would be good to know how I could help them.'

'Yes you have,' I said. 'I'll come along if you like and observe the men for a bit and then we can discuss what problems they have and how to do things differently for them.'

The next morning, I went over to the VP wing and asked if I could use the library for teaching Alex today. At first, they seemed unsure, then Miss Amey saw me and came over.

'Yes, that should be fine,' she said. 'It doesn't get used during the daytime.'

'Is there a computer there?'

'There didn't used to be, but since you made a request to the Deputy Governor, she's sorted it out so we can have one in there all the time.'

So I went along, got the computer going and loaded the Lexion software. Lexion is a brilliant Swedish programme especially designed for dyslexic learners and used in most Swedish schools. It consists of games and activities to practise skills in all areas of literacy, such as the letter sounds, spelling sequences, the ways words are used, visual memory and many more. At the end of each unit there is an assessment to show what progress the learner has made in that session.

When Alex arrived, he looked a little brighter than yesterday.

'I've been thinking,' he said. 'It's about time I learnt to read and write a bit better.'

'That's good. Shall we go through the dyslexia checklist first? You don't have to do anything except tell me your answers to my questions.'

As I took him through the twenty simple questions, the severity of Alex's dyslexia became more and more obvious. The first question was the only one he had no problems with. Everything else – all nineteen of the other skills – he had difficulties with. These included crucial things like not being able to remember two instructions – he could only cope with one at a time, which showed that he had a very poor sequential memory. His auditory memory was very low too as he had quite a delay sometimes between hearing something and understanding it. This was something I'd always found difficult as well, so I really understood that. He couldn't pronounce many long words, and could read very little and only haltingly. Indeed, he took so long to read a short paragraph in a picture book that he couldn't remember what came before it, so he lost the meaning. He couldn't follow any lengthy conversations and discussions, and could really only talk one to one, where he had time to think between responses.

Mixing up dates and times was a big problem as it meant he had often missed important appointments and could not be relied on. His other numeracy skills were poor too, not being able to work out simple sums in his head or use the number pad on a phone. He did some of the typically dyslexic things like muddling similar letters and jumbling the order of letters in words.

'I've always been terrible at sequencing things too,' I said in sympathy. 'Any kind of sequences are not good for me – times-tables, ABC, months of the year, times on the clock – I had problems with all of those. I still do sometimes, especially if I'm flustered or anxious.'

Alex nodded, smiling. 'I wish I'd known other people had the same problems as me. And you're a teacher too!'

'Yes, but only because I finally met someone who helped me to understand that what was wrong with me wasn't wrong – just different – and she helped me learn different ways to do things. Dyslexic people can learn, but they have to use other ways. That's what I'm here for.'

'You mean I can learn like that too?'

'Definitely, yes. We just need to find out what are the best ways for you, and that's what we're doing now.'

His smile lit up his face.

'So, let's carry on.'

Like me, Alex had always been good at thinking up loads of ideas but had difficulty explaining them and couldn't write them down. Alex had so many problems because of his dyslexia that we had loads to do. At least he was able to read at a very basic level, so that gave us a start to build on.

I did a short assessment with him, which showed his literacy skills were at the level of an average six-year-old (40% of the prisoners in this jail had literacy levels no higher than a seven-year-old), so Alex had done quite well to get this far with all the problems he had.

'Considering what your assessment shows, I think you've done brilliantly to read as well as you do. Let's go and work on the computer now.'

'Yeah,' he cheered. 'I like playing computer games.'

First of all we focussed on some of the simpler activities, to build up his confidence. I wanted to see how he connected the letters or letter-groups to their sounds and he soon started to get the hang of that. Next we had a bit of fun with some Spoonerisms, like 'par-cark', which he found difficult to put right, and so did I, but luckily he didn't find it too frustrating since we had the same problems with it, so we had a laugh.

'Maybe we'll be better at doing this,' I suggested, switching to a compound-word activity that put simple words together to make new words, like 'car' and 'pet' or 'foot' and 'ball'. When Alex got them right, the screen would show the picture to go with the compound word. He was much better with this activity and got nearly all of them right.

'This is good,' he said. 'I can do it right.' He was really pleased with himself, though knowing him a little by now I realised it might not last.

Sure enough, he was up and down in most of the lessons that followed, making slow but steady progress. Working at the computer was his favourite part of each lesson, so I made sure we did a lot of that each time. But it was getting frustrating for me that some mornings he seemed really slow and lethargic and I couldn't work out why. I asked one of the officers about it one day and he gave me the clue I needed.

'I've never known anybody drink as much coffee as Alex does, especially when he's playing on his x-box at night.'

I brought it up with him in our lesson. 'I hear you drink a lot of coffee?'

'Yes, I suppose so.'

'How many mugs of coffee would you say you drink each day?'

He stopped to try and work it out, using his fingers and mumbling his way through his daily routine. 'Maybe nine,' he said with a rueful smile. 'Yeah, it is quite a lot, isn't it? I didn't realise.'

'Well I reckon that affects your energy levels. Coffee is OK to drink occasionally, but not more than two or three cups a day. I know if I drink any more than that it slows me down, so I don't drink it much now.'

'But I can't have alcohol in here, so coffee is the only drink.'

'Well you could cut it down, and maybe have some healthier alternatives, like milk and fruit-juices. You could order both with your breakfast instead of coffee, that way you could have one drink at night and one in the morning.' I knew the prisoners had to order their breakfasts the day before and it would be given to them in the evening before lock-up. Often, as their evening meal was so early, they were hungry at night and ate their breakfast before they went to sleep. But that would be a good time to start, with a healthy drink to help him sleep better and another healthy drink to start the day right.

'Will you promise me to give it a try?'

'OK,' he agreed, with more than a little reluctance. 'If it's going to help me learn better.'

From then on, Alex began to make more progress in our sessions, which were once or twice a week, with him doing some practice in between. For homework I used to give him small words in spelling groups to practice in practical ways in his cell, spelling, saying, reading and playing with the words, writing them in the air, on the mirror, anywhere.

'Just five words a day,' I told him the first time. 'That way we will build up to your target of learning to spell 100 words.'

'I'll never be able to do that.'

'Yes you will. I'm sure you'll make your target, you'll see.'

While he was doing all this, Alex became so much calmer and more confident with himself that they moved him out of the VP wing.

'It's ace being in an ordinary wing,' he told me, when I had tracked him down. 'And I'm doing well with my learning aren't I?''

Alex reached his 100 word goal just in time, before he was moved to another prison. This was one of the most frustrating things about working with the prisoners in this jail as they were often moved on at only a few hours' notice, and I sometimes didn't get to know till two or three days later. But at least this time I'd had the chance to help him for a while before he went.

I was glad I'd been there to listen to Alex when he needed, which was nearly every lesson, and hoped there would be a good listener for him at his new jail. I said a silent prayer for him, wherever they'd sent him.

CHAPTER 4

PERRY

During my first few weeks in the prison I had got into trouble almost every time I tried to bring something in to use in my multi-sensory teaching sessions. The first time was when I brought some pipe-cleaners to make the shapes of letters. They weren't allowed because the prisoners could use them to pick locks. The next time was the plasticene – that can be used for moulding keys.

One day, when I'd run out of plastic bags, I wrapped my sandwiches with foil. Nobody checked my lunchbox when I took it through security and I didn't think to declare it, so it wasn't till I opened my lunch in the IT workshop, chatting with some of the men, that one of them suddenly started laughing.

'What's the matter?' I asked.

'The foil!' He pointed at it. 'Shut your lunchbox quickly. You'll get into a lot of trouble if one of the officers notices that.'

'Why?' I must have been so naive.

'A lot of inmates would pay you any money they could get for that bit of foil.'

'Really? What for?'

'Are you real? Do you honestly not know?'

I shook my head.

'For taking drugs.'

'Ohh!'

After that scare, I had to be extra careful and always checked everything with security – even the sandwiches themselves! I had managed to get a few multi-sensory materials cleared, such as sand and textured paper, but most of the traditional items used in infant schools were banned. So I decided to stop off at B&Q one evening on my way home. I strolled around looking for inspiration. Within ten minutes I was sitting on the floor with a reel of masking tape, having fun shaping letters on a carpet tile, when along came one of my neighbours.

'What on earth are you doing now?' she asked.

'Just trying some things out that I can use in the prison,' I explained, as if it was an everyday occurrence.

'You're always up to something different. What are you going to try next?' She laughed and walked on.

The masking tape was working well, so I took that and some carpet tiles, then gathered a few more bits and pieces to practise with at home. I even managed to persuade my younger son Stuart to help me experiment with things we had around the house.

We sat at the table and played with them together It reminded me so much of the times when I was a small child and my mother sat at the table with us and played games. We always had fun when she did that. It was my mum who taught me the importance of play in learning.

On B wing the next morning, an officer asked me to have a chat with Perry, a 43-year-old armed robber on his eleventh prison sentence. He'd just fallen down the stairs and was waiting for a doctor to come and check him over, so I sat and talked with him. The staff told me he was very bright but he seemed to have learning difficulties and to watch out because he could be very aggressive.

'I've just heard about your fall,' I began. 'Are you in pain?'

'My back still hurts, but I don't think it's anything much.'

'They told me what you're in for this time.'

'Yes, but it wasn't really my fault,' he said. 'I was in this gang and we went to do a robbery. It was in a warehouse and we knew they had insurance, so they would be able to claim for anything we took. There would be no old ladies there and nobody to get hurt. The gang-leader told me we had a customer lined up for one of their electronic items and to only take boxes of that. So we went in and I looked through everything on the shelves. I realised straight away that this would be a big problem, as none of the boxes had pictures on them – just printed labels full of writing. I couldn't read any of it, so I was flummoxed at first. Then I had an idea. I just had to look for the right size boxes and that should be fine, so I picked out all the appropriate ones and we loaded them into our van and got away easy.'

I had been listening with interest and realised that Perry must have a problem with reading, so he might be dyslexic.

'But that's when the problem really started. I had picked all the wrong boxes. It was daft, because I hadn't even realised that all the writing was in Japanese, so I wouldn't have been able to read it anyway!' He paused to laugh. 'It was ridiculous. Anyway, we didn't have a customer for what was in those boxes, so I piled them all into a garage I had rented for the gang. That was when I was caught red-handed. I got five years for that misunderstanding!'

'It sounds as if you might be dyslexic?' I said it as a question to prompt him. 'I am dyslexic and was such a failure at school myself, so I know what it's like.'

'Yes,' he agreed. 'I used to twist my letters all the time, but I didn't know I was dyslexic when I was at school. I was diagnosed during my first prison sentence, in 1984, but they never gave me any help for it. In all my stays in prison, nobody's ever given me any help with learning to read and write.'

'Well, that's what I'm here for. But first I'd like to hear more about how you got into trouble in the first place. Can you tell me about that?'

'Well, I left school as soon as I could. I'd always had lots of ideas for making money, so I started up by buying cheap fruit on the market and selling it for more. Soon I was able to buy a batch for £450 and sell it for £600. That was great – I got a real buzz from making a profit so easily. I realised I had a gift for making money and this was the first thing I'd ever been good at. I soon got enough together to start a café in Essex. Then I started three other businesses as well. The money was rolling in and I invested it in a new business each time to expand. I had people working for me and everything was great. But there was a big problem mounting up ... and I didn't realise till too late. It was my own fault I suppose. I started getting letters from the tax and VAT people, but I couldn't read them. I suppose they were demands for money, but I didn't understand them and thought they were just official papers, so I threw them away.

I knew nothing about tax or VAT at all, and didn't realise I would have to pay them.'

'People don't understand how someone like us can have loads of ideas and be good at business ... like Richard Branson,' I said. 'They wonder why we can't manage the paperwork that probably seems simple to them. I suppose you didn't want to hand the demand letters on to one of your admin employees?'

'No. I was the one who could make all these big deals and get the money rolling in. They didn't know I couldn't read or write. I never told anybody about that. I thought there was no need, and I wanted to be the man, the one who could do everything, so I didn't want anyone to know I had any weaknesses.'

'Yes, lots of people I talk to are just the same. No one likes to admit it, especially if they've been bullied at school.'

'Anyway, I started to get more and more of these demands and soon they were court documents and I began to suspect I might be in some sort of trouble. It all caught up with me eventually and I couldn't pay any of it, so I was convicted of fraud.'

'What happened after that?'

'Well, I'm no good with dates and times – they're just a muddle in my head, so when I got out again I kept missing appointments to do with the courts or probation and that got me more time inside. And the businesses folded with all that, so when I came out I had to find ways to try and pay off some of my debts. There was only one way I could think of to find that sort of money in a short time, so I got into the gangs thing I suppose, dealing drugs, getting into fights and doing more crimes. I didn't want to get involved with any weapons or anything, so I just stuck to the stealing, while other people held the guns. But I still got done for armed robbery. That was a shock.'

'I was just like you with my paperwork.' I commiserated with him. ' I started up various businesses, and I'd probably have got into the same problems as you with the taxman, but I took on a partner who was good at all that, so I didn't have to worry about it. The thing that really caught me out was many years later, when I was having some success working with unemployed youngsters and the local council offered me a huge amount of funding to expand what I was doing across their area. It was all going through great ... until they asked to see my business plan. I didn't have one on paper, only in my head. I knew exactly what I wanted to do and everything, but I couldn't write it down – I didn't even know what a business plan was. I'd never needed one before.'

'So what happened to the money they offered you?'

'They withdrew it.'

'It's a bugger, isn't it – this dyslexia thing?' We both laughed.

Far from being aggressive, Perry seemed bright-eyed and alert, despite the discomfort in his back.

'Do you want me to go and see where that doctor has got to?'

'No, it'll be fine. I want to stay and talk to you. I've never met anyone like you before. Do you think you can help me with my reading and writing?'

'Yes, I can. But the first thing I need to do is to assess you and find out where your strengths are and what we need to work on. Will that be all right?'

70

'Yeah. I'm up for that. It's about time, after all these years.'

'OK. Well I don't know how long we've got this time, so we can talk through the dyslexia check-list today and see what that shows, then if we have time we'll try the 'Skills for Life' reading assessment, to see where you have the most problems.'

'Great. I'm looking forward to this.'

Perry was alert and hungry for help as we started on the initial assessment, which showed that he experienced most of the typical dyslexic traits. I talked him through all of these and what we could do about them. Then he tried the reading passage. He was keen to start with, but it was very hard for him as this involved him in reading a paragraph of text out loud. Even though nobody but me could hear him, it was painful for him to go back to something he'd failed at so often in school. He persevered as far as he could, referring back when he was uncertain about words and this indicated a number of areas we could work on.

'That was a great help to me,' I said. 'So thanks very much for keeping at it. '

Next we got started on a sentence construction activity, which he was enjoying more, despite his confusion with the ordering of words. Then the officer who had been sitting outside the door of his cell popped his head around the door.

'The doc's here, so I'm afraid you'll have to go now.'

I packed away all my stuff in haste.

'Will you come back soon?' asked Perry.

'I'll try and come over to finish the assessments tomorrow and make a plan with you about how I can help you improve your literacy skills. Would that be OK?'

'That would be cool,' he smiled.

As I walked away from Perry's cell, along the landing towards the stairs, there was a bit of a scene with a temperamental Italian man, who was being accused of something. The prisoners gathered round the railings to look down and watch the argument building up. I could see from the onlookers' faces that this was the highlight of their day.

Whilst I had been gathering more multi-sensory materials to help prisoners learn by combining their senses, I had an idea, but I wasn't sure whether it would work, so I went along to the carpentry workshop to talk it through with Stan, the woodwork tutor.

'Would it be possible for you to get the men to make me some things I can use in my teaching sessions?' I asked.

'Well now,' said Stan, putting away some tools. 'That all depends what these things are. Not weapons I hope?' He smiled.

'No, nothing like that,' I replied in all seriousness. I don't know why it was, but I could never see jokes in the early days, nor when people teased me, which was definitely a handicap as most of the officers and men would have a banter and I always found it confusing until I realised that this was just to be friendly and pass the time. I always took everything seriously and they must have thought me very odd. It was a steep learning curve and now I understand better, though I still sometimes don't get it when someone makes a joke.

'So what have you got in mind?' he asked in a kind voice.

'I want to have some wooden letters,' I explained. Just the letters of the alphabet – maybe two or three alphabets, with textured surfaces so they each feel different. But the same letters in each alphabet would need to have the same texture.'

'Mmm,' he stood and thought for a moment. 'Like sandpaper, you mean?'

'Yes, that could be one of them.'

'We could stick on different grades of sandpaper, and we could carve some of them, and maybe used different textured paints, scatter seeds on varnish ...'

'That would be just great!'

'Lower case letters?'

'Yes, that would be best.'

'Leave it to me.'

Only a few days later, the letters duly arrived on my desk in the education department. I was very proud of this desk as, for the first few weeks, I'd been without anywhere to work on assessment papers and the like and to store my things. Now at last I had a base in the prison, a place to work late into the night if I wanted to.'

The letters were works of art. I couldn't wait to introduce them to the prisoners, along with some other materials I wanted to trial. I had begun to plan a course that I hoped to start running for small groups, and they would be perfect for that.

Meanwhile, I went from one wing to the next, teaching and assessing more men every day. I returned to B wing the following day as promised for a second session with Perry.

'Can we use a computer somewhere on the wing?' I asked one of the officers. 'I want to work with Perry today and do some assessment on the computer. Is his back OK?'

'Yes, it's a bit stiff and bruised, he says, but the doc passed him as fit.'

'Good. Where would be best for the computer?'

'There's already one in the library. Will that be all right?'

'Yes, can you ask Perry to come there while I go and set up?'

As the officer walked up the stairs to get him, I went to log on and install the Lexion software.

.Hi, Perry. How's your back today?' I asked as he walked in.

'Not too bad thanks,' he said. 'I just need to keep moving, the doc said, as it's quite stiff today.'

'OK. We'll make sure we don't sit down much today then.'

We started with another simple sentence construction activity, to follow on from the Learning Skills assessment we had started the day before. I noticed that, as well as trouble with sequencing the words, he had problems with the orders of letters for spelling even the most basic words.

'I've just had these letters made in the carpentry workshop,' I said, getting them out of their bag and spreading them out on the table. Standing up, I got him to turn them around to the correct orientation and feel each of them as he said the letter name and its sound. He enjoyed the tactile nature of this and seemed to think it was play rather than work, which was just what I wanted.

'Saying the letters and their sounds at the same time as feeling them helps your brain, your eyes, your hearing and speaking and your hands to work together to help you learn the letters better.'

'That's clever,' he said. 'How does that work?'

'Well, it's a bit like when you write your name. When you put a pen in your hand, do you see the letters in your head and maybe mouth them as well?'

He tried it. 'Yes!' he said. 'How did you know that? I didn't even know it myself.'

'Doing all that helps your hand know how to write the letter.'

'Wow!'

'Find the letters for your name.'

He selected the four different letters, and an extra 'r' for Perry, turned them round and placed them in order.

'This is cool,' he smiled, feeling the surface of an r. 'Both the r shapes feel the same.'

'Yes, that's to help you recognise them by touch. Now trace the shape and feel the surface of each letter as you say it.'

We did this with a number of basic words as well. Then we tried writing some of them in the air and on our hands.

'How do you think you learn the best?' I asked him. 'If you want to learn how to do something new, do you like to look at a diagram or pictures of how to do it, or follow spoken instructions one by one to do it, or do you prefer to have a go with your hands and see if you can work it out that way?'

'Definitely hands, and I'm quite good with looking at things to learn, as long as there aren't any words, but I'm not good at listening. I always forget what people tell me.'

'So you're mainly a visual and practical learner.'

'Really? I never knew that.'

'That's why school was so difficult for you, because most traditional teaching is done through listening and reading, and those are the things you find the hardest. Here you are going to learn through using your eyes and your hands, linked to your brain, just like we've been doing with these letters.'

I wanted to see if Perry could mirror the letters next, so I asked him to mirror the 'P' that I wrote in the air. I tried to do it for him first to show him what I meant, but I got in a muddle with that myself, so we had a laugh about it.

'OK, I can see I need some help with this too,' I said. 'Let's leave that for now and have a go on the computer instead.'

The Lexion assessment is a very positive and supportive activity, but also good at pinpointing the activities to use for helping someone to progress. This first assessment showed that while Perry had some skills of an average nine to eleven-year-old, his reading was at the level of a five-year-old and his spelling was the weakest of all, at pre-school level. At first that seemed to suggest he had trouble with visual memory, but I could see that with him it was more the combination of his great difficulty with sequencing letters and with 'hearing' the sounds of them in his head.

We finished the session standing up and moving around, shaping letters by walking them out on the floor. He seemed to really enjoy this activity. Finally I asked him if he'd found the session helpful.

'It's been enlightening for me,' he said, 'I could never understand before why I couldn't learn, but now you have helped me to realise what some of my issues are and how the ways I've been taught in the past weren't right for me. This way is. Now I know I can learn, and I like doing it this way. You've helped me to see what I need to work on so that I can use your approach to help me reach my reading and writing goals. It's wicked.'

I was really pleased with Perry and the progress he began to make. He was delighted to see that, after all those years, he had finally found a way forward that gave him hope for the future, even though he had a long journey to get there.

Once again, after a few sessions together, improving all the time, Perry was moved to another prison, but by now he had some ideas on how to help himself and I hoped he would be able to use this knowledge to continue moving forward with his literacy skills. If only we could have spread the use of these methods as well as the dyslexia software across other prisons, we could continue to help so many of our students wherever they went.

Fortunately, many of the prisoners I had assessed as dyslexic and begun to work with remained at the same prison throughout their sentences, so for them the learning journey could be uninterrupted, as long as I could keep the project funding going. This was an anxiety that dogged me from day to day now, as the months were passing by and I knew the funding would run out in the summer. I was looking for new sponsorship, but what would I do if I couldn't find any?

When I first started this project I was told that only 10% of prisoners were dyslexic – the same as in the general population, but I soon found this to be a huge underestimation. When I checked the figures from the first few hundred prisoners it remained steady at 53% of all those I had interviewed being dyslexic. On top of this there were another 16% with traumatic brain injuries – more than eight times the national average.

I was also shocked to see that only 21% of prisoners at that time and in that jail had the literacy skills of an average twelve-year-old or above, with 72% below the level of an average ten-year-old.

There were some other stark messages too, the most important being that 62% had not been able to pass or even take their driving tests because of the theory test being a written paper, and only 11% of those who had worked on building sites had been able to gain their Construction Skills Certificates, allowing them to work legally in the construction industry. This problem of paperwork barriers came up again and again in other areas too, such as filling in benefit forms or job application forms.

It seemed to me that I had a huge task on my hands if I was going to be able to reach as many of these prisoners as possible to help them, without it being in a classroom situation, and there were more men arriving daily. How was I going to be able to meet all their learning needs? I needed to think of a way.

CHAPTER 5

CARL and DON

'I'd really like to get these six men together in one room, and you're the only one that can make that happen,' I pleaded with the Deputy-Governor one morning.

'But Jackie, I can't do the impossible. These names you've given me are all high-risk prisoners on B wing and they each have severe behavioural problems – they are all highly violent men. Every one of them needs his own officer to guard him. I shouldn't let even two of them be in the same room together, let alone all six of them. You've got murderers and armed robbers amongst this lot – on long sentences for terrible crimes.'

'But they're all severely dyslexic, like me, and they all want to learn about how their brains work and what dyslexia is all about. They want to discuss and share their learning problems and the ways they can compensate for their dyslexia.'

'I know you have the best intentions, Jackie, but it really can't be done.'

'They've all promised me that they will be on their best behaviour.'

'And you believe them? Judging by past performances, even their best behaviour is worse than you can imagine.'

'But you know me. I always expect the best, and these men really want to do this, so I do believe them and I really don't think they'll let me down. They've all had so many failures in the past, so now they see this as their first chance to learn how to succeed.'

She sat there and smiled. 'Oh Jackie, you are a hopeless optimist!'

I laughed. 'Optimist yes, but why wouldn't they behave when this is all about them?'

'Well ...' she paused for thought and I breathed a silent sigh of relief that she might be wavering at last.

'We could meet in the glass room so the officers can watch us.' I knew this would be a terrible distraction for the men, but it was a compromise that might make it possible. 'You could even have the CCTV cameras on us if you like.'

'We'd have to have officers in the room with you as well.'

'No,' I said. 'This has to be an informal discussion, so that the men feel comfortable to share their experiences and concerns. They won't do that if there are officers actually in the room with them.'

'You do make my life difficult, don't you?'

I shrugged. 'If this is going to work, it has to be a free and easy atmosphere.'

'Free and easy? Are you joking?'

I ignored her comments. 'I've got six dyslexic men who see this as their big opportunity. They really want to understand themselves and their condition. All we need is the chance to make it happen. Can you stand in their way?' I said a silent prayer as she pondered my 'impossible' demand.

'Right. I'm going to talk to a few people and see what we can do. No promises mind.'

'Thank you, thank you, thank you!' I grinned.

'You'll have to be in the glass room, with security officers on the outside of the glass, plus CCTV cameras watching you.'

'Yes, that's fine. We'll cope with that.'

'But there's one more condition.'

'What's that?'

'You'll have to have a trusty in with you.'

My spirits sank a little. Who was she going to lumber us with?

'I want Don to be there for the whole session.'

Phew! Don was a volunteer mentor and I had already begun to work with him, so I felt relaxed about him being there. In fact, it would be really helpful to have him on board. 'OK,' I agreed. 'I know Don, so that will be fine.'

'Good,' she said. 'But remember, I'll have to speak to everyone before I can give you the go ahead. Come back and see me this afternoon.'

As I walked through B-wing, a tall, bald-headed prisoner rushed towards me, waving his arms around. Immediately, I stopped still and a small crowd began to gather.

'Hey, you!' he yelled at me. 'What you do about my brother?' He had a heavy accent and spoke with a surprisingly high voice for such a well-built man.

'Who is your brother?' I asked.

'Perry – he my brother-in-law. He need help. You need you help him. He no read. Why you no help?'

'I am helping a man called Perry,' I said. 'Maybe it's the same Perry. What is your brother-in-law's last name?'

Just then, the onlookers parted and a good-looking inmate, covered in tattoos, strode through the gap.

'Hey, hey, Marco,' he said, facing up to the man who was heckling me 'She's already helping him, so don't go on at her.' As this tattooed inmate stared at Marco, he seemed to crumble, then slouched off away and the crowd dispersed.

'Thank you,' I said, smiling with relief. 'But how did you know I'm working with Perry?'

'He's telling everyone how great you are – everyone except his brother-in-law, it seems!'

He paused long enough for me to notice how forbidding those tattoos made him look.

'I'm Carl. I've heard a lot about you already. Enough to know I'd like to help you. I know you have so many of the men wanting you to work with them and teach them to read and write. You can't do it all on your own, so If you need any help, I'd like to volunteer. I could work with some of them and encourage them. Most of the men know me as I'm a Listener, so I go into their cells and listen to their problems, as well as reading and writing letters for them.'

I could see an officer walking over towards us, and of course I wasn't really supposed to talk to prisoners openly like this, unless it was pre-arranged, so I knew I should move on to my next teaching session. 'Thanks for the offer, Carl. It's a good idea and I'll have a think about it. Maybe we could have a talk about it tomorrow?'

'Yes, OK.'

'I'll try and arrange it with the senior officer.'

At the end of the day I went back to see the Deputy Governor.

'Well,' she began, not giving anything away. 'I've spoken to the officers and they are very worried about your proposed session with the high-risk dyslexic prisoners.' She sat back in her chair. 'They are all scared rigid about this. These men are all enough trouble on their own, and we have never dared put any of them together, never mind all six of them. Why do you want to do this anyway? What's the point? Surely you can do more good if you work with them individually, like you've been doing so far?'

'Yes, I know they're high-risk, but they're always fine with me. And the point of having them together is so that they can share their experiences and talk about their dyslexia with each other. I really believe this will help them so much. It will help me too.'

She sat and looked at me with a steady gaze for a few seconds, that seemed like minutes. 'Dear Lord,' I prayed silently, 'please let her say yes.'

'Like I said yesterday, you'd have to be in the glass room, with officers nearby and the cameras on you all the time. I'll have to get a couple of the staff to monitor the cameras and everyone will be ready to act if there is even the slightest hint of trouble.'

'OK,' I nodded, knowing this was the best I could hope for.

'I've spoken to Don and he's worried about it too, but he seems to have a lot of respect for you and says he is willing to give it a go.'

'Thank you. I think Don knows all these men quite well, so that will be fine. I'll have a talk with him about it before the session starts.' Then I realised I hadn't asked.

'When can we do it? I'd like it to be as soon as possible, but I realise you have to make sure there are enough staff on duty.'

'I've checked the rotas and changed a few things around, so that you can do it on Friday morning at ten o'clock.'

'Thanks.' I stood up to go. 'Thank you very much.'

'I'm taking a big risk with this you know.'

'Yes, and I really appreciate it..

'If this goes wrong ...'

'I know. It won't.'

Driving home that evening, I kept thinking about these high-risk prisoners – was I right in thinking they'd all get on fine in a group, or was I being too naive? Maybe I hadn't really considered how much of a gamble this whole thing could be. If it goes wrong, it might mean the end of my project. It would certainly be the end of any help I can give in B wing. It hadn't even occurred to me that there could be a problem, but now I began to envisage all sorts of possibilities – arguments, fights, even a riot ... I shuddered at the thought.

It began to spook me so much that I knew I had to stop thinking about it. I switched my mind onto Carl and his offer of help. He seemed a really nice man, with a calm manner and a charming smile, though of course he is a prisoner and might be violent. I must find out what he is in for. I'll go and see him tomorrow and get him to tell me his story. The other prisoners seem to respect him, so he could be a great help.

I began mulling over some ideas I had about formalising the role of mentor. Up to now, I had assumed I'd need to use mainly volunteers from outside the prison to

84

support my project, but if there are more men like Carl and Don around the prison, in each of the wings, that could really take off. I could maybe set up a training course for them, to enable them to do some of my work. Then we could reach so many more dyslexic and brain-damaged inmates to help them improve their literacy skills too. I wondered if I could get this classified as a job within the prison, so that they could get paid, even though it would probably have to be a pittance, as the management wouldn't be able to exceed the amount they pay prisoners in other types of work. This was exciting – it could definitely be the start of something.

The next day, Thursday, I spent the morning teaching Perry, Fred and a couple of others, and part of the afternoon interviewing and assessing some new prisoners. Finally I found time to track down Don in his wing and have a quick word with him about the plan for Friday's high-risk group session.

'I was shocked when the Deputy Governor told me about this,' he said. 'If it was anyone else but you, I would have downright refused, but even now it scares me sick, just the thought of it – it would only take one of them to kick off and anything could happen!'

'Don't worry, it will be fine,' I assured him, but deep down my doubts were growing. I just had to quell any anxiety in its tracks and keep my belief in these men. I had to trust them, and show them that I trusted them. I knew if I could convince them I expected them to be fine, they would be ...but if they should pick up that I have the slightest concern or mistrust, it would all go pear-shaped.

I went through with Don what I hoped to cover and how he could help lead the discussion and encourage everyone to take part.

Finally, with everything else done, I could go and have a chat with Carl. When I arrived on B wing, I found one of the officers and asked him for permission to talk with Carl somewhere.

'Not today,' he said, shaking his head. 'He's banged up today.'

'Why?' I was disappointed. 'What happened?'

'I'm not sure. I was off-duty yesterday, but apparently he spoke to a visitor without permission.'

'Oh no,' I groaned. 'That must have been me. But I'm not a visitor. I work here.'

'Well you're on the education side, but you're not a prison officer, so it's against the rules.'

I knew this really, of course. It had been on that list of rules I had to learn when I first joined the prison. I felt awful. 'So can I see him in his cell?'

'No, I'm afraid not.'

'What kind of cell door does he have?' I asked. 'Is it one of those old ones with bars in it?'

'Yes. Why?'

'Well, maybe I could talk to him through the gaps?'

That wasn't against the rules, so the officer took me to the door. 'Jackie wants a word with you,' he said in a gruff voice. 'You'll have to speak to her through the door.'

Carl came and stood on the inside, looking at me through the gaps, with his cell window on the opposite wall. Being early summer, it was still light and the bright glow behind him contrasted with Carl's dark silhouette, so that he looked more frightening than when I'd met him the day before.

'Hi. Thanks for coming,' he said.

I strained to see his face properly, but the sunlight only accentuated the tattoos on his neck and head. 'Hello Carl,' I began. 'I'm sorry you got into trouble for talking to me yesterday.'

'No worries,' he said. I think he smiled, but I couldn't be sure. 'It's only for twenty-four hours, so I'll be back to normal tomorrow.'

'Thanks for offering to help. I'd like to talk with you about that, but maybe it will be easier if I come and see you tomorrow?'

'Yes, we'll be able to talk properly then, if you ask permission this time!' Now my eyes were gradually adjusting and I did see his smile, with the flash of his white teeth.

As I drove to the prison on Friday morning, I went over and over in my mind the reasons why I wanted to have this meeting today. Why wasn't I as worried about it as everyone else seemed to be? Yes, of course it was a big risk, but I was confident it would work. Was I deluding myself? Should I be more scared?

I went straight over to B wing to check out the glass room and where the cameras would be. If they had to be there, I didn't want them to be in the way, or to distract the men. I stacked a couple of tables and began to rearrange the chairs when Don came in, looking pale and shaky.

'Are you OK?' I asked. 'You don't look too good.'

'No, I hardly slept all night for worrying about this meeting,' he said. 'It's not too late to cancel it you know.'

'I don't want to cancel it. I can't – the men are all looking forward to it, and I'm sure it will be fine.'

'Well I'm terrified that somebody will kick off and the whole thing will turn into a smash-up, or even worse. You've got murderers here, you know.'

'Yes, I know, but I've told them all that if they want to be able to do this sort of thing they'll have to be on their best behaviour. I spoke to each of them about it and they all promised me they'd behave.'

'Well,' he rubbed his ear. 'It's your funeral.'

'I hope not!' I laughed, which broke the ice a bit. 'Can you give me a hand with the rest of these tables? I want them all stacked so that we can have the chairs round in a circle, so it will feel more informal.'

'I've heard some of the men calling you "Wacky Jackie. I reckon they've hit the nail on the head there.'

Just then, four surly prison officers came in.

'Why have you moved all the furniture?' asked one.

'Because I don't want this to look like a classroom,' I explained. 'It's supposed to be a discussion – more like a chat.'

'You must be off your head,' said another. 'You're asking for trouble having all those violent men in here together. I think we should stay in the room with you.'

'No, please don't.' I felt dragged down again, having to plead with them to let us have an ordinary talk without their overbearing presence. 'The Deputy-Governor promised me you wouldn't do this.'

'But she doesn't know how dangerous these men are.'

'We talked it all through and she agreed that I should give it a try and that you guys would stand outside and keep an eye on us through the glass. Please don't make things more difficult than necessary.' I was desperate not to let all my good intentions be foiled by this last minute hitch.

Finally, the senior officer agreed to let us start, with them watching from outside. 'But we'll be ready to come in if we see anything,' he said. 'If anyone looks like they're brewing trouble.'

So they went off to fetch the men, escorted them into the room, and sat them down, then spaced themselves around the outside to watch all parts of the room. I heard the click as the cameras whirred into action and it was time to start.

'I want to begin by thanking you all for coming today so that we can discuss how dyslexia affects each of us and how best to deal with it. We're going to have an informal discussion, but we will be watched by the officers outside and there will also be a couple more keeping watch via the cameras. I've told them that I trust you to act appropriately, to take part in the discussion and share your opinions with everyone else here in a friendly way, so that we can all learn from each other. The officers will be looking out for trouble, but we're going to show them – we're not going to cause any trouble, are we?'

All six men agreed straight away.

'I want to learn about my problems,' said one.

'I think we all want to have a good chat about dyslexia,' said another, 'Like what it is and how it affects our brains, like you said. Don't we lads?'

'Too right!'

'We don't want to cause you any grief, Miss.'

'Please call me Jackie. Like all of you, I am severely dyslexic and I was a complete failure at school. It still causes me problems, so I've been doing lots of research about dyslexia and I want to tell you what I've found out. But first, I want you to feel comfortable in here. I know it's difficult for some of you to sit still for long, so Don and I have cleared the tables away and it's fine if you want to walk around the room now and then, to help you concentrate, and I've also got some squishy shapes here that you can handle if you like, instead of fidgeting, to keep you focussed.'

'I'm just here to help,' added Don. 'And to learn as well.'

'The first thing I want to show you is this picture of the brain,' I began. I pinned the poster up on the board. 'This is how most people's brains work.' I pointed to each side of the brain in turn. 'Most people can use each side of their brain quite well for different activities, though they often have a stronger side and a weaker side. Scientists have found that most of us function best if we use the skills of both sides when we learn new things. So usually the left side is what we use when we learn to speak or read or write, or when we use number or tackle problems.' I pointed to the mathematical symbols, letters and words on that side of the diagram. 'Whereas the right side of the brain is best at creative thinking, imagining things, enjoying music and art, feelings, senses, emotions and social skills.'

I paused for everyone to think about what I'd said, then repeated it simply, to help them process this information. 'Many dyslexic people have to hear things several times over to fully take them in,' I said. 'Now, looking at this diagram, does anyone think they're equally good at everything?' Nobody moved. 'Ok, so what do you think you're best at?'

'I'm definitely best at the creative side, like ideas and music.'

'Yes, I'm best at the right brain things too.'

'Do any of you think you're good at the left brain skills?' I asked.

They all shook their heads. 'My left brain must look like a car-crash!' said one of the men and the others all laughed in agreement.

'Yeah, that's me too. No wonder I could never learn to read!'

'So, for most of you guys, and me too, this right, creative side is far stronger than the left, which is the language and maths side. The main reason we didn't learn properly at school was because the teachers tried to teach us using our weak side, instead of using our best side. So we need to use our strengths to improve our weaknesses and to help us learn. That means using our creative and spatial skills to improve our language and maths skills.'

Now I replaced the first image with a brighter, pictorial version of the brain. It showed a small, shrivelled-looking, monochrome area on the left side, with a few tiny mathematical symbols and a scattering of words. This contrasted with the large, colourful expanse of the right side, shown as a large green field, full of happy people and activity, making music, painting pictures, dancing and playing games. 'Now this is probably more what it looks like in our brains,' I said, and they all laughed.'

'Too right,' said one of the murderers.

'That's a great way to look at it,' said another.

Our attention now turned to how dyslexia affected us and we all started to share our experiences, going back to school days and also what was difficult for the men now. It was a great discussion, with everyone taking turns and listening to each other – much better behaved than the House of Commons debates I've seen on TV! It was quite a lively session, with everyone taking part and enjoying the chance to talk openly with others who had similar problems. The atmosphere was really calm and amicable. In fact it was all going better that even I had hoped.

Suddenly the door burst open and two security officers stormed in.

'Nobody move!' shrieked one of them.

Nobody dared – we all froze in the stunned silence that immediately followed their unwelcome intrusion. These men, dressed all in black with their hands on their belts, ready for action, were very intimidating. I was horrified. I could sense the men's anger boiling up, and was scared this would end in violence.

I took a deep breath and stood forward. 'Why have you interrupted our discussion?' I asked, in as reasonable a voice as I could muster, while quaking inside. 'There has been no problem here, until you came rushing in.'

'Stand still,' boomed the older one. 'There is too much moving around in here. This is supposed to be a lesson isn't it? You should all be sitting at desks.'

'And we saw somebody smoking,' added the other officer. 'Who's got the cigarette?'

The men were indignant. None of them had any cigarettes with them and there had been no lighting up. I was sure of that. I couldn't believe they were making up excuses like this to undermine our work in here.

'Nobody is smoking and there is no problem at all,' I insisted, realising this was just their excuse to stir up trouble, so that they could say they'd been right to worry in the first place. The silence lay heavy, and that worried me enough to face up to the officers. 'There's nothing wrong, so I don't understand why you came bursting in like that.'

'You need to be sitting still.'

'No, we don't. I explained to the Deputy-Governor that we would be having a teaching and discussion session and that some of the men would find it difficult to sit still for long, so they needed to be able to fidget and move around to help them think. That's all that was happening, and it was meant to happen. She gave her permission.' I paused, then continued, gaining momentum. 'This is my teaching session and we were all having an excellent discussion until you interrupted us. These men are all learning and enjoying their time here and behaving like the good citizens they are capable of being, if they were only given the skills to do that, which is what today is about. Or it would have been if you hadn't interrupted.'

For a moment I cringed – perhaps I had said too much and angered them more than necessary. Some of the men gave me a sly, admiring smile when I finished speaking. I was so fearful that the security officers would stop this discussion altogether, even though we weren't doing anything wrong.

'Somebody must have some cigarettes,' insisted the younger one as they both walked around the room, poking about and looking for anything incriminating, but they found nothing.

As this was going on, I watched the men for any danger signs. They all looked indignant and clearly resented this intrusion as much as I did. I did notice though that the younger of the two guards looked rather uncomfortable with his superior's aggressive manner. Eventually, to my surprise, he spoke up for us.

"I think they're fine. We ought to let it continue, because this is the only person who is really doing anything to help these men and the only one listening to them.'

'Huh,' grunted the older officer. 'It shouldn't be allowed. These scum don't deserve any help.'

I groaned silently, against the shuffling and fidgeting of the prisoners as they reacted to this insult.

Don stood up to speak for them. 'Please look at them. These prisoners are all really interested and engaged in what Jackie is saying about their dyslexia, as you can see.'

'Yes,' agreed the younger guard. 'This is the only woman giving them a chance. I think we should leave and let her carry on with the session.'

'OK, then,' nodded the senior officer, then added ominously: 'But remember, we're watching you!'

Thank goodness the men settled down once the security officers had gone and the discussion got back on track again. When we finally finished talking we realised that two and a half hours had gone by. I was astonished. Not one of these hardened criminals had gone out of line and I told them how proud of them I was.

'I hope you all agree that this has been a very helpful discussion and we've all learnt a lot, including me. You've helped me to think about some new ways to do things inside the prison and I'm going to go off and plan those straight away. I want to work with all of you as well, so I'll be back.'

'Yes,' said Don. 'And I've learnt a lot too. I'm not dyslexic, but now I know so much more about how to help you guys, so thank you for that, and thanks to Jackie too.'

They all gave me a cheer and applause. '

'It was great. When can we do it again?' said one of them.

'Thanks for really listening to us,' said another.

'Jackie went to a lot of trouble to get permission to have this session today,' explained Don, to my embarrassment. 'Everyone told her it wouldn't work and you'd all cause trouble, but you didn't. You've been brilliant, and I'm so proud of you for staying calm even when the security guys burst in. You did Jackie proud and you've helped her prove that she was right in believing in you.'

'Yes, thank you all for working together so well.' I was nearly in tears as they left with their escorts to take them back to their cells.

After lunch, I went straight back to B wing to find Carl.

'Thank goodness we don't have to speak through the bars today!' I said. 'So you told me you'd like to help me with some of the prisoners?'

'Yes. Being a listener in here, I talk with a lot of the men who have learning difficulties; some of the ones you're teaching. I read their letters to them and write letters for them too. They all go on about how great you are at teaching them, or how much they want you to help them, so I thought maybe

I could help you reach more of them and support what you're doing.'

'That sounds like a really good idea. I do have one or two literate prisoners like you in other wings who act as mentors for the men in between my visits. Maybe you'd like to do the same in this wing?'

'What does being a mentor mean?'

'Well, a mentor can go into a prisoner's cell, as you already do, and help him with his learning, maybe work with him on the computer if there's one available to use in his cell, or get him focussed on any practice or homework I've asked him to do. Or you could go with him to work on the Lexion dyslexia software on the library computer, or do some multi-sensory work with him, if I teach you how.'

'That sounds great.'

'This type of mentoring is called peer-mentoring, because it's one inmate helping another, with opportunities to talk and share experiences to support the work. Have you ever done anything like this before?'

'Not exactly, but as a listener, I am already trusted by a lot of the men who tell me their troubles and I help them talk things through. Also, before I came in here this time, I was trained by the Samaritans to take their phone-calls and deal with all kinds of problem situations.'

'Wow, that must have been interesting, but probably quite stressful too.'

'Yes, it was, interesting and sometimes very stressful, but it was satisfying too when you could help people through their worries.'

'So tell me about yourself.'

"I'm thirty-eight, this is only my second time in prison and I've moved about a bit. I lived in Holland for a few years, when my mother was there, to keep out of trouble really, but mostly in England.'

'What about your childhood?'

'That was OK, until my parents separated when I was twelve. I went wild and had to be put into care when I was thirteen. That was when things started to go wrong. I was in care till I was about seventeen, when I got into a bit of trouble and ended up in borstal for nine months. When I got out of there, I got into the drugs scene and they nicked me for importing drugs. I got twelve years for that and when I was released my mother persuaded me to go and stay with her in Holland. I worked in a restaurant as a kitchen orderly, then trained to be a chef. Later I got into the building trade.'

'It sounds like you began to sort your life out again.'

'Yes, I made good out there. I started my own building business and employed English workers.'

As he was talking I had a better look at his tattoos. I noticed he had some on his hands as well as the ones on his head and neck, and a teardrop tattoo below the corner of his eye. They did make him look quite scary, so I tried to focus instead on his engaging smile.

'Then I came back to England,' he continued. 'And joined what I thought was a legit importing business. They told me we were bringing in crates of Iraqi artefacts, but the police said the crates were full of heroin and cocaine – millions of pounds worth of the stuff.'

'How come you didn't realise?' I asked.

'Well, I don't know, really,' he shrugged. 'I suppose I must have been naive.'

97

'So what happened when the police found out?'

'Well, that was when everything hit the fan. One of my mates in the gang, well I thought he was a mate; he shopped me and said I was the leader and it was all down to me. He got off scot-free and the police gave him a new identity. It was all over the papers at the time.'

'So how long is your sentence?'

'Eighteen years.' His eyes dimmed as he said this and his shoulders hunched. 'It's a long time. I could be in my fifties before I get out, and my daughter will have grown up without me.' He paused, then his eyes brightened a little. 'My brief is putting together some papers for an appeal. I'm hoping that will shorten my sentence a lot. I've already been in here for more than a year.'

'When do you think the appeal will be?'

'Quite soon, I hope. The sooner the better, but knowing the courts, it might take a while, so I'm really keen to help you while I'm waiting. You're doing such great work with these guys.'

We talked for a little longer about Carl's circumstances. He told me more about his daughter, whom he adored, but she was ill in hospital, so he was very worried about her. They wouldn't let him go and see her. He looked so sad when he was talking about her, like any Dad really. I felt a real empathy for him, being stuck inside the prison, just a few miles away, and only able to phone once or twice a week to see how she was; never able to talk to her for more than a few minutes. So many of the men must be in a similar position with their families, and it must be even worse for the children, especially when they were young, like Carl's daughter.

'Let's think about the ways you can help me,' I said. 'You know a lot of the men and, from what I've seen, they obviously respect you. Do you know much about dyslexia?'

'No, not really. But I'd like to learn. I know there are many prisoners who can't fill in forms, so when they get out of here, they can't get jobs or claim any benefits and turn to crime to feed themselves or their families. I see it again and again. They leave one week and they're back in again a couple of weeks later. There's got to be some way we can help them get on their feet and prepare them for their release so that they can do something better with their lives.'

'You're right,' I said. 'I hadn't realised how often these men came straight back, but I reckon we can work on this.' I paused to think about it. 'The first thing is if I show you the computer software and you can see how that works, then you could use it with some of the dyslexic men on this wing. I already have a couple of mentors working on other wings, but nobody in B wing yet, so you'll be a great support in here.'

'How can I find out more about mentoring, and about dyslexia? I need to know if I'm going to be any use.'

'I'll bring in some information for you, some books about mentoring and dyslexia and some research work I did about different teaching and learning styles. Would you have time to read them?'

'One thing I'm not short of is time!' He grinned. 'That would be great. I'd love to learn about everything. I'm really excited about this.'

'Great. I'll bring them in for you on Monday. Meanwhile, let me write some names down for you. These are some of the dyslexic men in this wing. Maybe you could find them and have a chat with some of them over the next couple of days?'

That weekend, as well as looking out the books for Carl as promised, I worked on an idea I had been thinking about and started to plan a new mentoring course, tailor-made to the needs of the prisoners, with all the things they could learn. This could be a huge opportunity, extending my reach across the whole prison, with the help of mentors in each of the wings,

I could teach more people and transform more lives, like I had done with Fred soon after I started. I was still teaching him of course, but by now Fred's literacy was improving fast and he was writing short letters home every week, reading magazines and he could even read and write text on the computer, which was where I came in.. Now I was teaching him how to read simple instructions and fill in forms so that he would be ready for a new start when he got out.

CHAPTER 6

TONY

On E wing, I had heard there was a habitually self-harming prisoner called Tony. The staff were at their wits' end as they didn't know what to do with him.

'Have you had any training in working with self-harmers?' I asked a young officer one day. She was relatively new, so I hadn't spoken with her before.

'No?' she looked surprised at the question and curious about any possibility of training prison staff about prisoners' problems. 'I didn't know there was any training. Self-harming is quite rare, isn't it?'

'You'd be surprised,' I said. 'There are quite a lot of us about.'

'What do you mean?'

'I used to be a self-harmer.'

'No!' I saw the look of shock in her face. 'How ... I mean, why?' She was flustered now.

'Maybe you don't know, but I'm severely dyslexic, so I felt a real failure at school and I desperately wanted to learn. Nobody ever taught me the way I needed. One particular day, when I couldn't understand the lesson, I felt so furious and frustrated that I had to do something to ease the tension in my brain, so I slid my compass across the desk and down into my lap. I used it to score my arms and release my anger. It was such a relief when I saw the blood oozing out! And nobody noticed. That was the first time, and I did it almost every day from then on.'

'Really?' She looked aghast. 'Well, I was never any good at school either. I remember some awful lessons, but I don't think I was as badly dyslexic as you. And it never occurred to me to do that.'

'Well, for me it didn't stop there. Self-harming somehow let me feel alive. When I self-harmed it was something I could control, in a way that I couldn't control or understand anything else at school. So I was doing it for a reason. I think Tony must have a reason to do it too. What we need to do is to find out what that is. Do you think I could see him, and have a chat about it? I'm sure I could help him.'

'Yes, I think he's just in his cell this morning. Let me go and have a word with him. I expect he's heard about you – all the men are talking about how great you are, helping them with their learning. Maybe he will agree to talk with you.' She paused. 'But if he doesn't want to see you, I can't make him.'

'OK. I understand. But my guess is he will want to talk about his own problems. Tell him I'm a good listener.'

'Yes, I will. I've heard the men say you really listen to them.'

A few minutes later she came back. 'There's no spare office or room to use today, so I've arranged for you to meet Tony in the chapel. Is that all right with you?'

'Yes, fine. At least it's quiet in there and we won't have any distractions. That makes such a difference.'

I walked to the chapel with her. 'So he wants to see me then?' I smiled.

'Yes, He seemed willing, even keen, though I've not seen him enthusiastic about anything else.' She handed me a folder. 'This is the record of all his self-harming incidents since he's been here,' she said. 'Before my time.'

I re-arranged a couple of chairs in a corner of the chapel and sat down to look at the notes she had given me. As soon as I opened the folder I could see it was a very long document, with what looked at a glance like at least seventy or eighty dates, perhaps more, all with written notes beside them. But before I could attempt to read any of it, Tony arrived.

'Hello Tony. Come and sit down.' The initial part of our conversation was him telling me about his cell and his mixed feelings about the E wing staff, some of whom were sympathetic, such as Miss Amey, but most of whom seemed to berate him about causing a nuisance by drawing attention to himself.

Finally, I broached the main subject. 'I always had problems with reading and writing when I was at school,' I began 'I didn't know then that I had severe dyslexia. I just thought I was useless – a failure. They thought at school that I wasn't capable of learning, just because I couldn't read and write properly, or remember what the teacher taught us.'

Tony's eyes, initially dull, seemed to brighten a little, as if taking an interest in my story, so I carried on.

'But I was desperate to learn. I wanted them to teach me, but they didn't know how. So I was frustrated and angry with everyone. I wanted to shout and scream, but I couldn't do that in the classroom, so I self-harmed to let out the tension.'

'That's like me,' said Tony. 'I get so frustrated and angry in here, and there ain't nothing else I can do about it, so I cut myself. Look.' He rolled up his sleeves for me to see. His arms were a mass of scars, all shapes and sizes, crossing over each other, some old, white scars, some pink and fading, and several recent wounds, livid red. 'I did this one last night,' he said. 'But nobody's noticed yet.'

'Do they check you?'

'Yes, every day. I'm always cutting. It's so f'ing boring in here. I can't read or write and I get fed up with television all day long. It makes me angry, so I cut. I can't show you most of my scars – they're all down my legs and everywhere on my body. There ain't a place I haven't cut.' He seemed almost proud of that achievement, though I sensed that underneath he was very unhappy with his situation.

'Why do you have to sit in your cell all day? Is that for your own protection?'

'No. It's because there was nothing else I could do.'

'Did they ask you in the induction wing what you wanted to do, work or education?'

'Yes, but I can't do neither of those, can I? I can't even read my letters myself, never mind writing any. I can't read safety instructions, or laundry labels, or recipes or nothing, so I can't do work.'

'You've told me you have difficulties with reading and writing, but have you told the staff?'

'No, the screws never bothered to ask.'

I was shocked, after all the work I'd done getting the dyslexia check-list included in the prisoner assessments.

'Didn't they go through a dyslexia check-list with you when you first came in?'

'No, nothing. I think they've seen me so often in the past that they didn't bother to do any assessment with me.'

'So how many times have you been inside?'

'I dunno. But the judge told me at my trial that it's more than forty times since I was fourteen.'

'No?' I was genuinely shocked. 'You don't look old enough for half that!'

'I'm thirty-two,' he said, sheepishly. 'And it's true what that judge said. He was surprised too.'

'So, how long are you in for this time?'

'Four years.'

'What for?'

'Oh, just drugs mainly ... and a little bit of violence.' He seemed rather cagey about this, so I didn't ask him any more about it.'

'So, if you didn't choose to take a job in the prison, what about education?'

'Well, that's classrooms, ain't it? I can't do classrooms. They scare me rigid. I come out in a cold sweat if I go anywhere near a schoolroom. That's enough to make me violent. I can't do education.'

'You sound just like me,' I said.

He looked surprised. 'Are you taking the piss?'

'No, really.' I shook my head. 'I always hated classrooms. I hated school and couldn't wait to get out. School was my prison. I never had a good day in school for all those ten years. I just wanted out.'

'Me too. I got expelled from some of my schools. I had a terrible childhood – very unhappy, so I was always a

105

mess. I couldn't control myself. I still can't. The only way I can stop my aggression is by self-harming. That lets out my anger, just like you said.'

'But if you could have someone to teach you in new ways, to help you learn to read and write properly, but not in a classroom, would you be interested?'

He looked uncertain. I had already noticed, from his dull eyes, the way he dragged his feet when he walked and slouched when he sat down, that his self-esteem was very low. I gave him time to think it over.

'Maybe,' he muttered. 'But that's never going to happen, is it?'

'Yes it is,' I answered brightly. 'It's already happening. It's what I'm doing every day in my project – teaching men the skills in completely new ways. I teach them on their own to start with, in small rooms, or places like this, or the library. So I can teach you too if you like, and work with you to learn. And I can also arrange a mentor for you if you want.

He looked stunned. 'I've heard about you,' he said. 'They say you are the Florence Nightingale of prisons, except you don't have a lamp. But I thought they were having me on. How could anyone teach someone like me to read and write, when nobody could ever manage it before?'

'Well, I always thought that too. I was over forty years old and I tried masses of courses in all sorts of things, before I finally found just one tutor who understood. She was the one who first told me it wasn't me, it was the fact that I had dyslexia. That was the thing that was stopping me learning. After she diagnosed me, I got lots of help with learning and I loved it. I was even asked to help other students like me to learn. That's where I started with all this I suppose.'

'So you really think you could help me?'

'Absolutely. I know I can.'

'And I'll be able to read and write?'

'Yes, as long as you want to.'

'And I won't have to go into a classroom?'

'That's right.'

He sat forward, his eyes sparkled and he looked quite excited for the first time. 'When can I start?' He grinned at me. 'I can't wait.'

'OK. I'll come back tomorrow and we can start assessing your strengths and the best ways to work with you.'

That afternoon, I worked on my ideas for training the mentors and, when that was done, I started to think about running some learning workshops for the prisoners at the lowest 'entry' levels of literacy skills.

First I put together a list of inmates who I thought could make good mentors. Some, like Carl and Don, were men who had already come forward to work with me and were now helping individual prisoners with dyslexia or brain-damage. Others had volunteered to help and I recruited a couple more promising inmates that I had noticed as I went round the prison.

One of these was Tobe, an intelligent teenager whose parents were both lawyers back home in Ghana. He had come to England to go to university, but before he started he was accosted by a London gang. They threatened him into joining them on their crime spree, and he got a ten year sentence for murder. He was thrilled when I asked him to join the mentor training.

Another inmate I spotted as having potential to help others was Jazz. He didn't have dyslexia, but he had suffered accidental brain-damage as a child, which had given him some learning difficulties and had changed his personality from a lovely, caring child into an aggressive tearaway, always in trouble, going on to serve a string of prison sentences. Having grown up in a loving home, Jazz had that willingness to help others, and I thought this could be the saving of him.

Now I had my list of ten trainee mentors, I organised the course itself. First I had to find a room that would be available on the days we needed it. Next, I applied for permission from the prison management, through the Deputy-Governor herself, to release these prisoners from their various wings to be allowed to join the course, so that we could ensure their regular attendance, which would be very important, as they had so much to learn.

Finally, while all this was in hand, I set about planning the course in more detail. There would be eight modules. The first would be a general introduction to the role of a mentor, that covered peer-mentoring and how it worked, together with the different aspects and responsibilities of the mentoring role. The second session would be about hidden disabilities, such as dyslexia and brain-damage, what they are and how they affect people, how to identify and address them. This was a key module of the course.

Other sessions would be IT skills and using computers to assess and support dyslexic learners, multi-intelligences and learning styles, Neuro-Linguistic

Programming, Multi-sensory learning, and using DVDs to help teach prisoners to pass their theory driving tests and construction skills tests. We would also spend some time on working with prisoners to give them the necessary skills for filling in some of the most essential forms when they were released, such as benefits forms or job applications. Finally I'd got it all organised, with the help of some of the senior officers. Now I just needed to make sure we got off to a good start.

The first session was an eye-opener. Everybody arrived on time and they all seemed keen to begin. Some of them knew each other, but others didn't, so we started with the usual introductions session, which expanded into a very good discussion about peer-mentoring, comparing the experiences of those who'd been doing it and discussing the aspirations of the others to learn new skills and help their fellow inmates.

'Let's try a bit of role-play now,' I suggested. 'Let's have you in pairs, one as the mentor and one as the learner. You'll have to take turns with your roles. I'll tell you when it's half-time.'

'Will you bring round the oranges, Miss?' quipped one of the younger ones, football-mad.

It all went very well and nobody wanted to stop when our time was up. It seemed to be a great success so far. I just hoped they would all come back again the next week.

'That was great, Jackie,' said Don. 'I'm so glad you picked me to be one of the first.'

'I really love working with you,' added Carl. 'It's eye-opening. There is so much I could do in this role and I'm already learning new skills, even though I'm becoming an old dog at it!'

'Do any of you think you might be interested in taking on a mentoring job when you get out, with young people, say, or a charity organisation, or even ex-prisoners?'

They all put up their hands straight away.

'OK, that's great. I'll see you here again next time for the session on hidden disabilities.'

'You make it sound like a treasure-hunt!' joked Tobe.

'Jackie's the treasure here,' smiled Jazz. 'I've seen some mentoring myself, in the community, but it was nothing like as good as this.'

When I returned to E wing the morning after my first chat with Tony, I took with me some assessment materials and arranged for us to have the computer available in the chapel. First I ran through the dyslexia checklist with him and found that his reading and writing ages were very low, in line with an infant school child. However, he seemed to be quite bright. I took him through some of the early Lexion computer assessments and jotted down his strengths and weaknesses. We soon found out that his best learning style was practical, so I started him off, using a small, portable sand-tray and some plastic letter pastry-cutters. I asked him to make the shapes of letters and identify them, then to try spelling his family's names and some simple words. Then we tried writing them in the air and on our hands. Already he seemed more lively.

'You've made great progress this session, Tony,' I said as we were packing up. 'I'm proud of you. Shall we do some more tomorrow?'

'Yes please. This is the first time I've ever enjoyed doing letter-work.' He gave me a broad smile. 'I'm surprised at myself. I never knew learning could be fun!'

'I'll come again tomorrow, and leave you some things to do in between my visits. I won't be able to work with you every day, but if you like I could give you a mentor who could help you to keep going with things I plan for you. Would you like me to organise that for you?'

He looked a bit uncertain. 'It depends who it is.'

'OK, suppose I send you my top mentor, Carl? He's as good as I am.'

'He can't be! But if you think he's the best, I'll give him a try.'

The next day I worked with Tony on some other activities and left him with some computer practice tasks to do in the library and a variety of practical things to try out when he was in his cell.

'With all this to do,' he said, 'I won't have any time to watch the TV no more!'

Now I had to try and get permission for Carl to be allowed onto E wing to work with Tony. Being an optimist, I knew I could manage it somehow, especially if I went to see the Deputy-Governor herself. It took a bit of persuading but, sure enough, she eventually agreed.

'Why is it that you can always twist my arm?' she laughed.

'Because I'm worth it,' I grinned.

'Yes,' she said, thoughtfully. 'You can be a darned nuisance sometimes – the bane of my life. But you're right, you are worth it. You're doing a grand job here and the prison has never been as calm as it is since you came. That must say something!'

'Thanks.'

'So what's your next mission impossible?' she asked as I got up to go. 'I expect you've got some new, mad idea to reinvent the prison world?'

Should I tell her now? Yes, since she was in a good mood, it was the perfect opportunity, so I sat down again. 'Well, as it happens, I do have a new plan, to start some learning workshops ... and then I want to put on some family days on Saturdays ... and ...'

'Whoa! One thing at a time. What are these learning workshops about?'

I briefly explained my idea to her. 'Four or five of the most severely dyslexic prisoners, each one with their own mentor. We would need to have three separate half-day sessions, covering all the aspects of understanding their dyslexia, then identifying their strengths in other areas and building on these to develop their basic skills and equip them to manage their lives better once they get out. We would help them to develop their own personal action plans and set themselves targets they can work towards .' Phew, I thought. How did I think all that up so quickly?

'It sounds like a good idea, but I'd need to know much more. Do you really think it could work?'

'I know it could,' I said, with more confidence than I realised I possessed.

'OK, work out the details and give me something in writing.'

I gave her a look. 'Do I have to write it down?'

'Sorry, Jackie. I know it's difficult, but I won't be able to swing this without something concrete to go on. Remember, I'm on your side, if you can present it as a detailed plan.'

'OK. Thank goodness for computers and spellcheckers,' I grinned. I'll try and put it together for you over the weekend.'

When I came back the next Monday, I went straight to the management block and handed the Deputy-Governor's assistant my proposal to put on her desk. Now that I had the workshops planned out, I needed to put together a list of the five neediest prisoners and their mentors to join this first group. I don't think it ever occurred to me that I might not get the go-ahead, so it was fortunate that I did, within days, with full management support.

I started to go round and see the chosen learning workshop students and their mentors. I told the mentors first: Don, Jazz, Max, Tobe and of course Carl. I was a bit anxious about the students. What if I gave them the option to attend, and none of them said 'yes'? Fortunately, my first four agreed straight away – a great relief.

My final candidate was Tony. I knew how wary he was of any group-learning situation, so I explained it all to him very carefully. I didn't want to frighten him off before he even knew what it was about, so I just told him about what it would involve, without saying I wanted him to do it.

'There will only be four or five learners in the first group.' I said. 'I've got four, but I'm not sure about whether to have a fifth.'

'Why not?' He asked. 'Don't you have enough people who want to do it?'

'It's not that ...'

'Well, how about me? I reckon I could do that, if it's what you say, and if Carl is there. Or is he already booked in with somebody else?'

'No, not at the moment,' I said. Of course, when I had told Carl about it and said I wanted him to be there, I also explained about Tony and how I was going to broach it to him. I was relieved that my plan seemed to be working.

'Do you think you could handle learning in a group?'

'Well, it ain't school is it? And what you're going to do sounds good fun. I reckon I could learn a lot, with Carl there as well.'

'Yes, he'd be working with you, so that you could practise things and talk about it in between sessions.'

'OK. Can I do it?'

All we needed to do now was set the dates and get started.

Meanwhile the mentor training was progressing well ... until its 5th week. We were all ready and waiting to start that days' session, but where was Carl? There was always at least one officer outside the door and I asked him if he knew why Carl couldn't come.

'He's being moved to another prison.'

'What? When? ...' I was horrified. Carl was a key member of my team. He knew all the people to go to on each wing to get things done, or to work with the prisoners. He had read all the books I'd given him and developed some additional suggestions of his own to improve the way we did things. He was the man I always went to if I had any problems in the prison, and he had the greatest understanding of what difficulties prisoners would face on their release, and how to handle them. He was a star, and we all needed him there on our course, especially as we were hoping to put on our first presentation and awards ceremony in a few weeks' time, and he would have a big part to play in that. Yet now it seemed he might not even be there.'

As soon as the session was over, I raced across to see the Deputy-Governor. If anyone could sort this out, she could.

'I believe Carl's being moved to another prison, because his solicitor has lodged an appeal.'

'But why does he have to move now? Surely the appeal won't be heard for ages?'

'That's true, but it's just the way it's done,' she said.

'Well, can't it be undone? He's doing so much good here, and the men really respect him. He's my Head of Mentors. He even leads parts of the mentor training for me. We need him for the awards ceremony too – he's the mentors' leader and I was hoping he would be able to do a presentation for that. Can't you at least defer his move?'

'I can try ... if he hasn't already gone.'

That was what I was afraid of. So often a prisoner would not be given any advance notice that he was to be moved, so I desperately hoped it would not be too late.

Later that day, before I went home, I went back to see her. I knocked and popped my head round her door. 'Any news?'

'Come in,' she beckoned. I checked earlier for you and Carl is still here ...'

'Phew!' I breathed a sigh of relief.

'But the plan was for him to be moved this afternoon. I asked for a stay to be put on his move until at least tomorrow morning and I'm waiting to hear from his solicitor's office now. Have a seat and I'll call them.'

She picked up the phone and keyed in the number. I sat and listened to the one-sided conversation, trying not to react too loudly. 'So you are willing to agree to Mr Nixon staying with us for another few weeks? ... Thank you. He's one of our top mentors and I know he will be very pleased that he won't have to let anybody down and can complete the work he is doing to help fellow prisoners here. ... Yes, I'll get back to you with a revised transfer date, once it's been agreed. ... I'm very grateful for your help.'

As she put the phone down, I jumped up and cheered. 'Hooray! Thank you, thank you thank you. I said. I wanted to give her a hug, but maybe that would have been going too far. I was so relieved and excited that he could stay, at least till after he'd finished the course with me and after the presentation. Now I'd need to track him down and fill him in on what we'd done today, and discuss our plans to prepare for the presentation on the awards day.

Carl looked a bit down when I arrived. 'I was so depressed and frustrated when they told me this morning I couldn't come to the training because I had to be moved. I felt like kicking off. But then the Deputy-Governor came to see me herself.'

'Really? I didn't know she'd done that.'

'Yes, she came specially to talk it through with me,' he explained, breaking into a smile that lit up his whole face.

'So you knew before I got here?'

'Yes,' he said.

'You mean thing,' I teased him. 'You might have told me straight away when I arrived.'

'I couldn't resist having you on first!'

'I could kick you,' I joked, 'but that would be touching a prisoner, and I mustn't get into trouble for doing that!'

'I don't know how you swung it,' he grinned. 'But thanks. You're not just a teacher – you're a real friend!'

The Learning Workshops started well, with a module called 'What am I good at?' which caused some laughter, so I had to get them all back on track. Everyone did a learning-styles assessment to see if it matched what they thought about how they learned best. As expected, most of them had their greatest strength as practical learning, with some visual learners and very few with any strength in their auditory memory, which is often a hidden problem of dyslexia. We looked at qualities and skills, had half an hour with the Lexion computer software, which everyone always enjoys, and finally we talked about the 'Where am I now?' question, based on all that we had discussed that morning.

'I know where I am,' smiled Tony. 'I'm on the up. This was fun. I'm glad I came.'

The following two half day sessions went equally well and everyone finished with their own individual learning plan which focussed on their next steps to further improve their literacy skills, together with their personal action plan for how they would prepare to cope with rehabilitiation on their release, including a package for Perry on how to deal with the tax and VAT demands, and a set of forward targets to aim for. At the end of that last session, I asked them if they wanted to say anything about the Learning Workshops.

'Thanks for all your help,' said thirty-two-year-old Calum, with a reading age of seven. 'I thought I was good-for-nothing. I couldn't work or pass any exams at school, so I turned to a life of crime. Then these techniques of yours came along. I have amazed myself with how much I've improved' He paused and everybody nodded.

'Yes, you've made great strides with your literacy skills,' I agreed.

'I have been about for a long time,' Calum continued. 'But no one has ever sat me down and listened, or told me I had dyslexia. When I take my tests, it'll be goodbye to prison for ever!' We all clapped and cheered. I shall always remember the look of amazement on his face that his peers were applauding him.

'We have time for just one more...' I said.

Tony stood up and faced us all. 'I never had the help I should have been offered,' he began. 'I wanted to go for jobs, but I knew I didn't stand a chance. I always found paperwork hard. Jackie was the first person ever to have come to me and given me one-to-one help. It's about time something like this happened in jails. It's blinding!'

CHAPTER 7

WOLFIE

Anything that went wrong in the prison, they always used to call me in – 'Jackie will find a way. She's got the magic touch.' It was as if I was some kind of miracle worker. That's what they seemed to think I was. One time I was being hunted down all over the prison, and all the management staff were trying to find me.

Finally a senior officer located me.

'Quick, Jackie! You're wanted on the Hospital wing.'

'What for?'

'I've no idea. All I know is that a nurse over there has sent out an urgent call for you to go over there pronto.'

What a shock. I left everything and dashed across as requested, fearful of what might have happened. I assumed it was one of the prisoners I was working with, but who? Maybe someone had suffered a heart attack, or been injured.

I rushed through security as fast as I could and found the nurse who'd called for me.

'I'm Jackie Hewitt-Main,' I said, out of breath. 'Who is it?'

'What do you mean?' she asked.

'Well, I'm assuming that one of my learners or mentors has had some kind of medical emergency.'

'Oh no, it's nothing like that.'

'Then what ... ?'

'I have a patient here with a head injury and I've been trying all day to persuade the NHS to take him in at the local General Hospital. But every department I spoke to said no, they have no free beds. I'm pulling my hair out here. Can you use some of your magic and do it for me? Everyone told me you're the miracle worker round here and you'd be able to help. I need to transfer him right away.'

I was shocked. How was I supposed to be able to do that?

'I know I'm famous for being persuasive,' I said. 'But this really isn't part of my role, so I don't think it would be allowed.'

Arriving at security one morning, I was asked to go straight to Wolfie's cell, right into the cell to see him. This was a very unusual request, especially for a new prisoner, and I wondered whether it would even be allowed when I got to the VP wing. The officers there had to be so careful, with having mostly dangerous or vulnerable prisoners in their care. I went straight over and let myself in as usual. Not knowing his cell number, I had to ask an officer, so I was glad to see Miss Amey looking out for me.

'Thanks for coming,' she said, with a look of concern. 'I thought we'd better ask for you as we have a new prisoner who is very disabled and we don't know how to handle him or help him.' She paused. 'I'm hoping you'll be able to talk to him and assess his needs as we don't know where we're going with him at all, and he's getting quite stroppy because we're getting it all wrong and he isn't getting the things he needs. Can you give us a lead on all this?'

'Well, I know I'm special needs,' I sighed, then smiled at the double meaning. 'But I haven't trained to support people in wheelchairs with physical disabilities. I'm fine with going to see him and having a chat, but are you sure you want me to go into his cell?'

'Yes. I know we don't usually allow it, except for exceptional circumstances, but wheelchairs and Victorian buildings don't go together. That's why he has to be in a ground floor cell. It's very difficult to move him around in this wing – impossible in some parts of the building. We just don't know how to cope with him.'

'Mmm, I can see the problem. OK, I'll do my best – where is his cell?'

Miss Amey took me there herself and introduced me to Wolfie, who was sitting disconsolate in his basic, prison-issue, canvas wheelchair in the middle of his cell.

I began by introducing myself as usual, and explained that the officers had asked me to come and talk with him. I knew nothing about him yet, so I needed to find out.

'Tell me your story, Wolfie. How did you get to be in this wheelchair?'

'You're the first person who's asked me that since I got here,' he said.

'Did you have an accident, or is it since birth?'

'An accident – well, two accidents really. I used to be fit and healthy, great at sports and all that. That's why I joined the army when I left school. It was a great life in the Queen's Regiment. We all had a high old time, literally some days.'

As I listened to him tell his story, I began to realise that, whilst he didn't look it with his tattoos and scars, he was an intelligent man, though I didn't yet realise quite how intelligent he was.

'That's a coincidence,' I said. 'My ex-husband was in the army too. I used to live on an army base with our children while he was away on overseas service. We must compare notes. Maybe we've been in the same places.' I smiled. 'But go on with your story.'

'OK,' he nodded. 'Well, when some of us were asked if we would like to do some jumping – that's parachute jumping of course, I jumped at the chance – no pun intended! Luckily, I was accepted and went through all the training. I loved the rush of leaping out into the void, surrounded by nothing but the whistling wind, dropping for as long as possible before finally pulling the rip-cord and jerking into a float that buffeted me gently down to the ground. It was wicked!'

'You make it sound like a dream. In fact you almost make me want to do it myself, but I know I couldn't, I'm so frightened of heights.'

'I reckon you could. It's really kicking. It's so exhilarating that you forget about the height you're at, and the patchwork landscape of the ground beneath – everything really. It's more of a buzz than any of the drugs I've taken!'

'Wow. Maybe I'll have to try it out sometime.'

'It was all going great,' he said. 'I'd done loads of jumps and landed perfectly every time, until this one day in 1999. I jumped out from the helicopter as usual, and dropped as far as I dared. When it was time to pull the cord, it didn't seem to come like it should have done. I wrestled with it for several seconds before it untangled itself and the chute went up, but by then I'd dropped too far, and crashed with a searing pain on the hard ground.'

'That sounds awful,' I sympathised.

'It was awful. It was the end of my army career, right there, on the rock-hard earth of a foreign field.' He stopped to gather his emotions, but I noticed how watery his eyes had become and how a muscle twitched rather fast on the side of his cheek. He looked like a hard man, a typical army type.

'I broke my back,' he said. 'Simple as that. I think I knew it might happen one day, waiting so long to pull the cord. It was a great danger rush, but it ended up going too far.'

'Did you have to spend long in hospital?'

'Yes, I had an operation. Then I was in hospital for months, in a wheelchair at first, though a better one than this antique,' he sneered. 'I don't think they could have found me a more useless conveyance in a museum!'

'No, it's not up to much is it?' I agreed. 'I'll ask around and see if we've got anything better. There are all sorts of whizzy modern wheelchairs these days, aren't there, that can go up and down steps and everything.'

'Yes, but they cost thousands,' he said. 'I don't think they'll be getting me one of those!'

'No, they're too strapped for cash in prisons these days.'

'Prisons always have been. We're thrown into the sink and left here to rot.'

'So what happened when you left hospital?'

'Well, by then they had given me lots of physiotherapy and rehabilitation sessions, teaching me to walk again. I wasn't anything like as active as before,' he said with a sigh. 'But at least I was mobile. The only trouble was that I wasn't mobile enough for the army and I had to quit, as I knew I couldn't go on like that and I couldn't stand a desk job. So I was given a discharge, which helped. But it wasn't enough to set me up in civvy life. I'd never had to find my own place to live, or look after myself. I went to pieces at first, but gradually got myself sorted out, with a lot of help from my family. I had a home and people who loved me, but I hated not being in the army. I yearned for that comradeship, and the danger. Nothing could ever replace the life I'd had.'

'So if you learnt to walk again,' I said, to change the subject, as I could see his frustration building into anger. 'How come you are in a wheelchair now?'

'Like I said, I loved the danger rush. It was like an addiction. I couldn't parachute jump any more, so in 2003 I bought an old motorbike and pushed it to the limits.' He relaxed again as he remembered those days. 'It was mad – fast as the wind on those jumps. I needed the speed and the adrenalin. One day I was riding along the A13, at full throttle, when my brakes failed, just as I tried to slow down approaching a junction. Again, I'd left it till the last minute and the outcome was inevitable. I could see it coming, in slow motion, like freeze-frames in my brain.' Wolfie put his hands up instinctively, as if to shield his head, but then realised it was only a memory, not the real thing. 'It was the crash landing, all over again.'

'That sounds frightening.'

'I suppose it was, in a bad way this time,' he nodded slowly. 'I smashed into the back of a lorry, and was catapulted, head first, into a lamp-post. I could hear the crunching sound as I fell. I knew straight away it was my back again. That was when I blacked out.' He paused, recalling the details with a grave face. 'This time my back was broken in two separate places, and that wasn't all. I had 42 fractures altogether, broken bones all over my body. My left arm had the most, see.' He lifted his arm and rolled up his sleeve. It was so crooked and scarred that it made me feel nauseous. I had to look away before I was sick.

'When did you regain consciousness?'

'They told me I was in a coma for a month. All the medics thought I had brain-damage. They told my family that if I didn't die I'd almost certainly be a vegetable.'

'But you're far from that. It doesn't seem to have affected the cognitive parts of your brain.'

'No, when I woke up, I was fine that way, thank God. But it took another ten months for my body to recover from the accident, and this time they told me I would never walk again. I'm thirty-eight now ... and have to face the rest of my life in a sodding wheelchair.'

'Who told you that? Was it a specialist?'

'Oh, just the medics,' he said vaguely. 'Now I can't get that speed thing so easily.'

'Does that frustrate you?'

'Am I a snail? Of course it does. It used to be my raison d'être. Now I'm reduced to a maximum of three miles an hour in this bloody chair, if I can find someone to push me that fast!' He hit the arm of the chair with his fist, forgetting it was metal, so he had to nurse his hand. 'I'd rather be a vegetable,' he seethed between his teeth.

I didn't have an answer to that, so I changed the subject again.

'Is this your first time in prison?'

'Yes,' he struggled to recover his composure. I gave him time. 'My first ... and my last I hope!' he said in an attempt at light-heartedness.

'What are you in for?'

'I needed some excitement, so I got in with a gang. I had a mobility car, so they asked me to look after their weapons for them when they did a job. Suddenly, here was the chance I'd longed for – danger. I came alive when they put all their guns in the boot of my mobility car, ready for their next crime.' The spark returned to his eyes. 'I could say it never occurred to me that I'd get caught. But that would be wrong. It did occur to me. It was an ever-present possibility and it gave me that rush again when I drove to the rendez-vous that night, the night it happened.'

'What happened?' I didn't get what he meant.

'The police happened. They came into view on my mirror, right behind me, blue lights flashing. Oh that was so much fun. It's surprising how fast a mobility car can go! I led them on, then switched direction and shook them off for a bit, again and again, until finally they got me in a dead-end. That was when they found the weapons. I suppose it was, like they say, a fair cop!'

'So how long are you in for?'

'I don't know yet. I'm on remand until my case comes up.'

'How are you managing with things like meals, washing, and all that sort of thing?'

'I'm not managing. I get hardly any help and that means I can't wash every day or even eat sometimes, as this bleeding wheelchair won't fit through most of the doorways and nobody bothers to bring me anything or make everyday things possible, like they are for everyone else. They just take it all for granted and forget I need help.'

'Well, I can easily sort all that out. I'll get one of my mentors to help you. He can fetch your meals for you, help you to wash and shave, get you dressed and undressed and reach down the things you need. Will that be OK?'

'Yes thanks, That will be good – very good.'

Then I had an idea. This man needed his self-esteem lifting – something to give him a sense of purpose while he was inside.

'I need some help, too,' I said. 'And I think you can help me with that. We can help each other.'

'What do you mean?' He looked surprised ... and curious.

'I work with some of the men who have dyslexia, helping them to learn to read and write. We use lots of new approaches and make it fun, but the men often need mentors. I reckon you'd be really good at that. Do you think you could become a mentor?'

'I wouldn't know what to do.'

'That's no problem. I could train you and I'm sure you'd pick it up quickly. I have a lot of inmates who have been in the army too, and who need mentors with your kind of experience. What do you think?'

'OK,' he agreed brightly. 'I need something to do. I'll give it a go.'

Over the next few weeks, Wolfie did the training and started to work with a few of the men on the VP wing. Meanwhile I got one of the mentors to look out for him and help with all his daily needs, whilst I managed to source a slightly more comfortable wheelchair for him. It didn't go any faster or get through narrow spaces, but it looked smarter, with its black mock-leather upholstery.

Most days, after my first visit, I used to call in on Wolfie for a few minutes' chat before I went home. We shared our army stories and had quite a laugh. It seemed to cheer him up on his leaner days. Often though, I wouldn't find him in his cell, because he was mentoring one dyslexic prisoner or another. In fact, when I had to go into the prison one Sunday afternoon to pick something up, I popped into the VP wing to say hello. As I might have expected by now, he wasn't in his cell. I was pleased that he was able to get out and about a bit, now that I had arranged for there to be a computer with the dyslexia software installed and ready for him to use in the ground floor library, which was the only space he could access in his wheelchair. I went straight there, to find him engrossed in mentoring a new inmate with reading difficulties. He was so focussed on his work that he didn't see me arrive, so I tiptoed out again and found a member of staff to talk to.

'I've just found Wolfie mentoring a newcomer in the library,' I said. 'He's so into his work that he didn't even realise I was there!'

'You've given him a new lease of life,' said the officer. 'He loves helping the young ones, especially if they're ex-army like him. 'He's always helping them, right up to lights out some nights. He's much more cheerful now and less resentful of his situation, though he still needs so much help himself. Life is more difficult in here than it should be, to my mind, for someone like him. The prison really ought to have put him on one of the new wings and made sure he had easier access to things.'

'You're right there,' I agreed. 'I'm sure I'd complain more than he does, if it was me in that chair. I hate being dependent on other people. I'll see if I can arrange for him to be moved.'

I went back to the library, just as they were closing down the computer for the night.

It's good to see you working so hard on your mentoring,' I said to Wolfie, as his student left the library. 'You seem to be enjoying this new challenge?'

'Yes, it's great helping the youngsters,' he beamed. 'Perhaps I'll be able to do this when I get back on the outside.'

The dyslexia mentoring and teaching project was well-established after six months and we had already achieved a great deal, but there was so much I still wanted to do, so many ideas to introduce and so much work on the staff side of things to disseminate information and advice for dealing with learning disabilities.

I hadn't told any of the prisoners, not even Carl, who had become my right-hand man, but I had a great worry about how or even if I was going to be able to keep the project going, now that the first period of funding was up. It was only for those six months, and now I was without any financial support, for the project, for me or for my family. I wasn't even sure I could afford to keep my car going, and that was my only way to get to the prison, but somehow I kept struggling on.

Every day I was seeking out potential new sources of funding, but the summer stretched out with little immediate hope. I couldn't let the men down when they were doing so well. I had to keep it all going forward somehow. And that's what I did. But how much longer could it last? There must be somebody out there to save us, some charity organisation – I just had to find them.

CHAPTER 8

NEV

One of the complaints that kept coming up when I talked to dyslexic inmates was the problems they had with the menus. Every day, prisoners were given menus for the next day's meals and they had to tick whichever options they wanted. That was fine for the 47% of prisoners who were literate, and a few more were learning to read well enough to cope with some of the words, but about half the men in the prison were unable to understand the menus at all. Rather than admit they couldn't read a simple menu, most of them just ticked randomly, so of course they didn't know what they were going to get and often ended up with something they didn't like, or for those with health problems it might be something they couldn't eat.

I had an idea, and went to see Bob in the IT workshop to talk about a printing project.

'What I really want,' I explained, 'is a menu with pictures on it for each meal choice.'

'What for?' he asked, a little bemused.

'At the moment, prisoners who can't read well enough can't choose the meals they like. But if the menu had a picture of fish and chips, say, or of roast chicken for the main course, and apple or banana pictures for desert, they could easily choose what they'd prefer.'

'Oh, I see,' he stroked his chin. 'That's a clever idea.' He was deep in thought for a few seconds before he spoke again. 'But what if it's something like stew, how will they tell what kind of stew it is?'

'I'm sure if you ask your guys to come up with some ways to do that on the computer, some of them would, like maybe a casserole pot with a picture of a cow on the side?'

'Yes, you're right. That will make an excellent project to set them next week. Meanwhile I could work out the costings and so on. Would that be all right for you?'

'It would be great,' I said, with a sigh of relief. 'One more way that we can make the prison's routines more user-friendly.'

'Yep. I'll tell the lads about it tomorrow. That way they'll have some time to think about it.'

It turned out that it wouldn't cost much more and there was a spare bit of Bob's budget that would cover that, so he went ahead. Two weeks later the pictorial menus were in place and everyone was happy.

'This is kicking,' said one of the younger prisoners, when I took him one of the menus, hot off the press. 'Now I can choose what I like!'

Prisoners came inside for a variety of crimes and many of them had tragic stories to tell, but one of the saddest was 43-year-old Nev's story. I went to see him as soon as I heard about it.

The staff on the induction wing found a side-room for us and I met Nev there, with an officer outside the open door. It was always impossible to have true privacy inside, but that was about the closest we could get, so he seemed reasonably relaxed when he sat down on a comfortable chair I'd arranged at an angle to mine. That way we could talk without it seeming confrontational.

'Hi Neville, I'm Jackie Hewitt-Main.'

'Everybody calls me Nev.'

'OK. I usually talk to all the new prisoners when they come in here to see if they have any problems and how we can help. I gather you've had quite a lot of problems in your past?'

'Yes, you could say that. I can't remember a time when I didn't have problems,' he paused and gave me a sideways glance, as if to suss me out. Then he continued. 'Some people say that your life is laid out before you and whatever happens is fate. Well, I think that whoever planned my life must have been some schizophrenic comedian!'

'As bad as that?' I wanted to reflect back to him my sympathy without making any comments or judgements. This way I hoped he would open out to me.

'Yes. I'm not saying it's anybody's fault, but I never had anyone to turn to, or to share what I was going through.'

'Do you want to tell me about it?'

He gave me another look. Would he feel he could trust me enough?

'I'm a good listener,' I said. 'I had a few problems too when I was young. I always felt a failure and nobody listened to me. I wish they had, but maybe I could be that person for you?'

He still seemed reticent.

'How did it start?' I asked. 'Take me back to the beginning.'

That seemed to set him off. 'I was born in an institution for unmarried Irish mothers, unwanted, and spent the first five years of my life in a children's home. Then I was adopted by a couple who felt they should adopt a child because of their Christian beliefs – feed the hungry, house the homeless …' He stopped to compose himself. I said nothing, so he continued. 'They took me in, but they gave me no love, none of the love that every child needs. To me it seemed that I was taken away from my family, the children in the home, to a strange house on my own and no one to care about me.'

'How long were you with them?'

'Until they put me into a council-run boarding school when I was eleven. I'd been unhappy before, but that's when the real misery started.'

'What happened?' I prompted him, afraid that he would stop there.

'That's where I was first bullied. I was beaten up at night, too scared to sleep. It wasn't long before this led on to sexual abuse. At that time, it seemed easier to have the sexual abuse because at least I could sleep afterwards. The abusers would make out they were my mates. They gave me the attention I had never had, making me feel they cared about me, giving me presents and treats.' He sighed. 'But they were just using me for sex, for their own gratification.'

'Didn't you feel you could tell anybody about it?'

'There wasn't anyone to tell. They were all in it. Then one of these boys, through his own abuse, targeted me for his abusers, so between the ages of eleven and fifteen, I was used by him and by older men to do photos and films of us.'

'What happened after you were fifteen?' I asked in as normal a voice as possible, horrified by what he was telling me and hoping things would have improved for him.

'The criminal abuse just got worse, with the result that my anger and frustration went out of control. I would scream out to myself, to be heard, but sadly no one was there to listen. Then, as I got older, my trust in people went. I hated the way society was. I knew that some of these people that I should have been able to trust had positions of power that enabled them to carry on abusing kids like me.'

'What kind of people do you mean, the ones in power?'

'Teachers, older boys, some of the managers and important people outside the school. Well at least they told me they were important, to keep me quiet I suppose. Gradually I got involved in crime and it became a habit, a way to escape from the life I had. A cry for help I suppose.'

'Did that make you feel better?'

'No. But I was living day to day and I couldn't trust anyone. A girlfriend I had once said that her friends were my friends too, but I couldn't believe her. Even though I loved her, I still held up barriers because I didn't know how to tell her about me and my life. I couldn't bring myself to trust her.'

'Did you stay together?'

'No. In 1987 things got worse and I got six years for robbery. After serving three and a half years, I was given six months parole. But within that first month of freedom I got arrested for murder.'

'You certainly have had a hard life, haven't you? I know how close to crime so many people are who have been through bad things in their lives,' I said. 'My own son, after he suffered brain-damage in a car-accident, was getting into trouble with the police because he couldn't hack the difficulties that had affected his life. And he didn't have a quarter of the problems you've experienced.'

'I suppose life experiences affect everyone.'

'Yes. I'm sorry I interrupted your story. Can you go on with it? What happened next?'

'I'll tell you about the murder. I didn't mean to do it. It happened in the early hours of Christmas Day, 1990. I was just walking home, along the pavement, when a bloke came out of nowhere and tried to sexually assault me. I lost my temper and the result was that I had killed this guy within minutes.' He paused to take a deep breath. 'I never believed in red mist until that night. That's what I saw, a red mist. All the years of fear and abuse came back to haunt me and sent me wild. All the anger, frustration, hate and disgust came out of me. As I child I was never able to fight back. That night, my would-be abuser suffered the consequences of what all those others had done to me. In a way it was the crossroads of my life – a relief getting rid of the anger inside me. Yet, when I stood back and realized what had just happened, I couldn't believe that I had just killed this guy. I wasn't capable of killing anyone. So, for the first seven years of this sentence, I denied the crime. By not coming to terms with it, or admitting it, I was justifying to myself what I had done. I guess that's why the Judge gave me 99 years – a full life sentence.'

'That must have been a jolt, when you heard that.'

'Yes, but I had convinced myself I didn't do it, so I had no remorse or anything. I can see that now.'

'What helped you to see it?'

'It was just one day; I spoke to a senior prison officer on my wing, and told him that I had done it. I had killed the man. I knew it would open a can of worms about my past, but I put my trust in the prison to help me, and even more importantly, I put my trust in myself. Since then I've done three and a half years in therapy, talking and understanding myself. I started to do some courses as well. I did diplomas in fine art, art history and journalism, and several other courses too. I've even won awards for my art, writing and drama. Yet, prison becomes the children's home again. I will have to leave one day, if I live long enough, but hopefully I will be given some support this time.'

'So, you've been transferred here from another prison?'

'Yes. It's a bit like a new start, I suppose. But being here already makes me see that people do care, like you now. You and Miss Amey are helping me.'

'My project is about helping people, and I need someone like you to become a mentor. You've obviously got lots of skills and interests that you can pass on to others. A lot of the prisoners here are only just learning to read and write, through new ways of teaching, and they need to have mentors to help them. Do you think you might like to become a mentor?'

He smiled for the first time. 'Yes, it sounds good. I want to help other people.'

'I'll get some training organised for you. If you like, you could sit in on some of my sessions and see what's involved.'

'Thanks for listening to me,' he said. 'You were right.'

'What was that?'

'You are a good listener. I don't think I've ever told anybody as much as I've told you today.' He gave me a steady gaze. 'Thank you.'

Most of my time over the summer weeks was spent in my search for new sponsorship. To help this along, I started up an organisation which I called Mentoring 4 U. The mentoring that we'd done so far, and the training course which we'd developed here, were one of the major successes of these first few months and we needed to make it more available, not just to prisoners, but also to some of the prison staff who had expressed an interest, and perhaps involve community volunteers as well.

After my session with Nev, I called in on the IT unit, in the hopes of catching Bob. Sure enough, he was still there.

'Hi Jackie,' he said with a smile. 'Got any more jobs for us?'

'Yes, I have,' I laughed. It seemed my reputation always seemed to be ahead of me.

'What's it this time?'

'I want to have an advertising leaflet printed so that I can hand it all around the prison, to the staff as well as the inmates.'

He stopped what he was doing, grabbed a piece of paper and pencil and sat down at a table. 'Come and show me what you have in mind.'

'You know I'm not great at writing things down, or drawing pictures, but I can tell you about it. I'm very good at talking.'

'Yes, so I remember!'

I explained what I wanted and what it should include. 'Just a couple of folded A4 sheets will do,' I said. 'Maybe it could be on coloured paper and then we can just print in two colours on that, say black and red print on green?'

'Good idea,' he agreed. 'That will keep the costs down. By the way, who's paying for this?'

'Well, I hadn't thought of that. I was sort of hoping …'

'Not this time, Jack,' he said. 'I've used up all my budget now.'

'OK. I'll have to fund it myself, I suppose. How much do you think it will cost?'

'I'll work out some figures for you, but as it's you I'll keep the cost to a minimum. OK?'

'Great thanks!'

We finalised the leaflet over the next week and some of his prisoners did the designs and set up all the pages with the text written by Carl, Don, Wolfie and Nev. It looked great when it was done and I managed to persuade officers on all the wings to circulate to everyone. That brought us in quite a few more volunteers, so Carl and I ran another mentor training course.

I hoped this would help to attract one of the trusts who sometimes give grants or funds to a project like ours. I renewed my efforts and contacted everyone I could think of to plead our case. Sure enough, I finally managed to secure a new benefactor, 'Next Step', part of the Careers Service, and we were on track to continue with full funding again for the next nine months. Hooray! This was a huge relief and at last I could tell the mentors about it all. Of course they'd had no idea that there was a problem, although they did realise that I hadn't been able to spend as much time in the prison as before and had been great at filling in for me. But now, when I told them the history of this tricky stop-start funding, they were as thrilled as I was that our project was secure on its tracks again, for the time being at least.

CHAPTER 9

BARRY

I'd heard about a newly arrived prisoner on B wing with a lot of learning difficulties and disabilities, so I went over to find out more, hoping I could meet him and assess his needs. As I let myself in and walked a few paces forward, I was stopped in my tracks by a man I knew had a violent past, running towards me with a sharpened pencil in his hand. I began to walk backwards a few steps. Carl had told me about this prisoner's history, and the fact that he'd stabbed his last teacher in the neck with a sharply pointed pencil. I froze, petrified. Fortunately, one of the officers had seen this and ran straight over to me. At the same time, a number of nearby inmates rushed to gather round the man to stop him before he reached me.

'It's all right, Miss,' said one prisoner barring his path.

'Thanks,' I said, taking my first breath for several seconds.

The officer checked I was all right, then parted the crowd and pinned the prisoner against a wall with his arms behind his back.

'You've got it all wrong,' complained the man. 'I wasn't going to hurt her.'

'So what were you going to do?' asked the officer, with a degree of sarcasm, clearly doubting his words and holding onto him in a locked position.

'One of the guys was telling me last night what a good teacher she is,' the man explained, trying to turn his head. 'I just wanted to ask her to teach me. I want to learn to read and write.' Then he looked straight at me with a pleading expression. 'Can you teach me, like the others?' he asked. 'I never learned at school.'

I relaxed after that. 'I'm here to see another prisoner this morning, but if I have time later I'll ask one of the officers to come with me to have a chat with you.'

'Thank you,' he said. 'That would be great.'

As the man was marched off to his cell, two other officers came across to me, smiling broadly.

'Thank goodness you're here,' said one.

'We knew you'd come when you heard about Barry,' added the other. 'He's in such a state, and we don't know what to do with him.'

'I'll take you to see him,' said the first officer. 'But before that, there's somebody else I have to take you to meet.'

'I'd rather go straight to see the new prisoner,' I said.

'No, you've been summoned. You need to meet this man first. He's the top-dog prisoner, the real muscle of B wing, so what he says goes! He wants to vet you before you see Barry. If he likes you and wants to help you, it will make things a lot easier for your project in this wing'

I was annoyed at the delay, but had no choice, so off we went to a ground-floor cell, big enough for two, but used as a single room, all freshly decorated.

'Morning Henry,' said the officer. 'Here's the lady you wanted to see.' Then he turned to me. 'In you go. I'll wait outside.'

142

It was a most unusual situation. As soon as I walked in and saw this character, I felt as if I'd been dropped into an episode of *'Porridge'*! I remember a strongman type in that called Grouty, who held the prison in his vice, like a mafia boss. Well this man, Henry, was almost the image of him, right down to his swagger as he sat like a king on his 'throne', and the fawning way the prisoners had stepped aside for me to pass when I was being taken to his cell, the door of which was guarded by two of his heavies – one on each side. I imagined the throng gathering outside to try and listen in as we talked … and what Henry would do to them if he found out.

He motioned for me to sit down on his bed.

'Now,' he began. 'I wanted to talk to you about our new inmate – the boy Barry.'

I found this a strange idea, that a 45-year-old man should be seen as a 'boy', but perhaps in Henry's world anyone with disabilities was a child.

'I've heard nowt but good things about you, my dear,' he said.

It all felt a bit creepy to me – very uncomfortable. I couldn't wait to get out of here, but I knew this was a necessary obstacle, so I had to go with it. 'Thank you.' I looked around furtively, amazed to see curtains at the window and a coffee percolator like the Deputy-Governor's on his table.

'Now tell me about this little project you're doing.'

I cringed, but tried not to show it. I spent the next ten minutes telling him about the project and answering his questions as best I could. I think he must have been happy with my answers as he seemed quite jovial.

'I like you,' he said. 'You tell it as it is. I like a straight talker.'

I didn't feel I'd told him anything very much, other than the facts, though I suppose I was quite direct, which is unusual for me. Normally, being dyslexic, I can talk for England and I go all around the bush, but this time I just wanted to keep things short so that I could get out of here as quickly as possible.

'I'm going to get the top men on my wing to help you with anything Barry needs, so just you come and let me know, my dear.'

'Thank you,' I said, feeling as if I was in the headmaster's study. This whole situation seemed weird and I had no intention of going back to ask for any help from Henry and his 'top men'. Some of the staff on this wing were already quite helpful when it came to finding a quiet place, or moving the computer for me, so I didn't see how I would need any help from this self-appointed 'Godfather'. But I realised I would have to tolerate his interest and accept whatever help he offered.

'Now off you go,' he said, waving me away. 'Go and see the boy, now. Make sure you do your best for him.'

'I will.'

'Tell me a bit about Barry,' I asked the officer who walked me to his cell. 'What's he in for?'

'Shop-lifting,' he said.

'Really, they don't usually come in here for that, do they?'

'No, but apparently there was a bit of violence as well,' he replied. 'He got angry because he didn't understand what he'd done. He said he was going to pay but he couldn't see where the till was.'

'Do you think that was true?'

'Probably not, but I suppose it could have been. The trouble was that the shop assistant couldn't understand him properly and he was too deaf to hear what she was saying. The shop manager came out to see what was going on and Barry felt threatened, so he hit out – broke the man's nose I believe. That's what really got him arrested – common assault and shop-lifting.'

'So how long is he in for?'

'Two weeks on remand, then it will be up to the magistrate when he goes to court.'

'What are his main difficulties?'

'Where do I start?' He shrugged. 'They say he's autistic, he's partially blind, deaf and he slurs his words so much we can hardly understand anything he says. He doesn't seem to be able to read and write, but I'm not sure about that because he can hardly see. He's a drug addict too I think, like most of them in here. The main problem is, we just don't know how to communicate with him. We need to tell him what he has to do in the prison and find out if he can cope with everything himself, or whether he needs help. We can't even be sure he understands the basic rules.'

'OK. I'll try and talk with him and do an assessment as much as I can.

'You'd better see him in his cell, I think. You should be all right with him, but I'll have to stay outside in case.'

As we reached Barry's cell, I was a bit apprehensive about what I would find and how I would cope with his difficulties. But when I went in, he was sitting on his bunk, looking rather lost. I immediately felt a strong sympathy for him. It must be terrible to have so many of his senses impaired – not to understand what is going on and having nobody to ask for help, or anyone to understand him.

'Hello Barry,' I said brightly as I sat down. He didn't look at me, but his expression showed he knew someone was there. Perhaps he could see my shadow as well as hear my voice, even if it might be muffled or muted. I wanted to take his hand so that I could harness his sense of touch, which I thought might help him to know I wanted to support him. I might even have to spell out things on his hands. But, of course, I wasn't allowed to touch him at all. I just wasn't sure how this would go.

In my clearest voice, I spoke slowly and loudly. 'I've come to have a chat with you Barry. Can you hear me?'

He turned his head slightly in my direction, but kept his gaze fixed on the wall to my right. 'Yes, I can hear you a bit,' he said in a slow, distorted voice, like a soundtrack played at half speed. If I hadn't known about his problems, I'd have thought he was drunk and drugged. He definitely had a speech impediment, though I couldn't yet tell what it was. He seemed to have to work hard to say every word, so I knew this conversation was going to be long as well as difficult.

'Put your hand up if you can't understand me,' I said, very slowly, as I looked around his barren cell, with his black bag of clothes and possessions still on the floor where he had dropped it when he arrived that morning.

Barry nodded in response. I kept my eyes on his, but he didn't seem to want to make eye-contact. Of course, this could have been because his vision was too poor, but the officer had mentioned autism and I recognised lack of eye-contact as a symptom of some types of autism.

'My son had a bad car accident and he has some disabilities. Did that happen to you?'

'Not a car-crash,' he replied. 'I was electrocuted.' He separated out the syllables as he spoke, but I could see it was a big struggle for him to get his words out coherently. I listened hard and gradually I began to understand better as I got used to his way of speaking.

'That's what made me partially blind and deaf, and affected my speech,' he explained.

'Do you have any other problems?'

'Yes, I couldn't learn to read and write at school.'

'Well, that's like me.' I spaced out each short sentence to give him time to take in the words and give them meaning. 'I'm dyslexic. It made me a failure at school. Nobody understood that I had great ideas … and I wanted to learn so much.'

'Me too.' He brightened and his face became more animated. 'I'm great at doing maths in my head, and I know I'm intelligent.' Again, he sounded it out, syllable by syllable. 'They did a test on me once and it said I had an IQ of 160.'

'Wow! Was that when you were at school?'

'Yes, that surprised them. But the trouble was, it made them think I was lazy, as how can you have a high IQ and not learn to read and write?'

'That happened to me too. They never tested my IQ, but all the teachers thought I was lazy. They couldn't understand how I could talk so well, but not be able to write it down.'

147

'I love learning,' he said, with a spark in his eyes, 'and I know loads about some things. I used to be in the army and I learnt a lot about the world. I went to lots of different countries with the army. My last tour was Belfast, just before I left in 1981.' I sat patiently while he took his time to enunciate the words. It must have been so frustrating for a quick thinker like Barry to have to speak so slowly. If it was me, I knew I'd find it agonising not to be able to express my ideas quickly enough.

'That's a coincidence,' I said. 'Only a few days ago I was talking with another new inmate who used to be in the army. He has problems too because he is in a wheelchair.'

Barry seemed interested. 'Was he injured in the army?'

'Yes. A parachute jump went wrong and he broke his back.'

'Is he in this wing?'

'No, but I could see if I can arrange for you to meet him if you like? I can't promise anything though. The rules are quite strict in here.'

'That would be good. We can talk about our service days.'

'There are quite a lot of prisoners who have been in the forces. I'll ask an officer to get one or two of them on this wing to come and talk to you, if you like.'

'Yes please.' He smiled for the first time, then returned to a disconsolate frown. 'But they probably won't want to. Most people don't want to talk to me, because I can't hear much and I speak so badly. I don't expect anyone will want to bother with me.'

'We're talking all right, you and me, aren't we?' I wanted to encourage him and boost his self-esteem. 'I know it's difficult for you, but I'm getting better at working out what you say, now that I'm used to your voice. I can understand enough of your words to get your meaning, so I'm enjoying our chat.'

'Really?' He looked doubtful.

'Yes, really. You seem to be able to understand me better now, too.'

'Yes, but you speak really slowly and clearly so that I can differentiate the words.' I was glad that his impediment didn't prevent him from using a wide vocabulary.

'I was once married to an army man and we lived in barracks,' I told him. 'So we could talk some more about that. Maybe you knew some of my husband's mates.'

'Yeah,' he smiled again. 'Where were you based?'

'Aldershot.' I replied. 'Do you know it?'

'Yeah, I did some of my training there.'

'We must talk more about that some time.' I said. 'But for now I want to know about your story. Tell me how you were electrocuted.'

'Well, my problems started when I left the army. I got in with the wrong crowd and that's where it all went wrong. I got hooked on drugs, the hard stuff – heroin and cocaine.'

'So you were addicted?'

'Heavily addicted, yeah.' He paused. 'But I got off all that about twenty years ago. I did it myself. I only do cannabis now.'

'Well done for getting off heroin – that must have been a huge achievement.'

'Yes, I'm proud of myself for that.'

'What happened when you were in the gang?'

'They gave me the drugs to begin with, but then I had to pay for them and I didn't have any money, so they took me thieving. It was fine at first, but it all went wrong when we did a robbery in this factory. I was the guy who had to get the boxes down in the warehouse, and I was electrocuted by a live-wire. It shouldn't have been allowed, should it? I should have put the health and safety people onto them.'

'Why didn't you?'

'And tell them what I was doing there?'

'No, I see!' I was so naive – we both laughed at that.

'That's what turned me into this senseless body,' he said. 'The gang got me out somehow and took me to hospital – dumped me at the door of A and E, then drove off. I was in the hospital for weeks. The medics couldn't cure my hearing or my sight, but they did give me a speech-therapist. If it hadn't been for her, nobody would be able to understand me at all.'

'I think you're getting clearer as we speak,' I said. 'Maybe you just need practice.'

'My reading and writing were bad before, but now they're even worse. It affected everything.' He looked so despondent that I knew I had to try and give him some positive things to think about.

'Would you like me to help you with your reading and writing?' I asked. 'I could teach you to improve your literacy skills if you like.'

'No offence, but I don't like teachers.'

'I don't teach in a classroom,' I said.

'How do you teach then?'

'I can help you to learn in new ways, just you and me. It will be very different to any learning you've done before. And I can give you a mentor to help you when I'm not in the prison.'

'How do you mean, a mentor?'

I explained that a mentor is another prisoner. I could maybe find him one who was a soldier like him. I told him how a mentor would work with him and the sorts of things they would do.'

'I think I'd like that,' he said. 'But there's one big problem, on top of everything else.'

'What's that?'

'I can't see the print on a page. It's much too small and just blurs into a grey mess.'

I looked at his heavy-framed, tinted glasses with their lenses as thick as bottle-bottoms. 'Would better glasses help?'

'No.' He turned to face me directly for the first time, and lifted his glasses off his nose. They said these were the best they could make, and they do help. I can't see anything but shadows without them.'

'OK,' I said, thinking aloud. 'What about if I bring in some different sizes of large print to see which would be best?'

'Can you do that?'

'Yes, I'll try out some different fonts when I get home tonight and I can bring them in tomorrow. I'm sure we'll something find something to suit you.' Well, I hoped so anyway. I had an idea that there might be some sort of screen magnifier that you can fix to the front of a computer monitor, to enlarge the text, so I decided to try and track one of those down to order for him. But I thought I'd better not get his hopes up about that just yet.

We spent the rest of our time together talking, still slowly, about the prison rules, where things are on the wing and how to get help.

'I've been talking to B wing's top-dog prisoner this morning. He said he'd get his men to get things for you and help with anything you need. So that should be useful. I'll explain things a bit more to the officers too, because I know some of them are keen to help you.'

Once I'd answered all Barry's questions as best I could, I stood up to go. 'I see you haven't unpacked your stuff yet,' I said. 'Shall I get one of my mentors to come and help you with that?'

'Yes please, that would be great. Will you come back to see me tomorrow?'

I promised to come back the next morning and left to get things organized for him.

'In fact, I think I'll come back every day to start with, if you think you could cope with that.'

'You've proper cheered me up,' he said. 'I reckon I could cope. In fact, if your teaching is as good as you say it is, you can give me some homework too.' He laughed and looked straight at me again as I said goodbye and turned to leave. 'Thanks,' he called after me.

On my way out, I tracked down a mentor who I knew was ex-army to help and befriend Barry, explaining about his disabilities and how to communicate with him. Finally, I spoke to the senior officer at some length about what Barry would need and how we could help him.

That night I sat up late, experimenting with a variety of fonts and sizes, printing them all out to try with Barry the next morning. I also located a magnification screen on the internet and ordered it straight away. The next day I would be able to tell him about that and I was sure that working on a computer would be a great help to him, with all his problems. When I finally got to bed that night, I felt really positive about working with him and helping him to cope better with all his difficulties. It would be a learning curve for me and potentially a great help to other prisoners too, in the future, I thought, so I must make sure we note down everything we do.

When I reached B wing the following morning, the senior officer came straight over with news that Henry had been true to his word and got everyone rallying round Barry, and the mentor I'd found had been with him chatting about their army lives for most of the evening.

'He was so happy by lock-up time,' she said. 'I popped in to see him and he just beamed when he told me how helpful everybody had been and how well he had settled in. So thanks for getting all that organized.'

'It wasn't just me,' I grinned. 'I reckon Henry had something to do with it!'

'Yes, he really took to you yesterday,' she said. 'It was worth your going to see him.'

I went off to find Barry and listened as he told me with increasing fluency how well his first day had gone.

'And it's all thanks to you,' he said.

'And the big-boss Henry, and a few other people as well.'

The first thing we did was to try out all the fonts and sizes of text and found that he could manage with arial 18, which has quite a bold typeface, large enough for him to make out, but not so large that every few words would need a new page. My next task would be to convert all my handouts and practice sheets to that font for him that evening, so that I could leave him some homework to do. Not all of it would be on paper of course and I told him about the screen I'd ordered for the computer.

'That sounds great,' he said with a wide smile. 'I love computers. Before I was electrocuted, I used to play on them all the time.'

'Well, I've got a wonderful programme for developing reading and writing skills and it also assesses your strengths and weaknesses, as well as the progress you make. So, we'll get going with that as soon as the screen arrives and see how well you manage with it.'

'OK. So what will we do today?'

'I've got a check-list to talk through with you, to see what kinds of problems you have. I usually use it for people with dyslexia, but a lot of it might be helpful for you as well.'

'Maybe I am dyslexic, as well as everything else!'

'That's a point,' I agreed. 'It could explain your problems when you were at school.'

As I talked him through the list and noted down his responses, it became obvious that he did have some aspects of dyslexia, but they may have been related to his autism, or brought on through his electrocution accident.

I had taken in the textured wooden letters that the workshop had made for us and we spent quite a lot of our time, in his cell with the guard at the door, identifying letters and making words to 'read' out with his fingers, rather like reading Braille I suppose. He really enjoyed that, so I left them with him overnight to play with, as his sense of touch was clearly the strongest for him now.

'Tomorrow when I come, we can use the letters some more, and I'll bring in a couple of other practical activities that I think will help you. Tonight, I'll upgrade some handouts to the Arial 18 font we've chosen and you can try those tomorrow too.'

'Thanks Jackie. You're a star,' he smiled. 'See you tomorrow.'

CHAPTER 10

PADDY and SHANE

'So what would you like me to do?' asked Miss Amey as she met with Carl and me to plan the details for our awards presentation ceremony. We had agreed a wish-list of guests we wanted to invite, discussed how much space and what technology we would need, whether to have refreshments and of course, most important of all, the preferred date.

'Could you take the guest-list to the Deputy-Governor for her to check through?' I asked her. 'We really need management permission to invite all these people.'

'She might have to refer some of these to the Ministry of Justice,' The senior officer said as she looked through the names. 'This one in particular.' I looked to see and found, to my surprise, she was pointing at the name of a photographer from the local press.

'But we need a photographer,' I said. 'We must have some sort of record of the day, so that the men who receive awards and those who make presentations can keep a copy each.

'Well, as you know, my son Phoenix is also on the staff in this prison, so he has security clearance. And he's an amateur photographer and film-maker,' explained Miss Amey. 'If the newspaper photographer isn't allowed in, I'm sure we could get permission for Phoenix to take some photographs, and even make a video recording of it all as well if you like. In fact, I expect he'd be happy to do the video anyway, even if the press-photographer is able to come.'

'That's a brilliant idea. Can you ask him if he'd be happy to do the recording, and see if the management can arrange for him to be covered?'

'I'll ask him tonight, but I'm sure he'll say yes.'

'And could you ask the Deputy-Governor for a definite decision on the date and the best time to have it? We need to know that as soon as possible, so that we can get the workshop to print some posh invitations.'

'OK. I'll see what I can do.'

'I can ask Jazz if he'd be willing to design them for you if you like,' said Carl.

'Great idea!' I agreed. Jazz was one of our top mentors and he was well-known throughout the prison for his artistic envelope decorations. As well as mentoring, he wrote letters home for several of the old lags who had never learnt to read and write and, unlike our Fred, felt too old to bother now. From a small boy, Jazz had always had an artistic talent, though he'd never had the chance to follow it through. Over the past few years, he had decorated all the envelopes for his own letters home to his mother, and now more and more of the men in his wing were asking him to paint his designs on their envelopes too. He could have done this commercially, on the outside, but in the prison he just charged a couple of cigarettes-worth of tobacco for each envelope.

'I'm sure Jazz would feel honoured to do a job like that.'

Carl and I made a list of all the awards we wanted to present and in what order.

'Now we need to sort out the presentations,' I said.

'You mean who is doing what and when?' asked Carl.

'Yes. As Head of Mentors, you should do one of them.'

'Do I have to?' he grimaced, with a smile. 'I'm no good at speaking in front of people. I'd be better if somebody asked me questions and then I could just answer them.'

'Well we could do it that way if you like. But you'll have to think up some of the questions for me to ask. That way you will already have thought up the answers.'

'OK. I'll work on that then. Who else do you think?'

'Tony, maybe,' I suggested. 'He's come such a long way and is quite a new man now. It would be great if we could get him to speak. I'll go and ask him next time I'm over there.'

'Any others?' asked Carl. 'I know, what about Paddy Finch? He would be good – he's a whizz with his mind-maps. And we could ask Shane to tell the visitors what dyslexia is. What do you think?'

'Great. That's a good start to our list. I'll go and see both of them too.'

'Shouldn't we have an officer as well? We could ask Officer Harding? He's dyslexic.'

'Yes.' And maybe we should ask our sponsor for the first six months of the project, because the awards mainly come from that time. We could even ask him to help present them.'

Once we had a framework for the ceremony worked out, and a few more names on the list of potential presenters, we both felt we were well on the way now to the real thing.

'Keep your fingers crossed that Miss Amey can get us the permissions,' said Carl.

'And let's hope that none of our main speakers gets transferred at the last minute,' I added ruefully.

Later that day, after sessions with some of my learners, including Barry, who was now doing so well and making real progress every day, I went in search of thirty-one-year-old drug-dealer Paddy Finch. I knew Carl had assessed him as dyslexic, but otherwise I only knew what Carl had told me, so I was keen to have a good chat with him myself.

'I've never really had a proper chance to talk with you about your background Paddy, as you've mostly worked with Carl.'

'Yes, but I've heard a lot about you. He calls you "Wacky Jackie".'

'Does he? The cheeky sod!' I laughed. 'Well he tells me that you had an interesting life when you were young. Weren't you born in Malta, or was it Majorca? I'm no good with foreign place names.'

'Yes, Malta. That's where my parents lived when I was born. We lived there for my first six months, but of course I don't remember any of that. My older sister said she had to look after me because my parents weren't around much and we lived in the countryside, so we were all left to pretty well run wild.'

'So where did you all go when you were six months old?'

'I don't know. We went to lots of different places, so I'm not sure where we were after Malta. The first place I really remember was Margate. We lived there in a sort of commune, living with my Nan and Grandad, with all the aunts and uncles and cousins living nearby and in and out of each other's houses, so nobody really took responsibility.'

'Responsibility for you?'

'That's right,' said Paddy. 'Then we all moved to a huge house in Colchester. We just ran free in the area, but my mother must have been there, because when I started having headaches and trouble with my eyes, she took me round all the hospitals. When I went to school I was a bit wild, because I'd never really had any discipline, so I caused a lot of problems for my teachers. They said I had disruptive behaviour, so I had the cane a lot. Then they noticed I had problems with my reading and writing too, so they got me and four other kids a private tutor. But that didn't help much.' Paddy paused for a moment. 'My father died when I was young and I got expelled from school. Then my sister left home and we never saw her except birthdays and Christmases.'

'Was that the sister who brought you up when you were little?'

'Yes. There's only her and me in our family, and she went and left me behind.'

'That must have been difficult for you.'

'It was. But it was even more difficult for my mother. She couldn't handle my behaviour problems and didn't know what to do with me, so she put me into a boarding school.'

'How did you feel about that?' I asked.

'I didn't like being away from all my family and stuck in a school all day every day, when I'd never got on well at school. But it wasn't like my other schools.'

'What was different about it?'

'It was more relaxed. I really liked it there because it was very practical. It was like a farm. We milked cows and collected eggs. When we needed a new barn, we drew designs of what we wanted it to be like and wrote things down to help us work out how it should be built. Then we all got together and built it, and let the animals into it.' He smiled. 'That was great. We had clubs on Friday nights and girls from another school came and joined us.' Now Paddy's face clouded over. 'The trouble was, I missed all my family, so I kept running away.'

'Did you get home safely?'

'Sometimes I did, but mostly somebody would stop me and take me back to the school. Then when I was fifteen I joined a squat. That's where I got into drugs.'

'How did you pay for them?'

'I couldn't, so I got roped into dealing them. But I didn't get paid much, so I had to steal bread to eat and clothes to wear from the big supermarket. Before I knew it there were three police cars waiting for me outside. That was the first time I was arrested, three days before Christmas, when I was just fifteen.'

'What happened then?'

'My mum came with a social worker and picked me up. I got a bit of a telling off from that, mainly because she hadn't heard from me for two weeks and she was worried about me.'

'That's when they made me go to the local secondary school. It was OK, but I got very bored.. The social worker took me each morning and I was supposed to walk straight home after school, but sometimes I skipped off school and went out making money from selling drugs again.'

'What happened when you left school?' I asked. By now I was assuming that the recurring drugs element would get him into greater trouble.

'I got a job as a landscape gardener.'

'Wow! What a great job.'

'Yeah, I really loved it. I couldn't read or write much at all, but I found I was really good at thinking up ideas for garden designs and seeing what they would look like in my head.'

'That's quite a skill.'

'I know, but I was still selling drugs on the side. It was all going fine, but when I turned eighteen my mum got cancer and was on income support, so I was dealing more drugs. That was when I started to make myself get better at reading. I wanted to find out about the cancer, so I read as much as I could. But then the police started to get on my case. They found out I was dealing and they followed me around. One night they chased me and rammed my car, smashing the windscreen. That was when they found a stash of cocaine under my driving seat and I was arrested.'

'Did you have to go to court?'

'Yeah. That was my first time in jail. Soon after I got there, I was so worried about my mum that they let me speak to her doctor on the phone. He told me she would die within six months.'

'That must have been devastating.'

'You can say that again. I was in a terrible state. She started having treatment and losing her hair. She was a bit funny about that. But at the end of the six months she was still alive.'

'Where you still in prison then?'

'Yeah. I kept having to go to court, so I was in prison for a year. They took me to visit my mum in hospital the day before the final court case.' He looked close to tears as he remembered it all and paused to try and compose himself. He took a deep breath. 'She was the worst I'd seen her. I was only allowed to stay a short while and when I left her last words to me were "I love you and I'll always be with you." I was sentenced the next day. The day after that, I was sitting in my cell, praying to myself, thinking about my mum: "Please don't die. Please don't die." Then I heard footsteps coming to my door. I was escorted to the office to take a phone call from my sister and she told me that Mum had just died.'

'That must have been terrible,' I sympathized. Having a parent die when you're in prison and you can't be there when they need you must be awful.

'Yeah, it was.' His eyes were filling up with tears, but he fought to control them. His anger came out even now as he described how the frustration overwhelmed him and he started throwing things around the office.

'Did that get you into trouble?'

'It would have done, normally. But I must say, they were very understanding. The officer calmed me down and made me a cup of coffee. Then my sister rang back and we had a chat. That made me feel better. The next day they let her come and see me in the prison, on a compassionate visit. We had a cry and a cuddle. But when I went back on the wing, that was hard. I felt like I couldn't grieve with all these men around me.'

'Were you allowed to go to the funeral?' Not the date it was meant to be on, so my sister managed to rearrange it to the following week. It ended up being on my birthday and they took me up to Bedford in a police van. I couldn't believe it when I got out of the van and saw all my friends there. I had to be chained to one police officer on each side of me, and they weren't even going to let me sit by my sister, but I kicked off a bit and she pleaded with them, so they did in the end. But I was still chained up, so I couldn't give her a cuddle.'

'Were you inside for a long time after that?'

'Not too long because I'd already served a year on remand.

'How many times have you been inside altogether?'

'Five times before, and now I'm in for a year, unless I get parole. Last time I went out I had a dream of how it would be – I really wanted to go straight and start a new life. I'd been working with you and Carl and I'd really learned a lot. My writing and reading were much better and I wanted to have a life. I had lots of plans, but then it all went wrong.' I saw the disappointment in Paddy's face. 'That's when I got in trouble with the police again and ended up back in here.' He paused, then brightened. 'To tell you the truth, I just wanted to be back in here with you!' He gave me a cheeky grin.

'I remember you were doing so well with your learning and you had much more confidence when you left. I was really proud of you. So what happened to make things go wrong?'

'When I got out I had to sign for my £46, but I had nowhere to go, so one of my ex-girlfriends picked me up. She's a very good friend and we spent the day together. I stayed at her place for the next few days and had a couple of nights out with the lads, but I was being good.' He smiled. 'Then my money started to run out. I walked all the way into town because I had an appointment with the drug workers. But I met some of my old drug-dealer friends outside and they persuaded me to go for a drink and a score with them. They always hang around outside the clinic to catch people like that. When I was skint, I was a sucker for anyone who would buy me a drink. When I went back to the clinic later that day, I tested positive. They said I had to come back in another week for a repeat test, but I was still broke and had to go to the job-centre. I explained my situation and signed a piece of paper. Then they said I would have to come back in a week to look for a job. I said I couldn't wait that long. I didn't have any money left and I had to find somewhere to live and buy food and stuff. So they gave me an emergency £46. Out of that I had to pay my rent and feed myself, so the money went that first day. The only way I could live was to go back to selling drugs. I didn't want to, but I had no choice. The police turned up and arrested me again.'

'I'm sure I couldn't live on £46 a week either. That sounds like a nightmare.'

'Yeah. It was.'

'Well, in a way, that's why I wanted to come and see you,' I said. Because Carl says you're great at drawing things out, like charts and diagrams.'

'Yes, I suppose it's like when I sketched out landscape gardens. I designed them in my head and then I drew them on paper.'

'Have you ever done a mind-map?'

'I did one once with Carl, but I don't think I've got it any more. It was a kind of learning plan, to help me with my reading and writing.'

'Well, we're hoping to put on an awards ceremony in the prison. Carl suggested you could do a mind-map for us to show everyone.'

'What about?'

'We thought maybe you could show what your hopes and dreams were for going straight last time you were released, the changes you wanted to make in your life and how it all worked out,' I suggested. 'You could do a mind-map of it and put in some of the things that went right for you and the other aspects that made it difficult. You could also include what you want to do differently to try and make it go better next time. I'm sure a mind-map like that would help a lot of people in here, with dreams like yours to see how they could plan for their futures.'

'Yeah.' Paddy said. He thought for a moment. 'I can see it in my mind. I'd like to do that, if you or Carl can help me with the words. I don't want to make any mistakes. I used to write terrible letters to my sister. They took me hours and they were still full of mistakes. They looked like I was a five-year-old. But now I know I've learnt to spell and write better.'

'Yes, I reckon you have the best handwriting in the whole prison now.'

Paddy beamed with pride.

'We can help you with the spellings if you want, though you're really pretty good at it yourself now. The most important thing is that it must be your ideas and your design, because you're so good at all that. But what would be great as well is if you could show them your mind-map and talk it through for everyone.'

'I couldn't. I hate standing up and speaking in front of people, even in a small group, like when you did the learning workshops with us. Do you remember? They were kicking.'

'Yes, I do remember. You were on the very first one, weren't you?'

'That's right. But I hated it when you picked me to tell the others about something.'

'OK. What about if I ask you two or three questions about it and you can just give the answers? We could practise it beforehand if you like.'

'Well, maybe.' Paddy sat and considered that for a moment.

' Great,' I smiled. 'And thank you for agreeing to do the mind-map.'

'That's OK. I'll start thinking about it straight away.'

I left with a smile. I knew Paddy was reliable and now we had something definite to put on the programme.

The next person I needed to see was twenty-three-year-old drug-dealer Shane, who had already been in prison eleven times. He had suffered the most appalling sexual abuse throughout his childhood, by members of his own family, his teachers and 'friends'. Despite being an excellent athlete, Shane could never settle – he was always in trouble at school and was expelled twice, then got into drugs and a lot of other problems.

Carl had added him to our list because he had severe dyslexia, like me, and came in with very low levels of literacy, equivalent to a pre-school child, but now he was improving every day, with Carl's great mentoring skills to guide him. When I had first assessed Shane and told him that he had dyslexia, he was fascinated that there was something he could put a name to; a reason for his failures at school. I knew the feeling. We talked about it a lot and he was always wanting to know more about how the mind of a dyslexic person works.

When I arrived on E wing, Shane himself walked over to see me.

'How are you doing, Jack?' he asked. 'Have you come to see me?'

'Yes I have. That's amazing – I'm always coming over to this wing and I hardly ever see you, and now when I'm here especially to see if I can have a chat with you, here you are to meet me! Let's go and see if there's a room free somewhere.'

We found a corner in the library, with an officer nearby.

'So what did you want to see me about?' he asked.

'Carl and I are planning a special event in a couple of weeks' time,' I began. 'It's our first awards ceremony and we want to do a presentation about our work in here.'

'Great. Can I come?'

'I certainly hope so – that's what I've come to ask you. Ever since we had that long conversation together when you first came into the prison, you've talked to me about your drugs problems and all the awful abuse you went through, and then I diagnosed your dyslexia we used to talk about that a lot too. Do you remember?'

'Yes, you were the first person who ever really listened to me.'

'Well you had a lot of problems, didn't you?'

'You could say that.'

'But you've done so well since you've been in this prison.'

'Not like my last jail. I had a drugs counselor there, but she wasn't no good at counseling me.' He paused and a grin spread across his face. 'I don't think I've ever told you this, but she was much better at sex than drugs.'

I wasn't sure if I'd understood Shane right. 'You mean she was a sex-counselor too?'

'No, not a counselor. But she was a great lay. Every counselling session I had with her was a ball!'

I gasped. 'Didn't anyone find out?'

'No, why should they? That was the one time when I wasn't supposed to have an officer with me. He was outside in the reception room, but he couldn't hear a thing – we made sure of that!'

'Well, you're more of a rascal than I realised,' I said 'I can hardly believe it.' For a few moments, I was so shocked that he'd done this, and got away with it, and now told me about it, I didn't really know what to say. If it had been in this prison I would have had to report it, so I was relieved that wasn't my responsibility.

'So what do you want me to do for this presentation thing?' he asked.

'Well, I know you have learned a great deal about what dyslexia is, how your mind works and how it affects you, so I'd love it if you could do a short talk about that to our audience.'

'Who's going to be there?'

'Some of your mates, like Carl, Tony and Paddy. There will also be a couple of officers speaking, and we're inviting just a few people from outside who are interested in how well the project is going.'

'I don't mind telling some of the people in here, but I can't speak in front of strangers. I've never done it before. That would scare me shitless.'

'Well, it doesn't have to be very much, and I could stand with you and help you if you dry up or anything.'

'No, I really don't think I can.'

'But there's nobody that knows as much about dyslexia as you.'

'Yes there is. You know loads more than I do.'

'But I'm already going to be speaking a lot. We really need you to do that bit. I know you can do it. I'm sure you'll be brilliant. Please give it a try. I'll help you decide what to say and practise running it through. Will you at least give it a go?'

He shrugged. 'Well ... OK. But if I can't face it on the day ...'

'Don't worry. I'm sure you'll be fine, but I won't force you.'

'All right,' he grinned. 'Just for you!'

Everything was organised and all the invitations went out. The prison management were very helpful as they wanted to support the project that had done so much good, calming the prison down. Phoenix, the amateur photographer, got his camera rigged up to record the whole thing on DVD, and we had my laptop connected to a projector so that I could do a presentation to our invited guests. Now they were all arriving, the prisoners who were speaking or receiving awards were escorted across to the room where it was being held. Extra security officers had been put on to circle the room, with some of them inside with us as well. It was all quite fraught and I was very nervous until we started, but once I got going I got into the swing of it.

I started off with an introduction, talking briefly about how I had been helped by a mentor and tutors when I was at the college in my forties, doing literacy courses and my degree and how this project started. Throughout that first ten minutes or so while I was speaking, and in fact the whole presentation, the noise levels went from one extreme to the other. All the prisoners listened in attentive silence to me and to each other, with a great deal of mutual respect. We carried on speaking relatively unflustered, despite the continuous coming and going of officers, the doors clanking and creaking, keys clattering and clinking in locks, chains jangling on officers' belts, the loud walkie-talkie messages every now and then from the management to staff and the echoing footsteps and voices from outside the room.

Then Carl, Head of Mentors, talked about the stigma of dyslexia, what mentoring is – forming a relationship with a less experienced person, and how it works. He had looked up the dictionary definition of the word 'mentor' – 'a wise and trusted friend.'

Next up was Shane, who read fluently from his own notes, about his background, how the project had helped him build his confidence and self-esteem. 'Jackie has helped me to see that I am not alone, and she has given me all the skills I need.' He explained that I had recently given him a mock theory driving test to do, on which he'd scored a high percentage. 'Now I have the confidence to do my driving test and apply for jobs when I get out.'

Two other prisoners talked about different aspects of the project, one about assessment and the other about learning workshops and computer activities.

The last of the prisoners to speak was Paddy Finch, with his mind-map. 'Jackie's done a lot for me,' he began, and explained his situation. Then he held up his chart, beautifully drawn out and written. He talked us through each of his captions in turn, explaining what help he'd needed, what help he'd had in the prison, what help he would need outside, what help he could give others and what actions he would take to make sure he didn't come back inside again. These included keeping in touch with his family, to help him feel wanted and keep him going, starting a new life in a different town to keep him away from his previous bad influences, staying off drugs, and listening to people, trying to help them as well as himself. There was an enthusiastic round of applause for Paddy at the end of his bit. He kept a straight face while returning to his seat, but I could tell how pleased he was with the approval of his peers.

There were speeches too from Officer Harding, who admitted his own severe dyslexia and how it had affected him at school and afterwards, and three of our invited visitors, who were all said nice things about me and about the course, which is always good to hear. Then came the giving of awards. The Chairman of our sponsor group, presented certificates to about fifteen prisoners for their achievements in raising their literacy skills to higher age-levels. One of these was 67-year-old Fred, holding his certificate up for all to see, his chest stuck out and his face a picture of pride.

As I drove home that evening, I was relieved it had all gone so well, despite the odd hiccup. At least all the presenters were able to be there and most of the guests came and seemed really pleased with it all. Phew!

For me, the most important of these visitors, though she didn't speak during the ceremony, was Sue Blackburn, the tutor who had first diagnosed my dyslexia and enabled me to turn my life around. Without her, I would never have been able to study for my degree and my teaching qualification, and none of this would have happened. Other people to thank included Ken Lewis, Vince Hagedon, Sue Clayton and Val Rozga, all of whom had helped me along the way, and in some cases I think I had helped them too.

The security was quite intrusive throughout the presentation, and noise-levels were high, but I suppose that was the price for being able to have the award ceremony at all. I had worried about it beforehand, but now I knew it was a price worth paying. It had gone even better than I expected, so that was the main thing. A great tribute to everyone concerned. Now our new funding was in place, I had other ideas to develop and of course there were always new prisoners to work with, so I was feeling upbeat about the future of the project.

CHAPTER 11

GILROY

It was August Bank Holiday weekend, so no one was expecting me to come in for work, but I had forgotten to give some of the men the fresh homework they had asked for the day before. When I arrived at the entrance to go through security as usual, the officer on duty was astonished.

'What the heck are you doing here today? Have you forgotten it's a holiday?'

'No. I've got the new homework I promised to bring in for some of the men on my dyslexia project.' I suppose I must have seemed an oddball to be doing this, but I didn't want to let them down.

He put his head to one side, bemused. 'Do you realise you're the only civilian in the whole prison today?'

'Really?'

'I don't know why you're bothering,' he said. 'A waste of your time if you ask me.'

'Well, I'd like to go in and take it to each of the wings. I won't stay long.'

'Nobody is going to do homework without you in here, standing over them.'

'It's not like that.' I felt indignant, not so much for me, but for the men themselves. I was sure they were keen to do the work. 'I'll be back to collect it on Tuesday. They will do it, you'll see.'

Sure enough, when I arrived on Tuesday morning, every single prisoner handed in his completed homework. I piled it all up and went to find that same officer.

'Look,' I said triumphantly as I plonked down the papers in front of him. Every piece of homework done in time and handed in.'

He flicked through the papers in surprise. 'That's crazy,' he said. 'How did you do it – witchcraft?' I suppose that was his way of shrugging off the fact that I'd been right. His negative attitude was more unusual through the prison now than a few months ago, but there were still some officers who were against what I was doing and that was frustrating. I believed in the men and they rose to meet my expectations time and again so that more than made up for the occasional sceptic.

Later that Tuesday morning, I was called over to the management block. 'They want to see you straight away,' said an officer when he found me.

'What have I done now?' I said, light-heartedly.

'They didn't say,' replied the officer.

When I got there I went to the Deputy-Governor's office, a little apprehensive of what this would be about. I always seemed to be getting in trouble.

'Sit down, Jackie,' she said, with an anxious look. 'A serious security situation has arisen.'

'What's that?' I was worried now. I couldn't think of anything I'd done wrong.

'Remember Wolfie Baxter, who was released last week?'

'Yes, of course. He was one of my best mentors. He used to work all hours helping the men with learning difficulties.'

'We've had a call from the probation service. Apparently Wolfie had a meeting with his probation officer to talk about his work prospects and he said he wanted to work with you.'

'Yes, I know he'd love to continue with some sort of mentoring, but he knows he can't do that here, so maybe he means that he wanted to find another mentoring job.' I was puzzled. 'But I don't understand – why is that a security situation?'

'He said he had your phone number and was going to call you.'

'Here at the prison?'

'No, it's your personal number.'

'But he can't have that. I never gave it to him.'

'He says you did.'

'No I didn't. I'm sure of that. I know it's not allowed to give personal phone numbers.'

'So what does he mean? Could he have got it from anyone else?'

'Not that I know of.' I tried to think of any way this could have happened. Then I suddenly realised what it might be. 'Wait a minute. Maybe he has the number for *Mentfor* ... yes, that's probably it. They were our funder for the first part of the project, so I might have given him that. They are publishing my first project report.'

'Let's see if we can get hold of his probation officer and make sure.' She looked up the number and dialled it. I listened to her side of the call, but she didn't say much.

'You were right.' She smiled as she put the phone down. 'It was all a big fuss about nothing much! Wolfie wanted to go for a mentoring job and he suggested ringing you for a reference to support his application. He didn't realise the number he had wasn't your own number.'

I breathed a huge sigh of relief.

After lunch, just when I was planning to do some much needed paperwork, writing up new prisoners' interviews and assessments, I had a call to go over and see twenty-two-year-old Gilroy who was on suicide-watch in E wing.

'So tell me a bit about him,' I asked the officer on duty. 'What are his main problems?'

'It's hard to know where to start,' he said. 'Gilroy Barker has a lot of health problems, speech defects, brain-damage and, on top of all that, he's an alcoholic and on a lot of medication because he's psychotic.'

I tried to run that through again in my head to take it all in. I immediately felt a great sympathy towards him being in this old-fashioned prison, which must be a nightmare for someone with so much to cope with.

'What brings him in here?' I asked.

'Nobody seems to be quite sure.' He shrugged. 'From what I heard, he is suspected of being a paedophile, but it's all rather vague. Apparently he was hanging around with a group of under-age girls and the police assumed the worst. I'm not sure how they got the conviction, but maybe he did do something he shouldn't have. He doesn't seem to think so, and we think that's why he's suicidal. We're keeping a very close watch on him, but he's in such a muddled state of mind that none of us have managed to get through to him. He won't come out of his cell unless he has to and he won't talk to anybody.'

'OK,' I said. 'I'll go and see if I can get him talking.'

'First you might want to read this letter.' He handed me several sheets of handwriting. 'It's from his mother, about his medical history. She thought it would help us.'

I was taken to a quiet room off Gilroy's landing and I sat down to read. I'm not the fastest reader, especially when it's handwriting, and I have to concentrate hard to take it all in, but it was clear from the start that his health problems began at his premature birth, ten weeks early and with serious internal problems. Fortunately, the paediatrician was able to diagnose straight away that his oesophagus was connected direct to his lungs instead of his trachea.

Within hours of his birth, Gilroy was transferred to Great Ormond Street Hospital and underwent major surgery the next day. He stayed there in the special care baby unit for six weeks before he was allowed to go home with his parents, but he kept being readmitted until he had reconstruction surgery at nine weeks old – an operation that lasted seven hours. Then, only a few hours later, his heart stopped and he had to be resuscitated. In her letter, Gilroy's mother described the terrifying moments when this happened as she sat with him.

As a mother, I could empathise totally with her story and the awful effect it had on her. When I thought of my two sons, each with their own problems, especially my younger son's brain damage, what Gilroy's mother went through was even worse than my own experiences.

This tiny baby remained on life-support for several months until they cut a hole in his neck to fit a tracheotomy, so that he could breathe unaided and eventually be allowed home again. But of course he had to be monitored constantly and stay within sight of one of his parents at all times, day and night, in case it became blocked and he couldn't breathe. He had no way of letting them know he was in distress as the tracheotomy prevented him from using his voice. He also had a stoma bag fitted and had to have physiotherapy every day.

I imagined the strain all this must have put on his parents, not being able to have any respite except with someone trained to cope. When he finally had his tracheotomy removed, just before he started at his special school, they found his vocal chords had been damaged and now he would need speech therapy to help him learn to speak as best he could.

At school, his mother wrote, he had to have a full-time dedicated carer in case he had difficulty breathing or got food stuck in his neck. It was even more frightening for Gilroy himself than it was for everyone around him. At school, his co-ordination skills and balance were so poor that he couldn't do many things the other children could. During this period of his childhood, he had to have another major operation to shorten his oesophagus and this meant lifting his stomach into his chest to make them meet.

With all these problems, and especially because of his speech impediments, Gilroy was badly bullied. This improved at the start of secondary school, but accelerated badly and he had to be moved to another school. Here he was bullied again, so badly that he finally started to retaliate and hit out at the bullies, which led to him being unfairly labelled as a trouble-maker. He was moved to yet another special school and settled down better. He was the first teenager in there to pass his GCSEs.

On leaving school he had a succession of short-term jobs, most of them ending through no fault of his own. Gilroy became more and more depressed and got in with the wrong crowd who, unknown to him, were fleecing him of his allowance money by stealing and using his bank-card while he was asleep and replacing it before he woke. These so-called friends introduced him to alcohol and in his downward spiral, his drinking became a prop.

Finally, Gilroy's dad helped him to buy himself a motor-bike. It was not long before his first accident, in which he was knocked off and hit his head so badly the ambulance took him to hospital on a spinal board. But they didn't x-ray him and released him a couple of hours later. From then he seemed to become much more angry and aggressive. Unknown to them, he had sustained a brain injury. Soon afterwards, he misjudged a bend, was thrown into some bushes and blacked out.

The police asked him to do a breath-test, but this was impossible for him because he couldn't breathe for long enough. The police arrested him so, instead of going to hospital, he had to appear in court for refusing to give a breath-test. Fortunately, the medical evidence resulted in his case being thrown out. But this second accident caused another undiagnosed head-injury. Gilroy now fell into a deep depression, the drinking escalated and he began to have psychotic episodes, hearing voices in his head that told him he was a failure and no good to anyone.

At this point, I heard footsteps approaching, so I folded the long letter and put it away to finish reading later. Gilroy was brought in with his head bowed, shuffling his feet. I indicated for him to sit on the chair near me and the officer positioned himself in a corner of the room, out of Gilroy's direct line of sight.

'Hello Gilroy,' I began, with a gentle smile. 'I hope you don't mind, but I've been reading your mother's letter, which is very helpful. I am sorry to hear you have had so many health problems in your life. I expect it must get you down sometimes?'

He muttered something unintelligible, but I took that to be a yes. 'I believe you had a couple of accidents when you banged your head?'

A slight nod, with his head still bowed almost down to his chest. I could see the scars in his scalp, several of them. These were more than mere bangs.

'My son had a terrible car-accident when he was fifteen. He was thrown out and they couldn't even find him, until a bystander searched the undergrowth. He was in a terrible state with a serious head injury.'

Gilroy looked up slightly. 'That happened to me too.' At least, I assumed that's what he said.

'My son was in intensive care for a couple of weeks. He had a number of injuries, but the brain-damage was the worst. Luckily, they x-rayed him straight away.' I paused.

'Nobody x-rayed my head. I had brain-injury too,' he mumbled, but this time I understood it better.

'Did that make you angry, like it made my son?'

'Yes.' Now he looked up directly at me for the first time. 'My mum says I changed after my head injuries and argued with everybody.' He paused. 'I got into a lot of trouble and started drinking.'

'Yes, my son did that too.' Gilroy was listening with interest now, so I continued. 'He even got in trouble with the police for a while. And he couldn't get work. It's taken him a long time to move on from all that, but now he's in a job he enjoys and is able to control his anger much better.'

Gilroy said nothing, but seemed to be taking it in. His eyes were clearer and his expression less anxious.

'Are the officers being helpful to you?' I asked.

'Sometimes.'

'What about the other men? Would you like to make some friends while you're inside?'

'Maybe.'

This was going to be a one-sided conversation if I didn't change direction. So I began to ask him about the run up to his sentence.

'I know you're supposed to be in prison for a couple of years, but I don't know what happened. Maybe you don't want to tell me everything, but I'm a good listener, so you could tell me a bit about it if you like.'

'Nothing to tell. I was just hanging around with some friends.'

'The ones who got you into trouble when you were younger?'

'No. I still see them sometimes. But these were some girls I know.'

'School friends?'

'No. These girls are much younger than me.'

'How did you meet them?'

'Oh, just around. They live near me. We got talking outside the café to start with. They're good fun, so we had a laugh.'

'Where do they work?'

'I think they're still at school.'

'So, how did the police get involved?'

'I don't know really,' he began timidly. 'It was all so unfair. We were chatting and larking about outside the train station one night. The fuzz stopped their car and came over to talk to us. The next thing I knew, I was being taken off to a cell.' He paused, in some confusion. 'But I don't know why. We were just having fun. We weren't doing a crime.'

'So what did they charge you with?'

'I don't know. Something about abuse, but I didn't do anything wrong. They got me a brief, so he took on my case after that.'

I realised I wouldn't get anywhere further with this, and I'm not sure I wanted to, so I changed the subject again.

'Your mother says you passed your GCSEs. She sounds proud of that.'

'Yes, but they were my best subjects, so they were easy. I couldn't do much reading or writing. I always had trouble with that, probably because I learnt to talk very late, after my trachy was taken out.'

'Do you still have problems with your reading and writing?'

'Yes, it's worse now.'

'After my son's brain injury I had to teach him to speak, read and write again. It was a lot of work, but he eventually got there. Do you think you might have been a bit the same?'

'I didn't lose it, but I did find it harder to read and stuff after my accidents.'

'Would you like me to come and do some work with you, like I did with my son?'

'Maybe,' he said cautiously. Then he made eye-contact with me again, for only the second time and I held his gaze. 'Yes,' he nodded. 'As long as it's not with other people.'

'No, it will be just me to start with. We'll have some sessions together, and I'll be teaching you in different ways to when you were at school. But there is just one other person who could help you one-to-one as well. Because you're in E wing, I could ask my top mentor to come and help you practise your skills if you like, between my visits. He's also an excellent listener, so he could visit you as much as you want and listen to any problems you might have. Or if you are feeling depressed, you could talk it all through with him. His name is Carl Nixon. Would you like me to ask him to look in on you sometime soon?'

He thought about this for a few moments, then nodded again. 'Yes, OK. I'll give him a try if you're sure he wouldn't bully me. I haven't spoken to any of the other men yet.'

'Why's that?'

'When I talk with new people, that's when the trouble starts. Because I can't talk properly, people always take the mick, or start bullying me. I can't deal with that.' He stopped and gave me a look, as if sizing me up and deciding whether to confide in me. He must have made up his mind that he could take the risk. 'I'm a failure. I can't do anything right. My voices are always telling me that. I'm afraid of what people will say or do to me. They'd all be better off without me. That's why I don't talk to anybody, except my voices.'

I wished Carl was here. He'd know better than me how to deal with this. I didn't know what to say, but realised I had to say something.

'Do your voices bother you?'

'Yes, they're in my face all the time. Especially if I'm having an OK day. They keep telling me how useless I am, until I feel bad again.'

'Maybe they won't keep on at you so much if you have other people to talk to.'

He thought for a moment. 'I don't suppose it will make any difference, but I'll give it a try. I like talking with you. You're different to the officers.' He tilted his head slightly to one side. 'You really listen, and you seem to understand what I'm saying.'

'I can understand you fine if I listen carefully, so that's probably why you notice me listening. I'm sure anyone could understand you if they try.'

'But most people don't try.'

'I'll come back tomorrow morning to see you, if that's all right?' I looked at the officer who nodded and back at Gilroy, who gave me a slight smile, the first I'd seen. 'I'll bring some things with me to find out what your best learning style is and what areas we can work on first.' I paused. 'Do you like working on the computer?'

'Yes, but I'm not much good at it.'

'Well, I can show you how and I've got some really good activities we can do. We can try some tomorrow.'

When I returned to my office later that afternoon, I found several emails in my inbox, so I started to work my way through them. I was amazed and excited to find that some of them were replies to an email I'd sent out the previous day to some selected Members of Parliament. I'd done some research to see who might be interested in my dyslexia project and now I had some encouraging replies. Three of them asked if they could come and visit the prison in the New Year. Of course, I wrote back straight away and said 'Yes please,' even though I didn't know whether it would be allowed! I'd deal with that when I had the dates they wanted to come.

When I finally reached the last email, it was from our local radio station. They wanted to interview me! I was so excited and phoned them straight away on the number they gave me. They wanted to talk to me the next morning, live on their nine o'clock morning show. The idea was, because it was a phone-in show, they wanted me to tell people about my project and the way I taught the prisoners, which they thought would be of interest to any dyslexic people. They wanted my project to spark off some phone-in calls.

I could hardly sleep that night for excitement ... and worry. Would I be able to answer their questions properly? I'd never done anything like this before. What would they want to know? How much should I tell them? I didn't even know how long they wanted me to speak for. Would anybody be interested? What if they got no phone-in calls after I'd spoken? What if I made a fool of myself on live radio? This was scary. Finally I must have drifted off, but I woke even earlier than usual and started to get on my best make-up and everything, with a smart suit, before I realised they wouldn't be able to see me anyway! Never mind – it helped me feel more confident.

One of the problems with my dyslexia is time – I'm not good at telling the time or gauging a period of time, and if I'm late anywhere I get so flustered that I make a mess of whatever it is I'm supposed to be doing. Consequently, I always try to be early, to avoid being late. On the morning of the radio interview I arrived really early at the studio and had to wait in their 'green room'. (They had to explain to me what that meant.)

Finally, I was ushered into the studio where the host was about to introduce the programme, following the local news. I sat down opposite him and a good-looking young man got my microphone set up for me and checked it was working. Then the interview started and he welcomed me onto his show with an introduction to me and about my dyslexia project.

Then he asked his first question: 'Why did you choose to do this work in prisons instead of schools?'

'I've already done a lot of work in schools,' I began. 'And I've gone up and down the country to research hidden disabilities such as dyslexia, because when my son had a car accident nine years ago and suffered brain injury, it changed him so much that he got into trouble with the police many times. My fear was, and research has shown this, that many people with hidden disabilities, especially dyslexia and brain injury, end up in prison. So, I wanted to come and do research in the prisons. When I found there were so many men who needed help that they weren't getting, I started my project to help them.'

'So I suppose you start work with them in the classroom?' he asked. I wasn't sure whether he didn't know how I worked, or whether he asked it that way to provoke a better answer.

'No, I mostly walk the wings around the prison, talking to the men and finding out who has problems with their reading and writing and explaining how we can help them. I don't use classrooms, because most of these men have had terrible experiences of failure in classrooms when they were at school, so they are scared of classrooms and wouldn't agree to work that way.'

'So, you just talk to them as you meet them in the corridors? Do they come straight out and tell you they have literacy problems?'

'No. They won't admit they can't read or write properly in front of other prisoners. They have to be hard, or they know they could get bullied or ostracized, so I usually talk with the prison officers and they find a quiet room somewhere on the wing for me to chat with the men. I interview all the new prisoners individually when they come into the induction wing, so I know who shows signs of learning difficulties, and the officers sometimes tell me when a likely new candidate arrives, or which of the longer-term inmates they think I should speak to.'

I surprised myself – I was on a roll now. It was just like a normal conversation, and I was never short of words when I was chatting to other people, so the answers just flowed out of me, almost without my thinking about them. I guess that must have been because the interviewer's body language was encouraging as I spoke and he asked such good questions.

'So, if you don't teach in classrooms, how does your project work?'

'I find small spaces to teach prisoners individually, and I train some of the prisoners to be mentors, so that the men can help each other. I'm also hoping, if the prison lets me, to be able to run a new course to train some of our top mentors to become teachers of adult literacy, so that these prisoners can teach other prisoners.' I was glad of the opportunity to flag up my dream of leading this course and hoped that somebody in the prison's management might hear it.

The interviewer seemed impressed, then came up with the question I always get asked: 'Why are prisoners offered courses instead of being given a hard time while they're inside?'

That set me off in full-flow. 'I've been asked that question many times. If we can get to some of these young lads in their twenties when they first come into prison, or even better before they come into prison, and in schools, then they might not end up in prison. If we can help some of these young guys to understand their problems with dyslexia, which 53% of the population in my prison have, and give them the coping strategies, we might be able to stop them coming into prison. Or if they do come in, we can help them so that when they go out, please God, they don't come back in again. That's why it's important to offer them the training to help them stay out of prison.'

I couldn't believe how well the interview had gone and how easy it was. But then again, I always was a good talker. This was something I loved doing. It was almost like I imagined a drug to be – it left me on a high and I was buzzing as I drove to the prison. I couldn't wait to tell everybody about it, but a few people had heard and it was all round the place before I even got there.

'Well done, Jack. That was brilliant. Your really wowed them!'

'Great stuff, Jackie. Several of us heard how good you were.'

Even the Deputy-Governor came to find me. 'I didn't hear you on the radio as I didn't know you were going to be on, but everyone is saying how well you did, and what great publicity it is for the prison, so well done.'

I felt quite proud of myself. If I'd know there would be so much interest, I'd have let everyone know the evening before, but I was too afraid I'd say something stupid and get in trouble as usual.

Once the initial excitement was over, I assumed everyone would just forget about it and get on with their day's work, but it seems my interview sparked off interest in all directions. The local newspaper was onto me within the hour. They wanted to come to my house that evening and interview me for the next issue. I did that and it was a good article. This time I told people when it was coming out and somebody pinned it up on the main notice-board. That was a laugh, but it had a serious side too. Now, whenever I popped into my local shop or met a friend for coffee, or even in the library, people I'd never met before would come up to me as if I was their new best friend.

'I heard you talk on the radio. You were brilliant,' said one woman. 'I've got a cousin who's in prison in the Midlands. I've written to him about you. Now he's telling all his mates.'

'I read your fantastic article,' said another. 'My daughter is dyslexic and her school doesn't do much to help her. They don't do any of the things you do, like multi-sensory and all that. I'm sure you could help her.'

'You're Jackie Hewitt-Main, aren't you?' asked someone else. 'I heard you on the radio the other day and I just wanted to tell you how much I admire what you are doing with the prisoners. I'd love to support you in some way, if that's possible. Here's my phone number.'

I always stopped and talked to anyone with dyslexic relatives or friends and tried to help them if I could, at weekends. Some of them did indeed become friends and I'm still in touch with a few of them today.

Over the next few weeks I did a lot of work with Gilroy, and every time he seemed brighter and made more progress socially as well as with his learning. Using the checklist, we established that he really was dyslexic, so we got him going on the Lexion software, which he loved. I started him off with some of the basic activities and assessments, then Carl gave him daily practice sessions, as well as frequent chats to give him a more positive frame of mind.

'Every morning he comes out of his cell and asks me if the computers are up yet,' said Carl when we had a mentors' meeting a month or so later. 'He's really keen.'

'Yes, he always loves working on the computers.'

On one occasion, as I walked into E wing to work with Gilroy, the officer who first brought him to me stopped me.

'I don't know how you've done it, but Mr Barker is a changed man,' he beamed. 'I've never seen such a transformation! Before he would not come out of his cell unless forced to, and he would not talk to anyone, but he is now actually coming out and talking. I mean, he seems willing to talk to everyone. He loves the computers and pairing him with Mr Nixon was a genius move. Carl Nixon is always there for him, so if Mr Barker feels a bit low, he will go and sit in Mr Nixon's cell. Carl never seems to mind and will always sit and listen to Gilroy's woes, talk with him and build up his confidence. He's really come out of his shell.'

'Yes, it's great to see how well Gilroy's doing,' I agreed. 'He still has some anger to work through, but I think the voices have more or less gone now.' As I walked on, I said a little prayer that this would continue for Gilroy after his release.

CHAPTER 12

JOE

On arrival back in the prison after a short holiday break, I found a message from the management that a member of the House of Lords and two MPs had been given permission to make their own separate visits to the prison to observe the project in action. They each wanted to talk with me, some of my mentors and some of the prisoner learners. The dates and times had been agreed, so now I just needed to sort out where, who and what they would observe. I decided that we could change around the Learning Workshop sessions to coincide with each visit so that they could sit in with us to see what we did, then observe individual teaching and mentoring sessions and finally talk with individuals or a group of us, as they wished.

The first to come was Lord A, who immediately took a great interest in every aspect of our work. He stayed all morning and observed several aspects of the project, then stayed to talk with some of us before he left. I was a little concerned at his serious expression, so I plucked up the courage to ask him about it.

'Oh really?' He smiled for the first time. 'My wife tells me I always look too serious when I'm concentrating on something. It's just that I'm so interested in what you're doing here.' He asked me several thought-provoking questions about what he had seen, which showed he'd really taken it all in, and I answered every question with complete honesty, warts and all. I thought it was important for him to get a full picture of what we were doing.

'I'm afraid I have to go now to another appointment, but I'd much rather stay here and spend more time with you and the prisoners.'

'We've enjoyed talking with you,' I said.

'I must congratulate you on the impressive work you are doing here and I shall certainly be raising this project in the House of Lords at the earliest opportunity. You have my full support. Do please contact me if there is anything I can help you with as I'd like to follow you and the project over the coming year.'

'Thank you Lord A. I really appreciate your coming here and spending time with us today.'

He paused, as we shook hands. Then he tilted his head down a little towards me and lowered his voice.

'I have huge admiration for what you are doing here,' he continued. 'It's a complete eye-opener. You have shown that many of these dyslexic prisoners can be helped by the radical process of simply talking with them and getting them to engage. It's groundbreaking. Somebody should have done this long ago. I hope you can continue with your work and help it spread to other prisons.'

Sure enough, only a few days after his visit, Lord A emailed to tell me that he would be speaking about our project in a debate on the 1st of February and how to access *Hansard* to see what he'd said immediately afterwards.

When I read the *Hansard* account of his speech, I was happy to see that he'd praised our project as a 'new approach' to working with more than half the prison population who were dyslexic. He said:

> *'The real revelation here was successfully training other inmates to be mentors, to work with and support other prisoners' learning … prisoners are told they can help someone else because they have the same type of condition and so can understand the problem and explain it to others.'*

It was true that out of the forty men I had now trained to be mentors, about half of them had first been dyslexic learners with me and had later progressed to becoming mentors for others. They were often very effective in this role as they had experienced their learners' problems themselves and had learnt how to deal with them. And of course, the prisoner-learners had respect for them because the mentors had been in the same position, had made good progress and were role-models for those at the early stages of gaining literacy skills.

The next visitor was Mr B, a local MP who came to see what his constituency prison was doing for dyslexic inmates. He also took a great interest and promised to return for a second visit, which he did a year later. On both occasions he followed up by speaking in parliamentary debates and also asked a question at Prime Minister's question time, to which Tony Blair answered in a supportive manner.

In all of his five speeches promoting our project in the House of Commons, Mr B MP praised our project and several times called me *'that remarkable woman, Jackie Hewitt-Main'*, which led to considerable teasing from friends and family, who didn't recognise me in that description!

Soon after that, Mr B MP kindly agreed not only to attend the launch of my report of the project so far, but also to host it himself at the House of Commons. This was the first time I had been inside Parliament, so I was quite overawed by the venue, but once I was asked to introduce the report, my nerves disappeared and I went into top gear, speaking as enthusiastically as I usually do everywhere else.

The third visit to our project was by the then Minister for Prisons, who was very interested in what we were doing and also spoke about us in Parliament. Indeed, Mr.B MP arranged a meeting with the Minister after they had both visited our prison, and also with an Education and Skills Minister and myself in a private meeting room in the House of Commons, to see if they could find a way to finance the extension of the project.

It was all very hopeful for a few weeks and several of the prisoners wrote heartfelt letters in support of his initiative, including film-producer Max, in prison for kidnapping and my old friend, Fred Suggs, who proudly wrote his letter himself on the computer – a remarkable effort, with few errors:

> *Dear Sir/Madam*
>
> *My education is not too good. But the help I got from inmates and teachers gave me was very good.*

> *One day I spoke to a lady and that was Jackie Hewitt-Main and she told me about Dyslexia. I told her it was no good talking to me about reading and writing, because I don't even know my ABC.*
>
> *When I went back to my cell I thought that she was right in what she told me. I started to learn my ABC which I learnt in two days. I must say it's been a great help to me talking to Jackie which helped me with the F.T.C. I would like to say that we need a chance like this because a lot of people don't know what Dylexia is about.*
>
> *I thought I was dopey but it's not true because I am willing to learn so please help me and others and keep this going.*
>
> *Yours Truly,*
>
> *Fred Suggs*
>
> *P.S. I'm 67 years old, it just goes to prove you are never to old. Thanks for every thing and every ones help and lets keep the good work going.*

But, despite Fred's letter, and many others, the impetus of these parliamentary visits and support silently faded away as the money was not to be found. This was a very disappointing outcome for us all – the men as well as me, but we had plenty of other unexpected excitements to come.

The project had now been going long enough for our reputation to have spread with prisoners as they were transferred to new jails. *'Inside Time'*, the prisoners' newspaper, had done a feature on me and the project earlier in the year and I was unaware of this notoriety until I discovered, quite by accident, that there was a sheaf of letters addressed to me, at the back of a cupboard in the corridor of the management block. This intrigued me when I heard it from the officer who had let it slip.

'Oh, didn't you know about that?' he said, looking flustered. 'I'm sorry. I assumed you knew. Perhaps I shouldn't have told you. Now I'm going to be for it.'

'No, don't worry,' I reassured him. 'I won't say you told me. If anyone asks me I can just say I was looking for something else when I came across the bundle of letters.'

'Thanks Jackie. You're a diamond.'

I went straight over and explained to the Deputy-Governor's secretary that I was just looking for something of mine that was in the cupboard. She said to go ahead and get it, so I did. Inside the cupboard I found a pile of about twenty letters to me, bound together with elastic bands. They must have been there quite a while as one of the bands had perished and it fell away as I lifted them out.

Back in my office, I began to open and read the letters. Most of them were from dyslexic prisoners in several other jails around the country, asking to be transferred to this prison so that they could join this 'amazing' project. There was also one from a mother with the same request for her son, and the last was from a tutor at another prison requesting our materials to be sent to her. As I read through these often plaintive letters, I was appalled. Despite being addressed to me, they had all been opened by some unknown person, dated and marked as 'no reply needed', then slipped back in their envelopes and hidden away.

Why had I not received any of these letters, nor even been told of their existence over the intervening six months? My first instinct was to go straight to see the Governor or Deputy-Governor and demand to know why these letters had been kept from me, but I quickly realised this could be tricky as I would almost certainly have to explain how I came to know about them and I had to make sure I didn't get my officer friend into trouble. I decided to give it some thought, to make sure I broached it the best way, but I was so cross that these poor men hadn't even had a reply, and presumably they blamed that on me.

It was so unfair – I would have loved to respond to them. Of course it wasn't in my power to get anyone transferred, but at least I could have offered them some encouragement and hope. Waiting and waiting for a letter that doesn't come is soul-destroying to anyone, let alone a prisoner watching a chink of light that slowly dims into darkness.

Over the past few days, I had been hearing mentions of 41year-old traveller Joe, sentenced for 22 years for a murder everyone seemed to think he didn't commit. I was intrigued how this could have happened, and appalled that it might be true, so when I was asked to go down to the prison warehouse to see him, I was glad to go and find out more.

Joe had already been in the prison for two and a half years and was working in the warehouse as the store-manager for all the wheelchairs that were made or repaired there. He also looked after all the items of stock for everything else that needed repairs. The officer who greeted me when I arrived, told me there was not a piece of paper in the place, yet Joe knew where everything was – every tool and part, every nut, bolt and screw for the various different items, and he knew which bits went on each. The whole store-room was neat and tidy with everything in its place, but no labels, so only he knew where to find anything.

'Our Joe is a difficult man. He has a huge anger problem and can be very rude. He has often refused to work with teachers in the past, so I'm not sure how he will be with you. He got very angry with the last two who tried. Maybe I should ask him first?'

'No, I'd like to introduce myself to him and see how we get on. I'm not really like most teachers.'

'You can say that again!' He smiled.

'Where can we talk?'

'One of us will have to be close by and watch him the whole time, in case he kicks off, so the only place I can let you sit with him is the glass room at the end there, and I'll watch from the outside. He'll probably only last for about ten minutes anyway.'

'OK, we'll give it a try.' I went off to settle myself in the glass room while he went to fetch Joe. As I sat and waited, I was apprehensive about using this distracting environment, with loud music piped in, the brightest lights you can imagine and continuous movements visible through the glass walls. These are difficult conditions for anyone with dyslexia, including me. They made me feel as if my brain was buzzing, I didn't know where to look and I became quite fidgetty.

After a few moments the prisoner and his escort appeared. My first impression of Joe was one of shock. His face was slashed by a prominent scar and he was covered in tattoos down his forearms and hands. When he sat down, sort of folding himself awkwardly into the chair, I could sense him tensing up. Was it me, or was it the noise and light?

'Hello Joe,' I began. 'I'm Jackie Hewitt-Main and I hate this room, don't you?'

He flashed me a look of surprise, perhaps even bewilderment. 'Yes,' he agreed.

'I'm dyslexic, so I don't cope very well with the loud music blaring and the glare of the lights. They make my head buzz.'

'Me too,' he replied, with relief. 'It's difficult to think in here, with everything going on outside. My last teacher tried to make me learn in a room like this, but I told her to get stuffed after ten minutes.'

'Well, we'll have to try and make the best of it and see if we can have a bit of a chat. I'm not going to do any teaching today, so you needn't worry about that. I just want us to get to know one another a bit to start with. I never teach anyone until I've heard their story.'

Again, the look of surprise. 'OK.'

'Rooms are important to me. For example, I always feel uncomfortable in classrooms.'

'I thought you were a bloody teacher?'

'I am a teacher, but I don't usually teach large groups of people. I prefer to teach individually; for example, just you and me.'

'Funny sort of teacher!'

'Yes, a lot of people would agree with that.' I smiled and carried on. 'I like quiet spaces with solid walls, where we can move about and find the best way for you to learn. Everyone has their own best learning style. I guess, from your job in the prison, that you like practical activities?'

'Yes, I'm good at anything practical and I love my job.'

'I always tried to do the practical things too, because I failed at everything else in school.' I paused to assess his response, and was pleased to see his attentive expression, as if he identified with what I was saying, as I had hoped. 'I liked helping people too. I used to go and help at the Brownies every week and teach them to do their practical badges. I loved that. But I was no good at anything to do with reading and writing.'

'That's like me as well,' he said, nodding. 'I had problems with everything at school, even art and PE. I didn't like crowds. I still don't, so anything in a group is bad for me. And I knew I was thick.'

'Who told you that?'

'My father always said so.'

'I got called thick at school as well,' I said. 'And I thought I was thick for a while. I tried to commit suicide because I was so depressed at my failures.'

'Are you really a teacher?' he asked, incredulous. 'How can you be a teacher if you can't read or write?'

202

'That's a great question. In fact, when I was about your age, I found a tutor at college who was the first one to ever understand me. She diagnosed me as severely dyslexic and helped me to start learning. I mostly taught myself after that, with some help along the way.' I paused. 'It just shows, you're never too old to learn. I'm not great at reading and writing even now, but good enough to get by in most situations. I learnt how to fill in forms, how to use a computer, and all that sort of thing. All of that experience helps me to be a better teacher and to understand what dyslexic people like us need.'

'Am I dyslexic then?' He seemed surprised at the idea, but somehow pleased at the possibility of knowing what caused his problems.

'I think you may be, but I'll need to assess you properly to know. We could do that tomorrow if you like.'

'Yes please.'

'But in a different room. I'll see if I can get somewhere on your wing.'

He smiled. 'That would be great,' he said. 'But that's F wing – some of the officers aren't very helpful there.'

'I'll see what I can do.'

Through the glass wall I noticed a clock beyond where the officer was sitting and I was pleased to see that we'd already been talking for fifteen minutes.

'If we're going to do some assessments tomorrow, I want to know a bit more about you first. Tell me about your background. I believe you come from a traveller family?'

'Yes, sort of. My family are mainly travellers, but my parents live in a house nowadays. 'I used to live in the caravan in their garden.'

'Was that your choice?'

'No, they said they wouldn't have me in the house.'

'Was that because of your father?'

He shrugged, but said nothing, his face glum.

'You said your father called you thick. Didn't that upset you?'

'Not half. I kicked off about it the first time, but they carted me off into care for a couple of weeks to teach me to behave, they said.' He looked really sad. 'I wanted my dad to love me, but he never did. He only saw me as a failure at reading and writing, and never noticed the things I could do.' He paused, and a hint of a tear came to his eye, this strong man covered in scars and tattoos. 'It was my brother he loved. My brother could never do anything wrong in his eyes, but I could never do anything right. He kicked me out in the end, to fend for myself. I was only about thirteen - wouldn't have anything to do with me.' Seeing Joe's disconsolate face, I thought I'd better change the subject.

'What did you do when you left school?'

'This and that. I left without any qualifications and I had to steer clear of any forms or paperwork, so I started working in a toy factory, but I couldn't keep up with the work. My co-ordination isn't very good.'

'That's like me,' I said. 'I'm always getting in a muddle. What did you do next?'

'Agency work, filling in for people here and there. I could never keep a job down because in the end there would always be a piece of paper I had to read or write on, and I could never fill in an application form.' He stopped for a moment. 'When you tell people that you can't read or write, they look at you as if you're an alien.'

'I know exactly what you mean, I said. 'I always felt like that too.'

'Really?' Again that tilt of his head in surprise. 'And if I go for a job, as soon as they see me I get judged on my tattoos and the scar on my face. I can't do anything about that.'

'Have you been in prison before this sentence?' I asked.

'Yes, lots of times, always for drink-driving.' He looked a bit embarrassed. 'I've got a bit of a drink problem,' he explained. 'They did take me through some therapy in one prison and that helped a bit, but not for long once I was out.'

'And what about this sentence?'

He shifted in his chair. It was the first time I'd noticed him look uncomfortable.

'It's quite a long one isn't it?'

'Yes, twenty-two years.'

'I've heard a story that it was for a crime you didn't commit?' I said, as if asking the question. I wanted to see how he responded to that rumour.

'I got convicted of murder,' he said. 'It was my brother that did it, but my parents pointed the finger at me instead. They told me I had to take the rap because I was a failure anyway and it would ruin his life, and theirs too, if he got sent to jail for it.'

'So you went along with that?' I had the feeling I knew why.

'I didn't have any choice. I thought maybe my dad would think I'd done well if I took the rap, so I kept schtum and let them get on with it.'

'Do they come and visit you now?'

'No.'

'Never?'

'Never … but they do live quite a long way from here. I'm hoping for a transfer next year, if I can behave myself. There's a more open prison nearer home. They might come and visit me there, and that would be better for me too. I hate being stuck in buildings like this, night and day. I'm used to a caravan, and open spaces so I always hate being shut inside. Some of the other men don't seem to mind, but it's hell for me.'

Glancing at the clock again, I was amazed to see that we had been here talking for an hour. 'We've come to the end of our time for today,' I said. 'Thank you for talking with me like this. I hope it hasn't been too difficult for you?'

'No.' He looked surprised at himself. 'Not at all. It was good to talk. You weren't like the other teachers because you didn't push. You listened and you understood.'

The time had gone by so quickly that I felt we'd hardly begun. But I knew and understood a lot more about this rather sad man with the violent reputation, who had not shown any anger towards me, even though I was a teacher. And, above all, I felt indignant on Joe's behalf that his father refused to acknowledge his son's simple yearning for love and appreciation.

'How did you do that?' asked the officer in charge of the workshop, as Joe was being escorted back to his work area. 'I'm shocked that he didn't kick off once … for a whole hour. Joe's never talked with anyone for that long. He must have taken a liking to you.'

Now I had to set to and try to find both the time and a more suitable space to meet him the next day, so that we could begin his assessments. Time was an issue for him even more than for me, because he had to be on duty all day as manager of a group of other prisoners in the workshop. The only time he could be spared would be his lunch-hour, so I immediately changed a couple of things around so that I could have the same lunch-hour as his, then looked into the available spaces. It seemed there was no quiet space in the workshop building, so I checked out F wing, where his cell was. I had hardly ever visited this part of the prison, so I didn't know any of the officers there. When I went over to see them, they were very off-hand with me, so it was a struggle trying to persuade them to help me find somewhere we could work for an hour. Eventually, one of them suggested the chapel, as that would be the only quiet place we could meet during Joe's lunch break. I told them exactly what time I would arrive at the wing to see Joe and they reluctantly agreed.

On the next day, at the beginning of lunchtime, I arrived at the entrance to F wing as planned – 12.30 on the dot. Joe had already been escorted back to his cell from the workshop and was waiting for me. He told me later that he had looked for me out of his cell window and watched me do the long walk, about 300 yards, to F wing from the main buildings.

When I arrived, I was met by a female officer who seemed pleasant enough and took me to the chapel, then collected Joe and brought him to me. By now, we had already lost a few minutes from our allotted hour. We got straight down to the dyslexia checklist, which identified that Joe had sixteen of the twenty dyslexic traits.

'So it clearly shows that you have dyslexia,' I said.

He beamed. 'So now I know there is a reason why I can't learn things.'

'Yes. I can see that some of your weaker areas are definitely because of your dyslexia.'

We then looked at the learning styles questionnaire and found he was a visual as well as a practical learner. This seemed to surprise him. I then assessed his basic skills levels and found he was just above a five-year-old's level for literacy, and a nine-year-old's level for maths. We discussed this together and started to make a learning plan for him.

As we did this, with me writing down what we decided, he made a useful comment.

'I don't know how you can do that,' he said. 'White paper hurts my eyes.'

I always carried with me a set of coloured acetates, so I got them out and we played around with them.

'Do any of them help?' I asked. 'Which one seems best for you?'

He picked one out and placed it over the printed page again. 'This green one makes it much easier for me to read.'

'Good. I'll try and see if we can find some green paper for you to work on. If we do manage to find some, I could print out all the practice sheets on green and you could use it to write on too.'

'That would be mega,' he smiled.

'OK. I'll put out a call for green paper.' It was now nearly time to finish. 'They told me we could have the library every Tuesday lunchtime, from half past twelve,' I said to him. 'So we can use the computer in there. We can do some dyslexia activities on the computer to help you strengthen the skills you find hardest.'

I was surprised to see how downhearted he looked about that. Usually, this was what all the men wanted to do, but not Joe.

'You don't look happy about doing that.'

'I can't use a computer,' he began. 'I've never used one in my life. They're scary.'

'Ok,' I thought quickly. 'Well we can do lots of practical activities in the library, without even switching on the computer, and I'll give you some practice things to do in your cell as well. But how about if we sit at the computer at the end of our next session and do one activity? You can tell me what to type in, so that you don't have to touch it if you don't want to.'

'Well … maybe.' He looked uncertain.

'OK, so it's next Tuesday in the library and we won't use the computer if you really don't want to. We'll just play it as it comes.'

He smiled with relief.

By the following Tuesday, I had asked two or three friendly officers to look out for any green paper and by the time I arrived, it seemed the whole prison had been scoured! There was a huge pile of paper and card in various shades of green. Every wing had apparently been part of the now famous quest for green, all for Joe Miller.

Each Tuesday after that, I would take that long walk across to F wing and he would watch me from his cell window, giving me a cheery wave as I came nearer. I always looked out for him and waved back. But now would come the big problem. On that first occasion, a woman officer had let me in, but she didn't usually work on Tuesdays and the others were all men. I always timed it so that we could have the full hour to work together, but that hardly ever happened.

Once I'd let myself in, I had to find where the officers were having their lunch and ask if one of them could collect Joe from his cell and bring him to the chapel. But they were all sitting around, enjoying a good chat as they ate. Sometimes none of them would go and get him until they were ready, which meant I had to wait around for ages, and Joe would be sat fuming in his cell, knowing how much of our time was being lost. We had no choice but to wait until someone finally went to get him. It was very frustrating for us both. Eventually we might have as little as five minutes, or up to half or three quarters of an hour, depending on who would bother to get up from their lunch and collect Joe. On the rare occasions when the female officer was on duty, we would have pretty much the whole hour, which was a real treat.

These male officers could see how annoyed I was getting about this situation and, after lots of banter and teasing from them, I'd had enough. It made me so angry that I stood up in front of them all and said my piece, without holding back. I really let rip at them, telling them what I thought of their attitude and how badly they were affecting a man's chances to learn.

When I finished, there was a stunned silence. As I left F wing that day, I was subdued in the knowledge that I'd probably get into trouble with the management for that outburst, but I couldn't help myself. I just wanted to help these men learn, so that they could plan a future for themselves and not have to come back into prison again and again, as so many of them did. The more I recalled the stunned faces of those officers, the more scared I was that I would be banned from ever entering the prison again. I couldn't bear the thought of letting down so many of the prisoners if that happened.

All week I waited to be called in to the management block, but it didn't happen. That was a huge relief. Someone must have told the prisoners what I had done though, because when I returned to F wing the following week, a few minutes before lunch-time when most of the men were still milling about, there was a loud cheer. I looked around to see what it was for, then my face went red when I realised it was for me.

The funny thing was that a few weeks later, the whole of F wing changed. They had organised more computers for me on the wing and made it easier to work there, with staggered lunch-times for the officers and lots more co-operation. I never had any trouble at all on F wing after that.

Joe soon got used to the idea of using the computer and eventually came to love it so much that he decided to buy a laptop of his own as soon as he could. His learning progressed every week and soon he was working with a mentor and gaining confidence in his own abilities.

'You're doing so well now,' I told him. 'I reckon you'll be my star pupil!'

However, despite so many officers having changed their attitudes towards me, there remained one or two who regarded me with continuing disdain and did their best to frustrate my efforts.

So it was that one morning I was summoned to see the Deputy-Governor.

'I've had an official complaint lodged against you,' she said, with a look of genuine disappointment.

I was appalled. What was I supposed to have done now? 'What kind of complaint?' I asked her.

'A female officer says that she witnessed you touching a prisoner.'

I knew this was an absolute no-no. It would be a sacking offence for an employee of the prison service, except in self-defence or for security reasons. For me it could ban me from working here any more. 'Which prisoner? Where ... when?' I asked, incredulous. I knew I hadn't touched any prisoner. It was something I was always careful about. There were times when men were unhappy and really needed a hug, or even a touch on the arm, but I always had to refrain. It was hard, but I had always kept to that rule, so I knew this female officer must have a grudge against me – why else would she falsify such a claim?

'The prisoner in the complaint is Tony Tanner. The incident was apparently on the wing a few days ago.'

I knew I hadn't even seen Tony for a week or more and I was certain I had not gone close to him. 'That can't be right,' I said. I have never touched any prisoner, and I haven't seen Tony since at least a week ago.'

'Are you certain?'

'Absolutely,' I assured her.

'Leave it with me and I will investigate the context of this complaint and will let you know as soon as I can what the outcome will be.'

'I know what the truth is,' I said. 'So I have no fear about the outcome.' That wasn't quite true, of course, because I knew how manipulative some women could be, especially if they were jealous or resentful of me for some reason, so she might have bribed or persuaded colleagues to support her claim. But I was certain of what the outcome *should* be.

A few days later I was called back to see the Deputy-Governor.

'Sit down, Jackie.' Her face looked set in a neutral expression, but she couldn't hide the smile in her eyes. 'You'll be pleased to know … I have come to a verdict on this complaint.' She paused, then broke out in a grin. 'I'm sure you'll be glad that I have dismissed the case against you, which turned out to be no case at all.'

'Yes,' I let out a long sigh. I had never doubted the truth should win out, but I know life can be unfair, so I was highly relieved it had turned out right.

'On questioning her at length I found a number of discrepancies between her two statements,' explained the Deputy-Governor. 'So I have removed the complaint from the record.'

'Phew! Thanks.'

'How is everything going with your project?'

Here was my chance, so I took it. 'Fine, thanks, but we still don't have enough computers available to the men.'

'We don't have any more budget for computers this year,' she said.

'You don't need it,' I continued, with a smile. 'I came across a whole room filled with computers a couple of days ago and asked about them. Apparently they have never been used. Could I get them moved across to the wings?'

'Are you sure?'

'Yes. I asked in the IT workshop and they don't belong to them Bob said they were for the prisoners leisure and educational use in each of the wing libraries.'

'OK. I'll get them released and will organise for them to be moved to the libraries tomorrow. Will that be soon enough?' she teased.

'Yes, that will be great. Thanks.' I could have kissed her. It was her job to be fair at all times, but she had always been a great supporter of my project, and I was immensely grateful for her help.

I went home with a lighter heart that evening. As I opened the front door and stepped inside, there was a small white feather on my doormat. I picked it up and gave it a kiss. 'Thanks,' I said. 'Now I can get on with the next project initiative.' I knew this would be a great step forward, but I didn't realise just how great it would be.

CHAPTER 13

ARNIE

The *Lexion* software we were using was devised in Sweden and it was when I was on a visit to one of their prisons to observe what they do for dyslexic prisoners, that I had first seen *Lexion* in use. Since then, it had become one of the main elements of our project, crucial for assessing ongoing progress as well as initial assessment and a range of literacy activities at different levels, designed for dyslexic individuals. Annika Boreson Hallsvik, project leader for the development of this innovative software was one of our strongest supporters.

A group of officials in the Swedish prison service contacted me. They had apparently heard about the successes of our project and invited me to visit Skogome, their model prison, to help them develop a programme to screen their prisoners for dyslexia and other hidden disabilities and to establish what proportion of their prison population had specific learning difficulties.

I flew over to Gothenburg, where I was met and looked after by Annika, who accompanied me to meet the officials at Skogome. At the prison, I spoke with a group of educators from jails all over Sweden, then had a tour of the prison where I observed how they use the *Lexion* software. As I watched the men working on computers, the educators asked me what I thought could be bettered.

'Well, you are using it as a tool within a classroom situation, but we don't teach in classrooms. We use *Lexion* one-to-one, with individual learners.'

'How do you do that, unless you have a lot of teachers?' asked one tutor. 'Surely the classroom is the only way?'

'Many of our men refuse to learn in a classroom setting,' I explained. 'They have spent their school years failing in classrooms, so they are often scared of that sort of situation or just don't want to go through it again. I have trained forty of our inmates to be mentors and work with the men individually, right across the prison, sometimes in their own cells or perhaps in the library or other quiet spaces.'

There was a general look of surprise. 'How do you choose the mentors?' someone asked.

'There are two types of mentors,' I said. 'About half of them are quite literate and may have previous experience of doing something similar. For example, a couple of them are trained listeners for the Samaritans. But many of our mentors have themselves had problems with learning to read and write and have learnt with the project. Quite a lot of those have dyslexia, so are in the ideal position to help others with the sorts of problems they've experienced and learned to cope with.'

'Is being a mentor treated as a job in an English prison, like doing the laundry or working in the kitchen?' asked one of the officials.

'It is in the prison where I work, because I fought to make it so,' I replied. 'The men are paid 97p per day, just like men in other prison jobs. But this is not the norm in other prisons ... yet.'

'How do you persuade the right prisoners to become mentors?' Asked another tutor.

'I don't have any problem with that as many of the inmates who've learned with me volunteer to become mentors, and most of them make a grand job of it,' I said. 'I wish I could take on all those who volunteer, but I give them a long training programme of ten sessions, to make sure they are familiar with all aspects of our work and are ready for any situation a prisoner may present. Sometimes one of the officers will suggest someone, or occasionally I notice a man who is showing the skills needed to work with the learners, for example I spotted a couple of them working in the IT workshop.'

'That sounds a very interesting possibility,' commented one of the officers and everyone nodded.

The next day I talked through a variety of approaches to assessing dyslexia and other learning difficulties and gave them copies of my own checklist and various other forms of assessment. I demonstrated my approach when about to assess a new prisoner, using a variety of activities with one of Skogome's English-speaking inmates. They all watched with interest and made notes about some of the questions I asked and the things I said to help him feel relaxed enough to cooperate.

'You say that you found 53% of your prison population have dyslexia. How can we find out what is the percentage in this prison, and across all Swedish prisons?' asked someone at the back.

'I have interviewed and assessed about fifteen hundred prisoners so far in our prison, using the same assessment materials I have just given you copies of,

217

including my own checklist that I've trained officers to use in the induction wing when prisoners arrive. I keep a tally of the results of these assessments and it always stays steady around 53%. If you do the same here in your prisons, I'd be interested to know what you find out, especially if your results are quite different from mine.'

We all had a good lunch together and lots of animated conversation. There was a real feeling of excitement amongst the Swedish contingent and I felt encouraged that they were so keen.

In the afternoon, I talked them briefly through all the other aspects of our project and we finished with another question and answer session.

'You mentioned multi-sensory learning. Can you tell us about that?'

'Multi-sensory learning is particularly important for those who missed out on that at school; the ones who are practical learners,' I began.

'What do you mean, practical learners?'

'I use a questionnaire with the men to establish what is their preferred learning style. I find that most of the dyslexic prisoners are practical learners and a few are also visual learners. Hardly any of them are auditory learners, and yet that is the predominant teaching method in schools and colleges in our country.'

'It is the same here in schools, too,' said Annika.

'What do you mean, "multi-sensory learning"?' asked a Swedish tutor. 'Is it using all the senses at once?'

'It means using a lot of senses, but not all at once,' I explained. 'For example, you can learn the alphabet or the spelling of a word more easily and quickly if you use the sense of touch, with textured letters and tracing the letters in the air or in sand. At the same time it is important to make the sound of the letter and say its name, so that's the sense of hearing. You need to look at the letter and use various ways of writing it, such as on a misted mirror, with a wet finger on the floor, with toothpaste on a piece of card, in sand, on wet soap or using something like masking tape on carpet-tiles, always saying the letter sound or name at the same time. That's the senses of sight and hearing. If you can, encourage the learners to be active. They can walk round the shape of the letters, or make them in large, physical ways. The only senses you probably won't be able to use are smell and taste, but maybe that would be possible too in your prisons?'

'These are things that nursery teachers do in Sweden.'

'Yes, and they are the best ways to start the learning process for reading and writing at any age, but some of our English prisoners have never experienced this approach, or maybe they weren't ready for it when they started school.'

'You have opened so many windows and let the fresh air in for us today,' said one of the prison officials. 'Could we come and visit your prison to watch how you work?'

'I don't know,' I said. 'I'd love to show you what we do, but I think you would have to apply first to our Ministry of Justice, and to the prison itself.'

'We will do that. If they let us come, can we observe your project and talk to your prisoners?'

'I'd be very happy to host a visit from two or three of you, provided you obtain permission first from the Ministry of Justice as well as the prison.'

I was sitting in on a teaching session in the IT workshop one day, when I noticed one particular prisoner who kept asking the same question about how to do something, over and over again, as if perhaps he hadn't been able to understand the responses. When I watched him I noticed that he seemed very wary of the computer, so perhaps the questioning was also a form of evasion – putting off having to use his computer. Over the years I have developed a sort of extra sense that hones in on dyslexic people, and that's what happened with Arnie. I had the feeling he was dyslexic, like me.

I asked the tutor if she'd mind if I drew a chair up to Arnie's computer and had a word with him while I helped him get going. She seemed pleased, so I went over to him.

'Hello Arnie. I'm Jackie Hewitt-Main. I've always had problems with reading and writing and I didn't even know I was dyslexic until I was about your age. I couldn't help noticing that you had some difficulty with the answers to your questions.'

'Yes,' he turned and looked at me with a quizzical expression. 'I was diagnosed as dyslexic during one of my prison sentences years ago, when I was twenty-something. I've been in lots of prisons, but nobody has ever been able to help me.'

'That sounds like me too,' I agreed. 'I was a complete failure at school, yet I was always desperate to find a teacher who could teach me the way I could learn ... but I never did.'

'It's a bummer, ain't it?' he said.

I laughed. 'Why were you asking the same questions again and again?'

'When she was explaining what to do, I just couldn't get what she meant,' he said.

'I'm like that too sometimes. It's really hard to listen to the words and understand the meaning at the same time, especially if you are looking at the person's face as well. I find someone who changes their expression when they speak is really confusing when you're trying to listen and understand at the same time.'

'Yeah,' Arnie agreed. I noticed that his eyes had brightened since we'd started chatting, and his shoulders were up and his back straighter, as if a load had been lifted off them.

'Let's see if we can get this computer going,' I suggested, turning to face the screen. 'Do you know how to log on, or shall I show you?'

'I'd rather you do it. I can't cope with computers. The screen is too bright and I can't read the words. I've never really used one before, so I don't know how to log on.'

'OK. I'll do it first to show you. Then we can shut down and start again, with you logging on this time.' We went through that exercise and he actually did log on himself. He seemed pleased, but wary of the keyboard, as if frightened that touching it would break the whole machine.

'You said the screen hurt your eyes?'

'Yes, it's even worse than white paper.'

I got my set of coloured acetates out of my folder and spread them across his computer desk. 'Try these out,' I suggested. 'Pick each one up and hold it over the screen. Let's see if we can find a colour that helps you.'

One by one, he tried them all, screwing up his eyes for most of them and quickly discarding them. But he picked up the yellow acetate again and held it on the screen.

'This one helps a lot,' he said, in wonder. 'How does that work?'

'Most opticians know that some people who wear glasses find that slightly tinted lenses help them read more restfully. In your case, an optician could make you some yellow tinted lenses if you needed glasses. But I suggest you take this back with you to your cell and try it out on a few other things. If it really helps, I can order a yellow-tinted screen to put over the front of a computer when you are working on it.'

'Really? Thanks.'

'Now, let's try your acetate with this computer,' I suggested. 'What the teacher was telling you to do was to open the word-processing programme.'

'What's that?' asked Arnie. 'I can't be doing with words, not words that I have to read or write or spell. I don't do words, except when I'm speaking. I'm all right at that.'

We carried on with me showing him, one step at a time, then him trying it out. He seemed to gain a little more confidence, but it was slow-going, so I decided to stop while he felt good about what he had achieved so far.

Instead, as he said he was all right at talking, I started asking him about himself.   'You said you'd been in lots of prisons. How many do you think?'

'I don't know how many prisons,' he answered, but I do know I've been in prison thirty-nine separate times.'

I was astonished. 'You don't look old enough!'

'I'm 41,' he said. 'But I was only eleven the first time I was cautioned by the police, so I suppose I started young. It was all my big brothers' fault. They were always in trouble, so the police started to come after me too. It was the same at school. Because my big brothers had been so badly behaved and caused so many problems at school, the teachers expected me to do the same and they couldn't believe I might be different. So I didn't stand a chance.'

'What are you in for this time?' I asked.

'Drug-dealing. I've got two years and I'm half way through it.'

'So you might be released soon?'

'Well, if I am, I'll probably be on gate-arrest and straight back inside the same day.'

'Why is that?'

'Because I've got a few cases pending. I know one has been dropped, but I think they might charge me on one of the others.'

'Well, maybe they won't. Let's focus on your reading and writing for now. I can help you with that so I'd like to come and have a proper chat with you tomorrow and we could talk through your dyslexia, how it affects you and how to cope with it. Would that be OK?'

'Sure thing, as long as the officers agree. Nobody's ever tried to teach me about my dyslexia before. This is good.'

The next day I went to visit Arnie's wing to talk with him in the library. An officer sat outside as usual, but I don't think he was expecting any trouble. Arnie didn't have any self-confidence, and he'd been in a lot of difficulties through his life, but he'd never been violent as far as I could work out.

'What were you like at school?' I asked.

'I always tried when I was young,' he said. 'But my older brothers had been such hooligans at school, that all the teachers assumed I'd be the same. I remember once, when I tried to join in the discussion during a lesson, the teacher accused me of taking the micky.'

'How did that make you feel?'

'Very angry. I'm not usually aggressive or anything, but that day I could easily have hit out at the teacher for not taking me seriously. I had ideas, just like the others, so I wanted to contribute, but she thought I was a joker, about to make trouble, which I wasn't.'

'That must have been very frustrating. The same thing used to happen to me, only not as bad because I didn't have older siblings. I was always full of ideas, so the teachers couldn't understand why I didn't learn to read and write properly. They just thought I was lazy.'

'I was called lazy too, sometimes. They used to put me at the back of the classroom so that the others could get on better.'

'What did you do when you left school?' I asked.

'I did a City & Guilds course in brick-laying. I worked really hard and I was quite good at that. Then it all went wrong.'

'How do you mean?'

'I went right through to the end of the course. They reviewed all the work I'd done and I got a good grade. Then they said I had to do a final assessment to get the qualification. Well, I can't do written work, so that was a whole year wasted.'

'That's terrible.' I felt really bad about the way he'd been treated. 'Didn't you know you'd have to do a written assessment?'

'They told me I should have known because it was in the course details before I started, but I couldn't read them.,' Arnie said, despondently.

'Didn't anyone stick up for you and try to get the assessment dropped?'

'No, I just left. No point in making a fuss. My parents weren't bothered anyway. so what's the use?'

'Do your parents or any of your brothers have trouble with reading or writing?'

'Not as far as I know. My dad's a lorry driver and he can read, but he's not good at spelling. My mother is a machinist and I think she's fine with reading and writing. I have three brothers altogether and we are all different. My eldest brother isn't good at anything, unless someone shows him how to do it. The next one is good with his hands and can do anything practical. My younger brother is the bright one of the family. He can do practical things, but he is also good at written work.'

'The officer told me that one of your brothers is in prison, on this wing as well?'

'Yes. That's Keith, the youngest. He's not like me. He's the clever one.'

'Maybe I could have a chat with him too?'

Arnie and I started going through the dyslexia checklist together to find out what his strengths and weaknesses were and he showed a high number of problem areas, including many of the classic symptoms, such as confusing left and right, times, days and months, letters such as d and b, spellings and remembering messages. He was full of ideas, like me, but couldn't write them down. He liked stories but he couldn't read well enough to enjoy books.

'I hate having to read out loud,' he said. 'I always lose my place and feel like a proper dimwit when everybody gets impatient with me. All the loud sighs and tutting noises, and the odd giggle behind their hands.'

'Yes,' I agreed. 'I remember all that too. I dreaded having to read, and the teachers nearly always picked me. Maybe they wanted to show me up.'

Next I told him about learning styles and we went through the questionnaire, which showed the usual practical bias of someone with dyslexia, but with some visual strength as well. He seemed really interested in that.

'So, does that mean I learn best by seeing and doing things?'

'Yes, exactly right.' I nodded. 'So we need to choose the activities that fit those two things.'

His 'Skills for Life' assessments showed that he had problems with several letters when doing handwriting, but he was able to function in his overall literacy skills at the level of a nine or ten-year-old. However, his spelling skills were very low, in line with a five or six-year-old.

'Let's have a go at the Lexion assessment on the computer now.' I knew this would be a big step for him, so I took it slowly, showing and explaining all the things we did. The main thing that stood out was his problem with symbols, such as letters and numbers, so the software would now configure some practice activities for him to strengthen these aspects. We did a couple of *Lexion* activities together, with me keying in what he told me to start with, then gradually getting him to try. One of the things we tried was Spoonerisms – confusing sounds in words, such as 'nick your pose' for 'pick your nose', or 'no tails' for 'toe nails'. Arnie quite enjoyed those when they were explained to him, but he didn't find it easy to work them out.

He remained very wary of the computer itself, but began to do a little more, when he felt it was safe. I realised this would be a long slog and decided to get Arnie a mentor to help him get used to working on the computer and give him more confidence.

At the end of that first full session, just as I was thinking ahead to what we would do next time, Arnie dropped his bombshell.

'I'm due to move to an open prison tomorrow, to be nearer home.' He looked both happy and sad by turns. 'I was really looking forward to going,' he said. 'But now I don't want to. I want to stay here.'

'Why?' I asked, thinking it probably wouldn't be possible to change plans at such short notice. The prison service is not a flexible organisation.

'I knew I was dyslexic years ago, but nobody ever worked with me to help my dyslexia before. They just told me about it and left me. Now, I've found you and it's really good. You're the first person who has ever understood me. You're the only one who has shown me what I'm good at and what I need to work on, and you've explained my dyslexia to me. You really make me understand what my issues are and give me hope that I can tackle them at last. I don't want to stop now.'

227

I realised this was a huge speech for someone with as little confidence as Arnie and I was pleased I'd helped him to feel good about himself.

'I'm so glad I've given you hope,' I said. 'And that will always be there if you keep going with these things, but it must be too late now to cancel your transfer.' He looked so disconsolate that I wanted to give him a straw of comfort. 'I'm sure you'll be happier in an open prison. It must be better than this old place.'

'I got one of the officers to fill in a form this morning for me to ask for the transfer to be cancelled. I really want to stay here and learn with you.'

'Did he think you have a chance of cancellation, just the day before?'

'He said it might be possible. It has to be. I can't go now. This is my chance.'

The next day, I checked the plans for the day and Arnie's transfer was on the list, but it had a line going through it. I went straight over to see him.

'Have they told you whether you're going or not?' I asked.

He gave me a broad smile. 'I'm staying here,' he said. 'So I can go on learning with you.'

After a good chat with Arnie about what we would be doing next, we asked an officer if I could see his brother Keith. He was brought to me in the library and we went through the checklist. As I suspected, he too had some features of dyslexia, though not as many as Arnie.

The next time I saw Arnie I wanted to share that news with him. 'Have you seen Keith?' I asked him.

'Yes. He said he'd done a test with you, and that it went OK.'

'We went through the checklist, like I did with you.'

'What did it say?'.

'Didn't Keith tell you?'

'He said he'd got about half of the things on the list.'

'That's right, so that means he is dyslexic, though not as strongly as you.'

'But I always thought he was the clever one.'

'Well he is clever in some ways. You are too. We all are. But he is also dyslexic, so you ought to have a chat together about it all.'

After that, the two brothers talked it all through and began to realise that the whole family had some dyslexic type problems. This was quite a revelation for them.

Now that he knew he could stay, Arnie applied himself with enthusiasm to his studies, and especially to the computer. I got him a yellow screen to put in front of his wing's computer and his mentor worked with him on the *Lexion* activities and assessments between my weekly teaching sessions. Soon he was keen to show me how proficient and confident he had become with computers. This was quite a revelation for him and had obviously boosted his self-esteem. He could really see his own progress at last.

A few weeks after my visit to Sweden, not just two or three tutors, but a large group of them, together with officers and officials, plus Annika, came to visit our project for two days to see for themselves how it worked. They watched multi-sensory learning in a learning workshop, a mentor-training session on learning styles and multiple intelligences, and a whole range of other activities.

Some of our prisoners and mentors stood up in front of the Swedish officials and told their stories. Then the learners, including a couple who had recently graduated to become mentors, outlined their own learning needs and explained what they had gained from all the different parts of the project.

Next was Arnie's big moment. He had become so confident and proficient with the *Lexion* software that I had chosen him to show our Swedish visitors how we have developed new ways to use this software with the men. Arnie was a star and he proudly showed them his prowess by helping other prisoners to work on Lexion. As hoped, this was just the boost he needed. And the visitors, especially Annika, were clearly excited to see how we had found new ways to use the software in a peer-mentoring situation.

'I've never seen *Lexion* used in this way,' she said. 'It's inspiring to see how the mentors and the learners enjoy working together at the activities as a sociable experience, as well as making great progress in such a short time. We are all impressed by your whole project and I am keen to go back after this and try your approach out in our prisons.'

Members of the Swedish group talked with some of the prisoners informally to ask their responses to the way we worked, as well as talking with our prison officers and staff. It was a very successful visit and the start of an ongoing outreach relationship as Skogome prison changed their education programmes to incorporate what they had learned from our project.

Soon after the Swedish visit, I was called to the Governor's office. This was a rare situation. In fact I couldn't remember ever being summoned to see him before, other than by my own request on a couple of occasions. Now it was just a stark written order, handed to me by one of the officers on the wing where I was working that day. I read those few words over again, but there was no reason given. That made me anxious. What had I done that was so bad I had to go before the Governor himself? I was pre-occupied with the potential gravity of this situation, so may not have taken quite so much care as usual when locking the security door of the wing as I left.

Flustered, I automatically attempted to withdraw the key, perhaps a little clumsily, as I used to do when I was a child, which got me into a lot of trouble. The key broke in the lock. I was horrified as I looked at the top part of the key in my hand, with its jagged edge where the bottom part had sheared off inside the lock. Now what would happen?

I would have gone back inside to tell the officers, but I couldn't. And they wouldn't be able to get in or out either. I went straight to the management block and told the Deputy-Governor's secretary, who I knew quite well by now.

'Oh, Jackie!' She laughed. 'Whatever next?'

'I'm really sorry. I didn't mean to do it.' I sounded like myself as a child, trying to calm down my mother when I did the same thing with our front door key.

'Don't worry. It happens. I'll get someone to guard the door and our locksmith will see to it straight away. He'll just take the lock out and put in a new one, so no worries.'

'Thank you, thank you,' I gasped. 'I thought I'd be in terrible trouble.'

'I need to report it, of course, but I don't need to say who did it,' she reassured me.

'Thanks,' I repeated with a smile.

I walked along the corridor to the Governor's office and knocked on his door.'

'Come in,' he boomed.

I opened the door in great trepidation, trying to stop myself shaking. But clearly I needn't have worried. He broke into a wide smile as soon as he saw me.

'Sit down,' he said. 'I have some excellent news for you.' He leant across and pressed the intercom. 'Please send in Senior Officer Amey.'

'What is it?' I asked, in high suspense.

'I'll be able to tell you shortly,' he stalled.

Just then, the door opened, and in walked Miss Amey and gave me a broad grin. Clearly she already knew what this was about. I could hardly wait a moment longer.

'The great news is,' began the Governor, 'You've been nominated by Senior Officer Amey and have won the Criminal Justice Award for your outstanding contribution to working with offenders.' He paused for me to take it in. 'Congratulations!'

I looked from one to the other of them, quite incredulous. 'You're having me on, right? This is some sort of practical joke or scam? It must be.'

'It's no scam, Jackie,' said the Governor.

'I nominated you a few weeks ago,' added Miss Amey. 'They rang me up and asked more questions about you.'

'They checked it all with me too,' said the Governor. 'I must confess I was surprised, because I didn't know what

232

great work you have been doing here. But you are obviously doing a grand job for many of our inmates.'

'Wow,' I exclaimed. 'I can hardly believe it. I never win anything, let alone an award!'

The Governor reached for a large envelope and handed it to me. Inside was the award certificate itself, together with information about the award ceremony.

'We received a copy of your award certificate as well,' said the Governor. 'I gave it to Miss Amey to put up on display for all the staff to see. This is a very special occasion for us as well as for you. I'm sure you will enjoy taking your family and friends to the award ceremony.'

I was speechless for a few moments – a rare condition for me. Then I knew what I wanted to do. 'Can I put this on display too, where some of the men I work with can see it? I'd especially like to show it to the mentors at their next meeting. This award is for them too.'

'You have my permission to show it around to the men,' said the Governor. 'But I think after that you should keep your own copy to show your children, and your grandchildren too one day.'

'I'm not that old!'

'True, but you're obviously a remarkable woman, just as our MP called you in Parliament. A nuisance sometimes, I admit, but your project is doing a lot of good from what I hear, and everyone speaks very highly of you.'

'Thank you,' I smiled.

'No need for thanks. Just carry on with your good work.'

CHAPTER 14

REGAN

Most days I checked my emails while I was having a lunch break in my office. On one particular day I was surprised the find a message from *The Guardian* newspaper. What could this be about? I clicked to open it and read it through. They had heard about my Criminal Justice Award and the work I had been doing in the prison project, so they wanted to send an education correspondent down to see me at the prison. My spirits soared – this sounded an exciting opportunity to get our story out there again and attract more positive support for the dyslexia project, not only in prisons, but in schools and colleges too.

I replied immediately to say that would be fine, if they included some of the prisoners and mentors as well. I knew the men would love that, and it was only fair. They were all part of making our project a success. Of course I also had to explain to *The Guardian* how to obtain the necessary permissions.

The next day *The Guardian* wrote again to let me know the permissions were all agreed – so soon! Through further emails and a phone conversation, we arranged the details and I jotted down who I wanted them to speak to and what they should see, if they had time. It didn't even occur to me at that point that I should also think about what they might want to ask me and what I should say. Talking would be the easy bit.

The Guardian reporter duly arrived two days later and started by asking me questions. I suggested we do the questions later, when she had spoken to some of the men and watched part of an individual session. I had chosen Tony to work with me in a mentor session, mainly because he'd made such huge progress with me over the past few months and I thought he would enjoy it. They insisted on doing this session in his cell, having secured permission for that before they came. I checked with the management and they said it was OK, so I escorted the journalist and Tony back to his wing and we set up a short session in his cell, working with a coloured overlay, while the photographer took a photo of us, with the barred window in the background. I could see how well that would work in their newspaper.

Next, the correspondent interviewed Tony about his experiences as part of the project. He was a natural. He explained how he had never been offered support before for his reading and writing problems, and had become so frustrated by his failures that he used to be a habitual self-harmer.

'I wanted to go for jobs,' he said. 'But I knew I didn't stand a chance. I always found paperwork hard. Jackie was the first person ever to come and help me and she's given me one-to-one help. It's about time something like this happened in jails. It's blinding!'

'Tony has recently become a mentor himself,' I added. 'He made such good progress in his own learning that he volunteered to help others with theirs. He went through the whole training too.'

'How have you been finding it?' asked the journalist.

235

'There was a self-harmer who spoke to me the other day,' said Tony. 'He told me he was frustrated because he found it difficult to read and write. I calmed him down and am now going to mentor him. The governor praised me.' He smiled with pride. 'I used to be a proper rogue, but I'm turning.'

When the feature article came out the following Tuesday, with the great headline of 'Spelling out a Better Future', there was the photo of me and Tony in his cell. I bought a few copies of *The Guardian* on the way to the prison that morning and took one of them straight across to give to Tony. It was a joy to see his face when he opened the newspaper and saw his picture. It was a great boost to his self-esteem. So much so that it was difficult to think of him now as that depressed self-harmer who thought he was a failure when I first met him.

At lunchtime that day, just hours after the article had appeared in *The Guardian*, I was amazed to receive an email from a TV company. They had seen this morning's feature and wanted to make a documentary programme about our project for *'Teachers TV'*. They asked whether I had ever considered how effective my approach would be in schools, which of course I had, often.

They explained their plan of spending two days in the prison and to have a secondary school literacy leader to visit and observe the project, so that viewers would see how my approach could work in schools. I thought this was a great idea – a really exciting prospect. I'd always said my way of doing things should go into schools and colleges as well as prisons, but I'd never been given the funding for that. Here was the opportunity to reach thousands of teachers with new strategies to incorporate in their dyslexia provision.

I emailed back and said we'd be very keen to co-operate with them on this, but could they tell me more about the secondary teacher who would be the other main person in their programme? The reply came straight back that they already had someone in mind for this, the literacy and special needs leader in a Kent secondary school.

As with the Guardian, they would have to apply for all the relevant permissions, and more, since they would be bringing in a lot of personnel, with TV cameras, sound-systems, lights and the like, so it would probably be several days, or even weeks, before I heard back from them again.

As I walked across the yard that afternoon, I mulled over in my mind what we could set up for the TV crew, if they managed to get permission to film. I wondered if they would.

Another email in my inbox that lunchtime had been from a favourite member of the management team:

> *'Hi Jack. I've got a new customer for you – a gent by the name of Regan McRae-Smith on F wing. He's been turned down as a listener because he hasn't passed the security as he was caught with drugs when he came in. However, he is dyslexic. Just thought you'd like to know. I haven't told him yet, but I thought you could have a chat with him. Kiss, kiss.'*

I laughed at the sign-off – obviously trying to hide the fact that he'd asked me to do his dirty work in telling this poor guy the disappointing news. Ah well, maybe I could do it in a less demoralising way than if he said it.

I reached F wing and let myself in, walked through the security bubble and out the other side, into the wing itself, then found an officer.

'The management have asked me to talk with Regan McRae-Smith. I've got some disappointing news to tell him, and they say he's dyslexic, so I want to chat with him about that too. Maybe I can help him. Have you got a quiet room we can talk in?'

'OK, there's a small room I'll take you to down at the far end, then I'll go and get him for you. He's one of our high-risk prisoners, so I'll have to stay on the corridor while you talk, but I don't want to get in your way.'

'Thanks. Tell me about him. What is he in for?'

'A gangland shooting. He's nineteen years old and always up to mischief.'

I sorted out a couple of chairs and arranged them as usual, then sat and waited, thinking how best to tell this young man about being turned down as a listener. It wasn't going to be the best way to start our conversation, so maybe I should look for an appropriate moment to bring it up, once he's more at ease.

'Here's Regan,' said the officer. 'I'll stay close by in case you need me.'

'What's all this about?' asked Regan as he sat down where Jackie indicated. 'The screw wouldn't tell me anything.'

'I'm Jackie Hewitt-Main,' I began. 'I thought I'd come and have a chat with you because we have something in common.'

'Really?' He looked confused. 'What?'

'I've been told you are dyslexic. Is that right?' I didn't give him time to reply. 'I'm dyslexic too.'

He looked a bit startled now, and his eyes were alert. 'But who are you. You're not in uniform, so you can't be an officer.'

'No, I'm a teacher. I run a project across the prison for dyslexic inmates.'

Suddenly his face lit up. 'Are you Wacky Jackie?'

I laughed. 'Yes, that's me,' I said. 'That's what some of the men call me.'

'Yes, I've heard people talk about you. They call you the Florence Nightingale of the prison – the lady with the laptop!'

'Yes, there it is,' I said, pointing to it on the table beside me. 'I often carry it round with me in case we can't find a prison computer to work on.'

'Everybody says you're a great teacher, because you are dyslexic yourself, so you know how we feel and what we've been through. They say you don't act like a teacher at all, but the word is you're ace.'

'Well that's good. I was worried what you were going to say.' I laughed.

'I think everyone in here should have the chance to work with someone like you.' He paused and his previously cheeky face clouded over. 'When I was at school. They told me I was dyslexic, but nobody ever helped me like they should. Can you teach me?'

'Yes, that's why I'm here. But first we need to assess your strengths and weaknesses. I expect that, like me, you have a number of weaknesses that make it difficult for you to learn to read and write better, but if we can find out your strengths too, we can build on those to help you get going.'

'So how do you find out what my strengths are?'

'First we'll go through a dyslexia checklist and some computer assessments and all the things you don't have problems with will be your areas of strength. Also, we'll find out your best learning style, so that I can teach you to learn by using that approach. For example, if it's practical, like me, I will use multi-sensory activities to start you off with.' He looked uncertain.

'Don't worry about the names for things,' I reassured him. It's how we go about it that matters. But there is one more way I can find out your strengths, by going through the multiple intelligences with you.'

'What are they? I don't think they'll be much good for me. I was always told I was stupid.'

'You are intelligent, in your own way. Everyone is, but not necessarily in the same ways. For example, we might find you are strong at working out where things go, which is spatial intelligence, or you are good when interacting with people, that's interpersonal intelligence. There are several others too. I'm sure we'll soon see what kind of intelligence you have.'

'Can we do that now?' he asked.

'I've got a dyslexia checklist with me, so we could go through that first, and maybe a computer assessment on my laptop. But we'll do some more next time I come, including the multiple intelligences.'

'Great.'

'Talking of strengths, I believe you wanted to become a listener in the wing?'

240

'Yes, I put in for that, but I haven't heard yet whether I can do it.'

'Well I was asked this morning if I could let you know. I'm afraid you have been turned down for that. You could have done it, but they had to say no because they found some drugs on you.'

I could see he was disappointed.

'I thought that might happen,' he shrugged.

'How did you get into drugs?'

'It's a long story.'

I realised this was probably an evasion, so I asked him about his childhood.

'Well, I suppose that was where it all started. My father left us when I was very young, so my mother had a difficult time. She had to work two jobs to keep the money coming in, so I didn't see her much.'

'What about school?'

'That was really hard. The teachers never understood me and I remember always being sat at the back of the class, out of the way, I suppose. Every day was the same, until a new teacher came and she brought me in a tube of Smarties for me to sort out and count. That was my only good day. The rest of the time school was boring and I was rubbish.'

'You weren't rubbish – nobody is. As children, how we behave and how well we achieve in any area is at least partly down to how our parents bring us up and how well the school meets our needs.'

'It didn't meet mine at all.'

'Did that affect your behaviour?'

'Yes probably, but I was much worse out of school. My mum was working all the hours she could and she was never there when I came home, or in the holidays, so I wandered the neighbourhood and got in with the wrong crowd. I lived in London and there were a lot of gangs around, all warring with each other. That's when I got in with a gang myself. The police were always stopping me and giving me cautions.'

Regan did not tell me the name of the gang, but the office had a lot of information about the notorious post-code gangs across parts of London, so I assumed it was probably one of those. There was often some wild story or another in the papers about what they got up to, and none of it was good.

'Did you like being in a gang?' I asked.

'Yes. I felt I belonged to something. It was like a family. All my friends were there and nobody laughed at me, like they had sometimes at school. I was just doing the same as everybody else, so I didn't feel a failure any more.'

'I can understand that,' I sympathised. These guys were his friends and nobody criticized or bullied him. That would have been a seductive situation for him.

'One day I was carrying a gun for the gang …'

I waited to see what would come next, but he didn't continue – just seemed to withdraw into himself. Regan was so young and vulnerable and I wanted to help him. To be caught up in the gangs at an early age like that … he wouldn't have seen the future. With no qualifications and in a downward spiral, he couldn't see how he was harming his chances of getting a job and living a normal life.

'The officer told me you were in here for a gangland shooting. Was that what happened when you had the gun?'

He said nothing, but I noticed a slight nod, and a pleading look in his eyes, which suggested that maybe he felt ashamed of what he had done and didn't want to talk about it any more.

A plan had been forming itself in my mind, based on Regan's age and the fact that he had wanted to be a listener and seemed keen that he and others should have the chance to learn.

'I know you're sorry you can't be a listener,' I began. 'But I've got an idea that you can help me with.' He raised his head and his eyes lit up again, so I carried on. 'There are so many dyslexic youngsters like you around this prison. Wouldn't it be great if we can get some of you together and have some discussions about your experiences and maybe your futures?'

'Yes!' exclaimed Regan, without hesitation. 'That's a cool idea. I know a few on this wing. I could go round and tell them about it. I'm sure lots of us would enjoy that.'

'OK. I'll leave that with you shall I? You could tell me what interest there is next time, when I come over to assess you. If there are enough young men interested I'll ask the Deputy-Governor for permission to arrange some get-togethers for you.'

Over the next few days, Regan took charge, speaking to a lot of the youngsters on his landing and across the wing. He got all those who were interested to sign their names on his list and gave it to me at the beginning of our next session.

'Wow, you've been busy,' I said. 'I'll have to get the permission first, then find a room and fix a date, as well as extra security cover, but tell all these mates of yours that I'm on the case.'

'Will do. Thanks for being such a star,' he continued. 'Nothing as exciting as this has happened for ages. I really hope it works out.'

'Me too, Regan, so keep your fingers crossed.'

Over the following weeks, as we worked together on his dyslexia, Regan seemed to grow in self-assurance and became much calmer, as if happier in his own skin. While we were waiting for the permission to go ahead, he spoke to lots of the prisoners and told me the things they were interested in – mainly tattoos, sports, motor-bikes and cars, so I put the word around the officers and they started bringing magazines and books into the wing for the men to look at.

The young offenders in particular couldn't get enough of them, poring over the illustrations together, trying to work out the captions and comparing their preferences. Meanwhile, more and more officers were bringing things in for us along these lines, which really raised the boys' morale, and gave them a purpose to improve their reading.

Regan's big passion was football, so I encouraged him to try and teach me the rules and about the teams, but I struggled to learn it all.

The first youngsters' meeting took place on Regan's wing and was a great success, with everybody sharing their problems and learning from each other about how to handle them. Nobody causing any problems at all, so we held meetings whenever we could after that. Regan himself was flourishing and changing, growing in self-esteem and enthusiasm for life. He even started looking ahead to what he might do when he was released, though it was probably still a long way off at that point.

On the first morning of filming for the 'Teachers TV' programme, which they called 'Literacy Behind Bars', the production crew arrived early, closely followed by Laura, the literacy skills teacher from Kent. This was great as it gave us a chance to introduce ourselves and get to know one another a bit, while the producer was organizing the lights and cameras. We were both a bit prickly at first. I suppose she had probably had a long journey and as a specialist herself she maybe wondered what I could teach her that she didn't already know, and I was a bit on the defensive, with so much going on and wanting to protect the men from too much prying about their criminal backgrounds, as well as being worried all this activity would somehow break the rules for this visit, and thus get me into trouble. But as time went on, Laura and I relaxed with each other.

When everything was set up, Laura had to go out of the prison again, so that they could film her arriving and me letting her in through a security gate. Of course, this wasn't actually the entrance to the prison, but it looked good on the programme. I had to welcome her in for the cameras and take her through to the wing where we'd set everything up ready.

I had organised for various of the mentors and learners to join us at different stages of the filming, so that Laura could observe a range of project activities, talk with me, the men and a few of the officers and look at the learning materials with me.

One of the men I asked to be in the programme was Regan. He had made good progress and developed a great enthusiasm for learning, wanting to tell everybody about what we had been doing, so I thought he might come across well in the programme. I was right.

As we had a one-to-one session where he was writing words with toothpaste, he looked at me with a grin and said: 'Jackie, you're definitely wacky! I've never seen this way of learning before.' Then he turned to the camera, more seriously. 'But if I'd met someone like Jackie years ago, I don't think I'd be here in prison today. I'd have been able to concentrate and get somewhere in life.'

He hadn't told me he wanted to say all of that, and I was so proud of him. He was a real ambassador for our project and very keen to help the crew, all of whom warmed to him, his eagerness and his cheeky grin, to the extent that they bought him a lovely book as a thank you present.

'That's for being such a help to us in making this programme,' said the producer as she gave it to him. Sadly, whoever had chosen that book hadn't really thought about whether it might be the right sort of book for a prisoner to have, and the management took it away from him as they said it wasn't suitable for him to keep. I never did know why, and neither did he.

In between the filming of learner and mentor sessions, the Deputy-Governor herself, together with Senior Officer Miss Amey, both keen supporters of the project, were individually interviewed by the presenter about how our project impacted on the men and the prison as a whole. Both were full of praise for the work we were doing.

'Since Jackie has been working with the prisoners,' explained the Deputy-Governor, 'you can see a huge difference in them. They're much calmer and frustration levels are much less, which results in their being happier prisoners, and therefore much less problems on the wings.'

I didn't see her say this at the time, though I was glad when I found out what she said. I was aware that the prison staff didn't have to do so much overtime and there was less intervention needed from them across the prison, but I didn't realise it was all down to us.

Some of the prisoners were also filmed when talking to the presenter.

''Jackie has shown me things that no one else has ever been able to do before, like reading, writing and sums,' said traveller Joe Miller, who managed the prison's workshop stores. 'I learnt more in eight weeks than in 41 years of my life.' He beamed with pride at the camera.

When I watched that later, I thought back to all the troubles I had with the officers on his wing, the times we were left with only the last five or ten minutes of his lunch-hour for our learning sessions, and the fuss I'd had to make to sort that out. It was great to know that it had all been worth it.

Towards the end of filming Laura was shown outside a glass room, where I was working with a group of prisoners. She turned to the camera, impressed by what she saw. 'I was just watching Jackie and the boys through the glass and they're totally engaged in what she's talking about. They're animated. They're listening to each other. She's totally got them spell-bound.'

During a one-to-one session with young offender Danny, in which he was making words with pastry-cutter letters in the sand, I asked him to see what other words he could find in the word he'd made – *vegetables*. He then used his cutters to make the words *get* and *table*, concentrating so hard that it was as if he was in a bubble – unaware of the world, or the cameras. This was the boy who earlier in the programme had told the interviewer 'I set fire to my school and everything, just out of frustration.' Now he was learning fast and completely confident in what he was doing.

Next, Miss Amey was filmed talking to Laura. 'I think the cause of the majority of the prisoners' problems,' she said, 'is that their educational needs have not been met. Dyslexic people often have anger management problems, but that's because they're angry at themselves for being stupid or thick, or whatever other names they've been called. But once they've seen Jackie, they tell me "Now I know I'm not thick or stupid and that I have got the ability to go forward and change my life".'

Finally, the cameraman set up in the doorway of Danny's cell too observe him working with mentor Don, who was helping him to write a letter home to his step-mum. 'It's the first time I've done it for myself!' he said with pride.

Throughout the two days, Laura and I discussed her own students with dyslexia and how frustrated she felt that she and her staff weren't able to raise their skills sufficiently for them to gain some qualifications before they left school.

'I've tried everything I can to tackle my year 9 students' problems and they're still not making the progress they need,' said Laura. 'They don't have the levels to cope with GCSEs next year and I'm worried about their futures.'

At the end of the second day, as she left, Laura thanked me on camera and said how much her visit had helped her. 'I'm going to be in back in the classroom with toothpaste, sand, soap – whatever it takes' she smiled. 'I think I've learned a lot.'

'Keep in touch,' I said.

'Yes. Coming here has given me renewed enthusiasm. I'll let you know how I get on.'

The two days had flown by and we were all buzzing. I felt relieved and happy that we had done a good job and everything had gone well. When the producer sent a copy of the programme itself, I took it round the prison with me on my laptop and everyone enjoyed watching themselves or their friends.

The producer told me the programme was well received and I hoped it would help me over the next few weeks, as our funding came to an end and I had to go out and seek new sponsorship once more. I wasn't looking forward to having to work for nothing again, so I knew I had to get something organised as soon as possible to make sure the project would be able to continue for a few more months at least. I couldn't give up on people like Regan, Joe and Danny.

CHAPTER 15

PETE and GREG

The news of an impending Ofsted inspection spread panic all around the prison, although for us it was not so much panic as apprehension. I was quietly confident about the project, but keen to make sure we were working well while the inspectors were here. We had very little notice so I immediately started work on getting the paperwork up to date – my least favourite job.

I had no idea whether they would want to observe the project in action, so I worked on the assumption that they might and began rearranging things to hold a learning workshop and a mentors' training session to happen during their visit. The rest of the time I would make sure that I was either teaching, mentoring or assessing prisoners, so that they would have plenty to look at.

One day, whilst visiting the IT workshop to talk over an idea with one of the officers, I noticed a man who seemed to be helping a group of young inmates with their computer skills, going from one to another of them, and they looked as if they really valued his help.

'Who's that prisoner helping the others?' I asked.

'That's Pete Askey. He only arrived a few weeks ago, on a six and a half year sentence for wounding with intent which surprises me as he seems quite a gentle man. I think it's only his second prison sentence, and he asked to join an IT course here, but now he seems to be leading it single-handed!' He laughed. 'These young guys really appreciate him helping them. He may be more than twice their age, but they feel he's one of them and he gives them confidence.'

'Do you think he would make a good teacher for men with literacy problems?'

'Yes. I'm sure he'd be great. He just seems to love helping these youngsters to learn and he actually does teach them a lot.'

'Thanks. If I come back at the end of the session, do you think I could maybe have a word with him?'

'Why not ask him?'

I went over to talk with Pete. 'Hi, I'm Jackie Hewitt-Main and I run a project across the prison to help men with dyslexia and other learning problems. I'm looking for more mentors from different sections of the prison to make up a group of ten men to do a new course I want to put on.'

'What sort of course?'

'It's the City and Guild PTLLS course for training people to be adult literacy teachers.'

In a split second he showed his pleasure at being asked. 'That sounds cool, but I'm not really a teacher type. Do you think I could do it?'

'Well, your IT tutor thinks you can, and it looked to me as if you were doing a grand job with these guys, so you could be an ideal candidate for my course. Would you like to join it?'

'Are you kidding?' he smiled. 'Yes please. I'd love to do that.'

'OK, I'll come back at the end of this session and perhaps we can have a quick chat about it before you go back to your wing?'

I returned twenty minutes later and sat down in the IT suite with Pete. 'Tell me about yourself, Pete.'

'What do you want to know? I'm forty years old and I've only been in prison once before, for just two weeks.'

'What were you in for that time?' I asked.

'A drink-driving offence. It was nothing really, but I was well over the limit.'

'So what happened this time?'

'It was stupid really. I stabbed my neighbour, but it should never have happened, and I didn't even start it.'

'Did you have a fight or something?'

'Sort of. I've had a hard time for years, drifting through a series of relationships and into drugs. That was my worst move, the drugs. I ended up on the streets, but a social worker found me a place in a hostel, and then just recently I was given a flat in a block , away from all my druggy friends, so I could try to get clean and make a new start.'

'That sounds like a positive move.'

'Yes, it was, or it could have been. I liked my flat and I got an allowance to kit it out, so I settled in well. But my neighbour was an obstreperous bastard. He kept getting at me for playing my music too loud.

'Was it loud?'

'Yes, of course. I love music that's got a good beat. You have to play it loud to get the enjoyment from it. But he's just a killjoy, out to make trouble. He doesn't want anybody to have fun, so that's why he was always coming round and complaining. He even threatened to report me to the housing association if I didn't turn it down.'

'So did you ever turn it down when he asked you?'

'A bit, sometimes.'

'Didn't anyone else complain? Like old people maybe, or families with young children?'

'No. Nobody said anything to me. I don't think it was loud enough to disturb anybody.'

'Except your neighbour?'

'And that was only because the walls were so thin. It was a cheap building that was built with rubbish materials. No wonder he could hear my music. If I'd turned it right down to almost nothing, he still would have been able to hear it. He would never have been happy, whatever I did. He just wanted to make trouble.'

'So what sparked things off?'

'Well, ' continued Pete, 'one particular day, when I was coming up the stairs after doing some shopping, he marched out of his flat and barred my way on the stairs. He was being very bolshy and it ended in a big argument, pushing each other around, until I managed to get past him and into my flat.'

'Was he OK when you left him?'

'Yes, angry but OK. I didn't hurt him. But a few minutes later there was a loud knocking on my front door. I suppose I shouldn't have opened it, should I?' He looked at me ruefully.

'No, you probably shouldn't,' I agreed.

'But I did open it and there he was, with a large kitchen knife in his hand. I saw red. I immediately slammed the door shut, went into my kitchen to get a bigger knife and went back out onto the landing. That was when it happened. I just wanted to defend myself, but he lunged at me and I dodged, we had a scuffle and the next thing I knew he was lying on the floor, moaning, with a pool of blood spreading across the tiles.'

'What did you do?'

'I ran to get my phone and called an ambulance.'

'Presumably the police came too?'

'Not straight away. I think the ambulance people must have called them, so they came to my flat later,' he said. 'There was no point trying to hide. I knew I'd done wrong, stabbing him like that, but it was in self-defence. I told the police that, but there weren't any witnesses and they didn't believe me. That's how I came to be in here again.'

'Well now that you are here, I'd really like you to join my adult literacy teachers' course. It's going to be a long course that goes on over thirty separate sessions, with a lot of work to do so it's quite a commitment. Do you think you could cope with that?'

'Blimey,' he said. 'That sounds a lot, but I'd love to give it a try.'

'Are you sure?' I asked.

He paused as if to check his thinking, but only for about two seconds. As I hoped, he nodded his agreement. 'Yes please, count me in,' he said. 'When do we start?'

I laughed. 'As soon as I can find a suitable room that's available at the same times every week, and get the permissions for all those prisoners who want to take part.'

He looked disappointed.

'But don't worry,' I said, with my fingers crossed. 'I'm sure I can get all that sorted out, and it will start as soon as possible, hopefully in the next two or three weeks.'

'Ace! I'm glad you came to the workshop this morning, or I wouldn't have met you and I would never have known about your cool course. Thanks for including me. I can't wait to start!'

I went over with the officer to escort Pete back into his wing, so that I could pick up something I'd left with one of the staff. When I arrived, I heard someone call my name. I didn't immediately recognise the voice so I turned round to see a tall, young man with a huge grin, walking along towards the stairs.

'Jack, Jack,' he called again. 'It's me, Greg.'

Suddenly I realised who he was, a cheeky boy of 15 I had taught at the training centre two or three years before.

'Remember?' he asked. 'You used to chase me down the alley when I skived off to earn a few quid at the market.'

'Of course!' I laughed at the memory of it. 'That was about three years ago, wasn't it?'

'Did you really think you could catch me?'

'No. But I wanted you to know that I cared enough to try.'

'Yes, we all knew you cared. Like when you used to buy us breakfast with your own money, just to make sure we had a good start to the day.'

'I brought in newspapers too, remember? To try and tempt you to read the sports pages.'

'Yes, I never met a teacher like you before.'

'You must have been about fifteen then, and you were already so tall that the market porters thought you were grown up and you conned them into giving you a job early morning and after lunch to set up and clear away the market stalls.'

'Yes, I couldn't give up the chance. I was earning good money for a fifteen-year-old, but you were very good about it.'

'Well, I enjoyed teaching you all. You were always fun.'

'Yes, we had a laugh, didn't we?'

'And I seem to remember you were very dyslexic?'

'Yeah. That's right.'

'But you were a quick learner. You soon raised your reading and writing levels.'

'Yes, thanks to you and your weird methods!'

'Didn't you do some other courses too? Bricklaying, wasn't it? And computers?'

'Yes, I became really good on the computers. If you want any data doing, I'm your man. I help a lot of the other guys in here, reading and writing emails for them, and stuff like that.'

'Great. It's really good to see you, Greg. But I'd rather it had been in different circumstances. What are you doing in here?'

'I shouldn't be here. I got three years for assault, but it was all a big mistake.' His expression turned serious.

'How come?' I asked.

'Well, I was just walking past the shopping mall, minding my own business, when this man ran out in front of me, and I heard someone shout out to get him. "Rape, rape!"

256

they shouted. So I chased him down and grappled him to the ground.'

'Was that all? It sounds like a tricky situation.'

'Yes, it was just instinctive to go after him, knowing he had raped a girl.'

'So why did you get three years? Did you beat him up as well?'

'Well, yes, sort of. But I had to do something to keep him there while someone called the police. When they arrived, I was sitting on him and his nose was bleeding.' He paused. 'The guy said he hadn't done anything wrong and I had just attacked him for no reason.'

'Didn't you tell the police about the cry of "Rape"?'

'Yes, but they didn't believe me. The girl had run away and there were no witnesses who had heard her by the time the police arrived, so they charged me and I was found guilty. That was it!'

'Well, I'm doing a project in the prison now, so if you'd like to join us, you could be a mentor if you like.' I had a sudden idea. 'In fact, if you're already helping prisoners, you could even consider becoming a teacher yourself. Have you ever thought of that?'

'But I haven't been to university or anything.'

'No, you don't have to if you're teaching adult literacy, as long as you've done the course for teaching in adult education.'

'I wouldn't have a chance to get on that. And I don't think they'd do it in here anyway.'

'As it happens, you're wrong.' I grinned. 'I'm about to start leading a City and Guilds course called Preparing to Teach in the Lifelong Learning Sector.'

'That's a mouthful.'

'Yes, it's PTLLS for short. I'm about to make a list of candidates for that. I can only take ten. I know you're a keen learner, and there's no market here to skive off to! But it's a long hard course – thirty days, with work in between. Do you think you'd be interested?'

He put his head to one side. 'If it's you teaching it, I'd love to, as long as you promise not to chase me down any more alleyways.'

'I don't think I could these days,' I laughed. 'It's a deal. But I will have to come and observe you working with other prisoners first, perhaps doing some mentoring for me.'

'OK. That sounds good.'

That afternoon I sat down with pen and paper to finalise my list of ten of the best prisoners to train to be adult-literacy teachers. I started the list with Pete and Carl, plus Tony, who had made such brilliant progress that he had become a mentor and was doing really well. Also on the list would be Wes, Tobe from Ghana and kidnapper Max. I added young Greg and another three names and that was it. Now I needed to gain permissions for each of them to come. I knew that wouldn't be as easy as I'd made it seem when I first talked about it with Pete.

I typed out the list and my plans and printed it all out to deliver to the Deputy-Governor hoping she would allow them all to attend.

Next I embarked on the mammoth logistical task of finding and booking a room for thirty sessions, ordering enough course materials for them all, ensuring appropriate escort and security arrangements, registering the course and arranging to have an external assessor come to one of the sessions. Was there anything else I needed to do?

I gave Greg a short course in being a mentor, then observed him with another inmate on his wing. He was a natural, so that confirmed my judgement was right in adding him to the list. He carried on and became a very good mentor over the next few weeks, before the PTLLS course began.

Up till now, I'd managed to turn around most of the staff's negative attitudes and many of the officers had become my staunch supporters. But when I started trying to make the arrangements for this new course, I encountered surprising scepticism from nearly everyone. Even the management seemed to be putting obstacles in my way.

'Are you crazy?' asked one senior officer. 'These men are prisoners – some of the most dangerous men in Britain. How can you even think of training them to be teachers?'

'They are going to be the best teachers for other prisoners – some of them are dyslexic themselves, and have learnt how to cope with their learning problems, so they are in the best place to teach others how to do it, and be role-models for them.'

'There's no way any of these names will last the course,' said another officer. 'You're wasting your time.'

'Why don't you just stick at what you do best and stop reaching for the moon?' asked the Deputy-Governor. 'You have done a brilliant job in this prison up to now, but I think this is going too far, even for you!' She paused, then a grin spread across her face. 'You're incorrigible … but if you're dead set on it, I'll support you. What do you need me to do?'

I gave her the list of men. 'Could you please check the names on the list and give your permission for them all to come on the course?'

I arrived early on the first day of the Ofsted inspection to find the inspectors were already there, and looking for somebody to talk to, so one of them came straight to my office and I showed her my assessment materials, the data I'd collated on the findings of interviews and the progress updates I gathered from the Lexion software.

She seemed quite impressed and asked me some questions about how the project worked and how this was different to the approaches adopted by most other prisons, which used a commercial scheme, but little mentoring or multi-sensory work, let alone any of the other things we did. I told her briefly about the press and political visits earlier in the year, the Swedish prison's adoption of our approach and the recent '*Teachers TV*' programme.

'So you see, nobody else is doing what we do,' I summarised. 'I did a lot of research across the world before I set all this up. The men are engaged and most of them are making great progress. Best of all, they really enjoy all the practical things we do and a lot of them, when they have improved their own skills, want to help other inmates to do the same, so I train them to become mentors as well.'

'It sounds like you have a lot to be proud of in your project,' she said.

'Thank you. Yes I am proud of the men and especially the mentors, who are all doing a great job. I hope you'll be able to visit some of our sessions. I've made a list for you of what we will be doing over the next two days.' I handed her the timetable.

'Thanks. I'll try and make sure I can come to at least one of these.'

It all seemed to be going well and she came to see a learning workshop in action. She watched for the first few minutes and then went around, talking with some of the men about what they were doing, what progress they were making and what they thought of the project. I heard the men give her some great answers.

'I'm very glad I came to observe this learning workshop,' she said to me afterwards. 'I think it's a wonderful opportunity for the prisoners to help and learn from each other. I've not seen anything quite like this before and I enjoyed talking to the men. I'm sure you'll be pleased to know that I've graded you highly on everything I've seen.'

Phew! As I reflected on how well that session had gone, everyone else in the prison was still flapping about, and I could feel the tension everywhere I went. There was a lot of whispering in corners and dashing around, a mountain of papers being moved from here to there, and panic was rife. I wished I could help them and calm them down, but I knew there might be problems in some areas, so there was nothing I could do.

When the report came out a few weeks later, it slated the prison overall. However, our project gained praise:

> *The very well-managed project ... Training for learners to become mentors and carry out the initial dyslexia screening is particularly good. Mentors develop a*

261

good understanding of dyslexia and are skilled at
reassuring potential learners and encouraging them to take
part ... A very skilled tutor uses a wide range of learning
resources to provide highly individualised learning
support. Learners make significant developments ... and
build on their existing abilities to help them achieve tasks
they have previously found difficult and frustrating. Many
increase their confidence and self-esteem and progress to
other classes or work."

At first, I was disappointed with this judgement. I wanted us to be 'outstanding'. But when I met another Ofsted inspector a few months later, she told me that when an institution does badly in its inspection, as our prison did, the inspectors are not allowed to grade any aspect of its work as outstanding, so we did well in the circumstances. When I gave our section to her to read, she said it suggested a grading of 'very good', which was the highest that could be given in that situation. I felt a lot happier when I knew that.

The Deputy-Governor had given permission for all those on the list to attend and the day finally arrived for us to start on the PTLLS course. I had ten students signed up for this and eager to start. I had watched them all doing their work with other inmates and selected them for their potential as teachers, so nothing to do with qualifications. In fact, five of them had first become known to me as prisoners with learning difficulties – six if I counted Greg from our time at the training centre.

For all of us, arriving together in the room that first morning was a strange experience, charged with a mixture of apprehension and enthusiasm. And I don't just mean the lads – I felt the same as they did. I started off by explaining the aim of the course, which was to help them all to gain a greater knowledge and understanding of how to work with challenging learners in a group or classroom environment. This was a daunting prospect for anyone who had failed in classrooms at school, as some of these men had themselves experienced, but this course would show ways to help learners conquer that fear.

I was just about to launch into giving them an outline of what we would be covering over the thirty day-long sessions, when Pete put up his hand.

'Hey,' said Carl. 'You don't have to put your hand up with Jackie. Just say what you want to say.'

'OK,' grinned Pete. 'You keep telling us this is a PTLLS course, but what do those letters stand for? I think you told me, but I've forgotten already.'

'Good question,' I replied. 'It's Preparing to Teach in the Lifelong Learning Sector. OK?'

'Yeah, thanks. It sounds rather grand for us lot.'

'No, you guys are exactly the right people for this course, and I assure you it will be far from grand, if that means elitist,' I said. 'However, I hope it will be grand in terms of being interesting, enlightening and enjoyable.'

'You bet,' nodded kidnapper Max. 'Everything is more fun with you and your Wacky Jackie style!'

'That's what I used to say when she taught me at the training centre,' agreed Greg. 'We had a lot of laughs.'

'Yes,' added Carl. 'Most of us wouldn't have dreamed of doing something like this without you teaching it.'

'You're blinding!' agreed Tony.

'Stop it lads,' I pleaded. 'You'll give me a big head.'

'Fat chance!' said Greg. 'You're too down to earth for that.'

That first day was all about the role and responsibilities of the teacher in adult literacy. When I planned this day and had to read the recommended course materials I groaned. They were so boring. So I thought up lots of ways of geeing the course up to make it more engaging and fun. We did some hilarious role-play to kick off with – how not to teach adult literacy. That got everyone loosened up and in the mood. I was amazed at how quickly the day passed, and I think the men were too, judging by their reluctance to stop.

'Thanks Jackie. That was an ace day,' grinned Pete.

'Roll on next Friday,' added Tobe.

The course continued and all ten of the men stuck with it, working hard in between sessions on their homework tasks and working through all the modules. I was so proud of them.

One day, about half-way through, we had an external assessor to observe a part of the day. At the end of her visit she seemed really pleased with what she had seen and gave me a copy of her feedback about us, which ended with:

'It was obvious Jackie had fully prepared them and built their confidence enormously.'

For several weeks, officers would stop me and ask how many of my students had dropped out, and seemed amazed when I told them none had – they were all working conscientiously and their enthusiasm, if anything, had grown alongside their confidence. We finally reached the end of the course. The men had to take an externally marked test to gain their qualification and we were all on tenterhooks, waiting for the results.

Finally one day the envelope arrived and I opened it with trepidation. I was confident myself that they had all done well enough throughout the course, but when it came to tests, anything could have happened. I could hardly contain my excitement when I looked at all their final marks. Ten prisoners had started this course, ten had persevered and completed it ... and all ten of them had passed! I couldn't wait to tell them, so I went straight over to the Deputy-Governor to ask if I could get them all together to share the results as a group, with a bit of a party.

'That's wonderful news!' said the Deputy Governor with a wide grin. 'I don't think anyone thought you could do it, not even me, but you did. It's brilliant!'

'Yes, I'm very proud of the men,' I said.

'And I'm proud of you too,' she clutched my arm. 'It's a wonderful tribute to all the hard work you put into this ... and your unique style!' She paused. 'I didn't tell you before, but do you realise that this is a first for prisons. It's never been done before, training serving prisoners to be adult literacy teachers!'

'Wow!' I said. 'That's good isn't it?'

'It's not just good. It's great.'

'Thanks. So can I get the men together and have a bit of a party to celebrate?'

Her smile turned to a frown. 'What do you mean by a party?''

'Don't worry,' I reassured her. 'Nothing alcoholic or anything like that. Just some fruit juice and biscuits. Maybe even a cake. Just for half an hour or so. They've worked so hard for this – please say yes.'

'Well … OK,' she nodded. 'But we'll have to keep an eye on things.'

'That's fine. In fact, why don't you come along and join in?'

CHAPTER 16

DEAN

'You wanted to see me?' I asked the Deputy-Governor as I went into her office, soon after I arrived at the prison one morning. Although I knew she was genuinely supportive of our project, any call to the management block still had me quaking.

'Yes,' she said, putting her pen down and sitting back in her chair. 'Thanks for coming over straight away.' She smiled.

'What have I done now?'

'Nothing, that I know of. But I'm hoping you will do something.'

'Oh really? What is that?' I was rather wary – it could have been anything, and I didn't want to jeopardise the project.

'I thought you might be interested in this.' She handed me a sheet of paper with a lot of print on it and I could already see some very long words.

'What is this?' I looked up. 'You know I need time to read things like this. I can't just take it all in straight away.'

'It's an international conference,' she began.

'Yes? That's what politicians do, isn't it? What has it got to do with me?'

'OK, pass it back and I'll read out the relevant bits to you.'

I gladly handed it over to her and she ran her eyes down the page.

'It's being put on by the European Prison Education Association. There's some information here about the delegates coming from prisons and prison education services in lots of different countries, mostly in Europe, plus the USA and Australia.'

'Where is it?'

'In Ireland. They are going to have speakers on all different topics related to education in prisons, especially adult literacy.'

'And you'd like me to go to it? To represent this prison?'

'Yes, sort of.'

'What do you mean, sort of?'

'Well, I would definitely like you to go, but that's not all.'

'How do you mean?' I was confused now. Either she wanted me to go or she didn't. What else could there be? I'd never been to Ireland, so it would be nice to see something of Dublin and hopefully the countryside too, but I wasn't sure I would learn an awful lot from it. 'Who's the main speaker going to be?'

'They call it a keynote speaker here.'

'OK, whatever they call it. Who will it be?'

'Well, that's the thing.' She picked up another sheet of paper that looked like a typed letter. 'They want you to be the keynote speaker at the conference.' She looked up to see my reaction. 'What do you think?'

Now I was really confused. 'I think they must have made a mistake. They've probably got the wrong Jackie.'

'No, apparently one of the organisers read about your project in the *Guardian*, then looked you up online and watched your *Teachers TV* programme. They want you to do a forty-five minute talk about the project.'

'Forty-five minutes?' I was astonished. It sounded like an age. 'How could I talk for that long?'

'No problem,' she grinned. 'You could talk for forty-five hours if you had to. The challenge would be how to cram it all into just forty-five minutes. And they'll probably have trouble stopping you, once you've started!'

I had to laugh with her. She was quite right of course. Even though, like many dyslexics, I don't have much concept of time, I don't usually have any trouble talking. 'OK, you're right,' I said. 'I'd better do it then.'

'Great! I'll write back straight away and tell them, shall I?'

'Yes, I suppose so.' I gulped. What had I let myself in for?

'Do I have to go over on my own?' I asked, realising I would have to fly. That meant airports. It wasn't flying that frightened me, it was what happened at either end of the journey – airports are scary places for dyslexics, with all the confusing, difficult-to-read signs pointing in all directions.

'They'll only pay your expenses, as you're the speaker, but I'll see if we can pay for you to take someone with you, as long as they're employed here.'

'Ok, thanks.'

'How about Sue?' she suggested. 'She'd probably find it useful for her work here anyway.'

'Good idea.' I stood up to go.

'I'll give the conference organiser your contact details shall I, so she they can make the arrangements direct with you?'

'Yes please, that will be fine.'

The conference a few weeks later was great. Together with Sue, I managed to negotiate the airport fine, thank goodness, and arrived at the hotel where we'd be staying. I insisted that we get up really early the next morning, as I didn't want the worry that I might be late. The organisers had laid on a taxi to take us to the venue and I could see on the programme that my spot was mid-afternoon. In one way that was good, as I'd have time to get used to the place and the people. The only problem was that I was already nervous, and the whole day stretched out in front of me, with lots of time to get even more anxious. I'd never spoken to such a large and important group of people before in my life. What would happen if I forgot my words or lost my place? Would they provide me with a glass of water in case my throat dried up? What about if I got a coughing fit?

I tried to listen to all the other speakers and watch their video clips, but I couldn't concentrate as well as I wanted to, with worrying about whether the video would still work when it got to my turn, so that I could show a clip from the *Teachers TV* programme. The lunch was good and it was lovely to be able to talk with people from so many different places and find out about their prison education systems.

Finally, my time came and I stood up to speak, my hands shaking as I put my notes down on the lectern. I don't know why I'd written myself some notes, because I knew I wouldn't be able to read them very well, with so many people looking at me. I suppose I must have thought that having notes would give me confidence and make me look more professional. But once I'd got started, that was it. All my nerves faded away and I was doing my favourite things – talking to people, telling them stories and explaining all about my project. I loved it. Everybody was smiling at me and I had a great time.

At the end of the day, several delegates from different countries stayed on to talk with me and everyone seemed enthusiastic. That was exciting. It was a real buzz to know I had helped them to think about how to improve things in their prisons.

One of those people was from a jail not far from Dublin, inviting me to visit her prison, which I did on the next day as our flight wasn't leaving till the evening. But first I had to go back to the conference venue and lead a workshop for 20 Irish prison educators. Fortunately, that went very well. Then Sue and I were driven to the delegate's prison, a forbidding nineteenth-century building, where we were shown around and saw a lesson going on in a classroom. I talked with some of their staff about ways to incorporate elements of our project into what they were doing for prisoners with learning difficulties. I always love going round other prisons and can always see so many things that could be improved. But I always have to be careful I don't say too much and frighten them off!

Within days of my return, I'd received several emails from people who had enjoyed my talk at the conference and wanted to know additional information about the project or the materials we used. I also had a phone call from Australia.

It was a guy who was the head of training in a number of prisons, wanting to ask me about some of the things I'd talked about at the conference. He had a lovely accent and we chatted for a while.

'I think our prison system must be ten or twelve years behind yours in some respects,' he said. 'Our school education system is very good, but we have a long way to go with the prison education service.'

Then he dropped the bombshell. 'If only you could come here and visit one of our prisons yourself. Then you could show us what you mean.' He paused for only a moment. 'I don't suppose you could come over could you?' He made it sound as if I could just pop round the corner, instead of travelling to the other side of the planet.

As it happened, Dawn Amey, one of the senior officers had by now become a good friend of mine and we had decided to go on a holiday abroad together. We had been discussing what kind of holiday, but hadn't decided yet.

'I'm due a holiday,' I said. 'And now I know where to go!'

'Really?' He sounded genuinely pleased. 'That would be great for us.'

I suddenly realised that this might be much more expensive than a budget flight to Cyprus. I had no idea how much it would cost to fly to Australia.

'The only problem.' I blurted out, 'is the airfare.'

'We could pay towards your travel costs,' he offered. 'If that would help.'

'It certainly would.'

I smiled as I put the phone down. I hadn't had a proper holiday since before the project began, eighteen months before, so I was really excited at the prospect of a trip to Australia. Dawn and I could have a holiday as well as visiting a prison, which of course she would be interested to do as well.

I hadn't realised how long and tiring the flight to Darwin would be. We were exhausted when we arrived, and jet-lagged for days. Fortunately, we'd decided to have a couple of days relaxing first, before we visited the prison the guy on the phone had told me about.

I was expecting a smart, new, airy building, so it was disappointing to see it was quite old-fashioned, presumably built around the time settlers first arrived in Northern Australia. But once we got inside, we were give a warm welcome from the friendly staff and shown all around, speaking to prisoners and officers, as well as having a meeting with the training manager and some of his team to discuss aspects of what we did. It was great to visit the place and I always loved to talk to interested people. They were all eager to learn about our approaches to working with dyslexic inmates and seemed to lap up everything I said, then asked lots of good questions.

I remembered what the Training Manager had said when he first spoke to me on the phone, about their prison system being so far behind ours. I don't know if he meant just in that prison, or all the prisons, but I had to agree. However, since then I think they've introduced a lot of my ideas, and perhaps some others too, so maybe things are going much better over there now.

While I'd been away, Carl had been running things, and doing an excellent job, from what the officers told me. This was a great relief, although I knew he would be fine. The only problem would have been if they'd decided, as they could do from time to time, to deny him access to the other wings or, even worse, if they'd suddenly moved him to another prison. Fortunately they didn't ... not then, anyway.

One morning, one of the senior officers told me about a new prisoner on the VP wing who was already causing trouble.

'Nobody likes Dean,' he said. 'And he's so angry all the time that the officers find him hard to handle. Do you think you could maybe go over there and have a word with them. I think they might be glad of some advice from yourself?'

Always intrigued by new prisoners' stories, especially those with problem behaviour, I went straight across to the VP wing and found a couple of officers to talk to.

'Your colleague John, over in B wing, told me about your tricky new prisoner. I think his name is Dean?'

'Yeah, he's tricky all right,' said one.

'More than tricky, if you ask me,' added the other. 'They say he's a snitch. He grasses on other prisoners, so none of them like him.'

'What do you know about him?'

'Well, his name is Dean Wilson, he's 38 and he's a murderer,' said the first officer.

'How long is his tariff?' I asked.

'99 years.'

'A very angry man, is our Dean,' explained the second officer. 'A wind-up merchant and a proper waste of space if you ask me.'

'Can you take me to meet him for a short chat?' I asked.

'OK. I'll escort you to a spare office while my mate finds him for you. I'm afraid I'll have to stay with you while you talk.'

'That's fine. I think we'll just have a brief chat to start with, so that he can get to know me a bit before we talk for any longer.'

The officer walked me through the open ground floor area, past prisoners as they moved around the wing. Suddenly I was aware of a tension in the air. I don't know how I knew it before anything happened, but there was a hush, almost a stillness as all the movement seemed to slow to a stop. I looked towards the old metal staircase. That's when I saw the focus of everyone's attention.

A large man, who looked like he was from the 'A Team', sat on a step, a few up from the bottom. He had a big pot of margarine and was smearing it all over his head, neck and chest, then his arms and his legs too. I was stunned. I'd never seen anyone do this before. I couldn't think why. Fuming with barely controlled rage, he sat and seethed until he could contain himself no longer. Suddenly he stood up on the step and stuck out his chest.

'Come on,' he bellowed. 'Who's for a fight?'

I was rooted where I stood, too afraid to move. From every direction, officers ran past me towards the stairs.

As they reached the bottom step, Carl and Wes, both mentors, stepped out of the room where they had been

275

working, through the crowd that had gathered nearby and walked calmly towards him.

'Hello Dean,' Carl said as he climbed up to his level. 'I can see something's bothering you, mate. Let's have a talk about it.'

I was impressed to see the way Carl handled this angry giant, known for his physical violence. He just seemed to treat him as if he was a good friend. He didn't show any fear at all. But then of course I remembered his training as a Samaritans listener. That must have helped him.

'Come on,' coaxed Carl. 'Let's go back to your cell and get you cleaned up.'

'Then we can talk if you like,' added Wes. 'You can tell us what's bugging you.'

The prison officers surrounded them as they slowly moved back to Dean's cell.

It was the next day before I was able to go back and see him. Dean was brought into the room by the first officer from the previous day, who sat in the doorway, just behind him, but out of his vision. As I watched Dean sit down and settle himself, I noticed he didn't make eye-contact with me and seemed subdued. I would have thought him a different person from the margarine-greased strongman of the previous day.

'Hi, Dean. I'm Jackie ...'

'Yes, I know.' He looked at me for the first time. 'Carl told me about you yesterday. He said I should see you because you'd listen, and maybe you could help me.' His expression seemed to be pleading, but I didn't yet know why.

I had to find out more about him and try to understand his problems before I could tell if I might be any use to him.

'What did he tell you about me?'

'He said you are dyslexic and you have a son who had a brain injury.'

'That's right.'

'I have both of those things. They make my life hell, and nobody understands.'

'Well I understand. I was a failure at school and I know the problems my son had because I looked after him and had to teach him everything, all over again.' I paused to evaluate his response. He was clearly taking it in.

'I saw you on the stairs yesterday,' I continued. 'I could see you were very angry and frustrated. Did something happen to fire you up like that?'

'I didn't mean to kick off,' he said. 'I just couldn't help it. I felt like I needed to explode some energy to get rid of the anger.'

'So what caused it?' I persisted. 'Did you have a letter, or ...?'

'Yes,' he interrupted, with a quizzical look. 'I had a letter from home. How did you guess?'

'I just had the feeling it would be something like that. I know how difficult it is to receive bad news in here. Or maybe it was difficult to read?'

'No, I am dyslexic, but I can usually read OK when I know the person's writing. It's my writing that's worse – especially my spelling.'

'So was it bad news?'

'Not exactly. But they're all so difficult, my lot. And they never think of how I will take things, stuck in here,

277

knowing that they're all happy and getting on with their own lives. They don't even send their love or anything.' He kicked an invisible spot on the floor.

The officer shifted slightly, leaning forward in his chair.

'It's all right,' said Dean. 'That was yesterday. I don't expect they'll send me another letter for months. I reckon I'm better off without them anyway.' He half grinned to try and hide how much their letter had hurt him.

'Did you have a difficult time when you were a child too?'

'Yeah, not half.'

'Were you an only child?'

'No, I have a brother. He's two and a half years younger than me, but we're very different. I've always been the one in trouble, the angry one who gets nicked. He seems to manage to stay clear of any bother, so he's the blue-eyed boy to my father and I'm the villain.'

'What about your mother?'

'She died when I was a nipper, and I don't remember much about her. The dominant one in our house was always my father. He was an aggressive bully – still is.'

'What about at school?'

'I was always in trouble there too, right from the start. I suppose I was quite a handful and I couldn't sit still. I had to be active. I used to be a top long-distance runner. I should have been an athlete, but it never mattered enough to me. There were always problems that got in the way.'

'What sort of problems?'

'Well, to begin with it was the dyslexia,' Dean explained. I couldn't seem to learn like the other kids. I always got into trouble for that. The teachers said I was lazy.'

'I had that too, and I know how wrong that was. I reckon I worked harder than any of my classmates to try and learn things, but I never could.'

'Yes, me too, I suppose. Well, I don't think I worked all that hard, but I did as much as the others and I wasn't lazy. But I was always in trouble for something. Then, when I was about ten, I was larking about and bashed my head on the ground. Then a few weeks later I fell off my bike, head first. Luckily it was on tarmac, so not quite as hard as concrete, but both times they reckon I had a brain trauma. That's what they called it. After that, it was like I changed into a different person – angry all the time, shouting and swearing, frightening the little kids, hitting out at anyone who crossed me, and some that didn't. They said I was disruptive, though I didn't know what that meant at the time.'

'That's similar to what happened with my son,' I agreed.

'And the angrier I got at home, the worse my father was. In the end the council sent me away to a boarding school to get me out of the way. I hated it there too.'

'You said you were good at running?'

'Yes, that was the best thing there. Every week we went out on a proper cross-country run. I always came first in my class. Once the best runners in the whole school did a run together and I was the winner. I beat all the lads older than me, when I was just 13.'

'Were there any other things at that school that you liked?'

'Yeah. I was rubbish at reading and writing, but they found out I was good at maths. I started to really look forward to maths lessons because I was quick at that. I was in the top group for maths. But then it all fell apart.'

'Why?'

'Somebody must have decided that because I was already good at maths I should stop doing it and spend all my time at reading and writing, so that really make me cross. What was the point me being there anymore if I was only going to be allowed to do the things I was no good at? So I ran away. They brought me back, so I kept running away, and they gave up in the end.'

'Then what did you do?'

'As soon as I was old enough, I applied to join the Royal Marines, but they wouldn't take me. So then I joined the army with an old school friend.'

'My husband was in the army and we were based in Aldershot. Where were you?'

'All over the place to start with. Then I did a long stint in Northern Ireland.' He choked up. I waited for him to be able to speak again. 'But my mate was killed, right in front of me. I went to pieces.'

'How awful.'

'Yeah. I couldn't take it. I had a nervous breakdown, and they gave me a medical discharge. That was when I went along with the wrong people and got into drugs and alcohol.'

Where were your father and brother while all this was going on?'

'Oh, they'd buggered off to Australia, so I didn't have no one. How could they do that? They just upped and left without a thought about me. There they were in their happy new life, while I was stuck in sodding England with no job, no home and a heap of troubles.'

'You had a hard time, didn't you?'

'Yeah. And I couldn't even find anyone to help me get my reading and writing better, so that I could apply for jobs and benefits and stuff.'

'Did they diagnose your dyslexia at school?'

'No, that was years later. When I was at school they just thought I wasn't putting enough effort into it, I suppose. Nobody thought of testing me to see if I had a problem.'

'So when did you find out?'

'When I did my first prison sentence. That was when they tested me and found out I had dyslexia and ADHD.'

'And what did they do to help you?'

'Nothing.' He paused, scowling with frustration. 'Nobody's never done anything.'

'Well, we can do lots of things to help you here. My project is all about helping men with dyslexia or head-injury related learning difficulties, so you are exactly the person we need.'

'Really?' he said, with a look of surprise. 'Nobody's ever told me they needed me before.' His face broke into a grin. 'You mean you can help me with my reading and writing and stuff?'

'Yes. There are a lot of ways we can help you. We could make a start tomorrow if you like.'

He looked me straight in the eyes and it was the first time during the conversation that I felt he was fully engaged. 'Yeah, I'll give it a go.'

As Dean was escorted back to his cell, I was stopped by Dawn Amey, who told me she'd heard about the previous day's incident with Dean on the stairs, when he was trying to pick a fight.

'I was very proud of your mentors,' she said. 'Proud of the way they handled a very tricky situation with Dean yesterday. It sounds like they averted a lot of problems.'

'Yes,' I nodded. 'That was Carl and Wes. They're both great at calming things down. I was very proud of them too.'

It would be good to be able to say it was plain-sailing with Dean from then onwards. It was very up and down, but we gradually made progress, working together, and he did seem to calm down and focus a bit more, though he was very unpredictable and it was hard work sometimes.

'You're an absolute saint to put up with him,' said Carl one day, when Dean had been particularly demanding in a group session.

The breakthrough came after several weeks, when Dean decided he'd like to train to be a mentor in our project. I knew he'd changed his attitude when he committed himself to that and he did very well, so that I was able to assign him to his first learners. One Sunday evening, two or three weeks later, Dawn Amey did her rounds to check on everybody and found Dean still working at the computer in the library.

'What are you doing in here so late?' she asked, and went over to look at what he was printing out.

'I'm just designing some new handouts for a couple of the guys that I'm going to be mentoring this week,' he grinned. Dawn told me later that she'd never seen him look so calm and confident.

'You look like you're enjoying this?' she asked him.

'It's great,' he said. 'I love doing something like this. Jackie says she needs me. Nobody has ever needed me before.'

When Dawn was telling me about this the next day, she said it was the first time she'd ever known him do anything for someone else. 'I was amazed!' she said. 'You've done it again – turned round a difficult prisoner and made him into a positive member of the community.'

'Thanks.' I smiled and was glad, but somehow I didn't have the energy to be excited, like I would usually be. I seemed to get tired so easily these days.

'Are you all right?' Dawn asked me, with a concerned expression.

'I'm fine, just a bit tired. My asthma has been keeping me awake the last few nights. That's all it is.' I tried to look more cheerful than I felt. 'A mug of cocoa and a good night's sleep will put that right.'

CHAPTER 17

JACKSON

For a long time I'd been thinking of introducing our project to another prison, if they were willing, and then perhaps more widely. I knew I couldn't lead it personally in more than one prison at a time, so I needed to think of another way of extending our reach. I had to put this plan to the back of my mind for now, but I was determined to come back to it when I could.

Meanwhile, another long-standing dream of mine was to introduce a day for dyslexic families on Saturdays. So many of the dyslexic prisoners I had interviewed and assessed told me about their fathers or brothers, and a little less often their mothers or sisters, who also had dyslexia. In many cases, it was handicapping whole families and preventing them from accessing jobs, benefits, driving tests and many other everyday challenges. Sometimes, prisoners' relatives were actually jealous of how much help their convicted sons or brothers were getting from us inside, developing ways to cope with their dyslexia, whilst they themselves were floundering from day to day in the outside world.

Carl helped me to put together a proposal for Saturday family days in the prison, to support whole families together – inmates and their relatives. Each Saturday would be an activity day, including things like dads using recipes to cook with their children, playing board-games, cards and other games together, doing sports, sharing picture books with their little ones, doing craft activities and using the dyslexia software together on computers.

The prison required us to submit a formal application to the Ministry of Justice, which we did, with the help of a charity funding body, followed by a long wait for the verdict. We really didn't know which way it would go, but being so positive, I just assumed we would get the go-ahead, so it was a great disappointment when it was refused.

One morning I was called over to the IT workshop where the officers and some of the prisoners there were having problems with a new arrival in the group. As I walked over I was thinking was this going to be another Dean – the one who made himself unpopular with everyone?

'Are you all right, Jack?' asked Bob, the main IT tutor, when I arrived. 'You look a bit pale today.'

'I'm just a bit tired,' I replied with a smile. 'I'm fine really.'

'It's Jackson, that one there,' said Bob, the main IT tutor, pointing at a short young man who was trying to take over another inmate's keyboard. 'We call him "the little professor". You see, he thinks it's his job to tell the others what to do. I'll have to get back in there, before one of them kicks off.'

I went into the room with him and sat at the side to watch Jackson, who had his back to me. I noticed what a loud and belligerent voice he had and how he wasn't listening to the other guy at all; just being a mister know-it-all.

'You can't do it like that,' he was saying to the man next to him. 'This is what you have to do. It's easy.' He quickly clicked on various keys and whizzed through the windows to reach the page he wanted, without making any attempt to involve the man who was supposed to be learning from this task.

I went over to Bob. 'Is he always like this?' I asked.

'Yes, he gets up everyone's nose. He deliberately winds us all up and is very rude to tutors as well as the other men. Some of the staff have already refused to work with him.'

'Yes, I can see how the other prisoners react to him,' I said.

'He reckons he knows it all, and maybe he does, but he has no social skills.'

'Is it all right with you if I go and have a chat with Jackson?'

'Yes, be my guest. Everybody's on edge when he's here. We'll get a lot more useful learning going on without him. Take him into my office if you like. But he's in for GBH, so you'll have to have an officer with you.'

Bob sent him off with me to the adjacent room, where an officer sat outside the open door. I watched Jackson as he sat himself down at the table with me, his shoulders hunched and his expression churlish. I noticed he didn't make eye contact with me and everything else I had learnt about him in the past five minutes suggested he might be a classic case of Asperger's Syndrome. That would certainly explain a number of apects of his behaviour.

'Sorry to take you away from the computers,' I began. 'I can see you're confident in using them.'

'Yes,' he snapped, his gaze fixed on the skirting board.

'All you young guys have such an advantage over me,' I continued. 'Both my sons are great on computers too. You must be about their age, I guess?'

'I'm twenty,' he replied.

'My elder son is one of these people that's good at everything,' I smiled, with a shrug. He's dyslexic, but he's such a know-all that he used to really annoy his teachers at school when he knew things they didn't. He's very bright so he knows all the answers.'

Jackson's expression relaxed a little. 'That sounds like me,' he said. 'My teachers used to get cross with me, and so did the other kids. They weren't as intelligent as me, and I don't like people anyway.' He still wasn't making eye-contact with me, but he raised his head and his eyes were brighter. 'I'm dyslexic too. I can read quite a bit, but my writing is bad.'

'Richard finds that so frustrating. I expect you do too?'

'It's hard when I think so fast and I can't put it down on paper, or even on the computer.'

Now that Jackson seemed to feel more at ease with me, I asked him about his background. 'So, what brought you into prison?'

'It wasn't my fault, what happened. I was just minding my own business at the time.'

'Were you working?'

'Yes. I had my dream job, in the British Army Intelligence Corps. I'd just done my training and was on the way home, on leave, walking along a road from the station, with my army rucksack on my back, when a gang of lads that were in my year at school spotted me and came over to taunt

287

me. They walked along behind, shouting insults and laughing at me. I tried to ignore them at first, but then they started prodding me and trying to pull off my rucksack.'

'I bet that made you feel cross?'

'Yes, I could feel myself getting angrier and angrier. Finally I just exploded. I turned around to face them and they jeered at me. I just went for the nearest one, while the others stepped back and watched me pulverize him. They were gathered all round, but nobody tried to stop me. I suppose all my army training had made me physically stronger than I'd been at school, so I think they were surprised. They just stood back and watched. I didn't realise my own strength until it was too late.'

'Did you hurt him badly?'

'Yes. When I finally stopped hitting him, he was unconscious. One of the boys called for an ambulance and he was taken to hospital. I got 10 years for assault.'

'How do you feel about that?'

'It was their fault for getting me all riled up, but I suppose it was me that did the damage. It doesn't feel right though. I don't understand why I got all of the blame. It just wasn't fair.'

'I used to feel like that too. Because I'm so badly dyslexic, and I think I might also have had some other problems, I always felt things were unfair when I was at school. I always got the blame for being the way I was, and I didn't know why. I felt as if I didn't belong, like I was from another planet or something. I remember standing in the playground, upset because nobody would play with me and everyone seemed so different to me.'

He nodded and his expression seemed quite animated now.

'Do you sometimes feel as if you're an alien, like I did? Like I'd been dumped on Earth from another planet – do you feel like that too?'

'Yes,' he agreed. 'Yes, that's just how it is for me too. I'm always a misfit. I've never met anyone else who understood me.'

'Even in here?'

'Especially in here. I wish I knew why everyone gets at me for knowing so much. I can't help it.'

'Maybe it's not so much about what you know, but about the way you tell them. We could work on that. There's nothing wrong with knowing things – it's good . With my son, Richard, I showed him ways to deal with that. I reckon I could help you too, if you like.'

'Really?' For the first time, he made fleeting eye-contact with me. That felt like a huge step forward.

Over the next few weeks, I assessed him to see what aspects of his dyslexia we should work on first. I could see how frustrated he was that his literacy skills were so poor, when he had such a huge thirst for knowledge. He could never get enough of learning new things and his memory for facts was excellent. In some ways, his Asperger's Syndrome made him a difficult character, cutting him off from the social side of prison life, but I found him interesting. He was always telling me things I didn't know.

I helped him channel his intelligence to learn some coping strategies and improve his social skills. He soon felt much happier with himself, which made it easier for him to live as part of the prison community, though I wouldn't say he ever felt comfortable with it. I couldn't teach him to like people, but he did learn to interact with them less confrontationally.

Ever since I'd had a bout of pneumonia in 2004, I'd tired more easily than I used to before and I often suffered from asthma after a long day or when I had a cold. But I always ate healthily and I'm sure that made a difference. However, just recently I always seemed to feel worn out and everything was an effort. More and more people began to notice. My breathing was becoming difficult too.

It was very frustrating that I couldn't find the energy to be my usual self, so I went to see the doctor and he referred me for tests at the hospital. One of these was on a new machine and the operator had to follow the instructions on a wall-chart on how to use it and what the findings meant.

'Just blow steadily into this, Mrs Hewitt-Main,' she said, smiling as she handed me a tube thing attached to the machine.

I blew as steadily as I could, which wasn't easy and I went into a coughing fit as I handed the tube back to her. I noticed that her smile disappeared as she looked up at the wall-chart. Feeling anxious, I followed her gaze.

'What does it say?' I asked.

'The consultant will tell you,' she replied, assuming a vacant expression. 'I will refer you to Mr Scott, who will explain your results.'

Fortunately, the writing on the wall-chart was big and bold, so I looked back at the bit she had scrutinised and read what it said: 'A classic case of obstruction in the neck.' I would have been worried about this, but I knew that my neck had got bigger and I'd had a lump in my throat for years, so it was no surprise really. I just assumed it was to do with my old problem of an under-active thyroid, so I didn't give it another thought once I was back in the prison.

Later that day, I was leading a Learning Workshop for five inmates and their mentors when an officer came and popped his head round the door.

'You'll have to leave I'm afraid,' he said. 'Someone else needs this room. You'll have to relocate.'

'But I booked it ages ago. It's booked for the whole afternoon.'

'Sorry.' He didn't look it. 'I'm just following orders.'

This was so frustrating, but there was nothing I could do about it. 'Where have we got to go?' I asked.

We've found you a room in B wing.' This was another building, across the yard.

I tried to pick up all our papers and learning materials, together with my laptop, but I was struggling to hold everything. Some of the men stepped forward to help me, but the officer intervened.

'Stand back, lads,' he ordered them. 'You can't carry anything for a member of staff. It's not allowed.'

A couple of officers escorted us as we started to make our way through the security gate and into the yard, with me weighed down and struggling to breathe, and them not helping at all. Finally, Carl and Pete stepped forward again and picked up a couple of things I'd dropped.

'Leave them!' barked the first officer.

'Get back,' said the second, picking them up and trying to balance them again on top of the pile in my arms. It felt like 'Crackerjack' and I was about to drop all my cabbages!

'Please let us carry something,' said Pete to the officers.

'Jackie's not well. She needs help,' added Carl. 'We could carry some of her things for her. You can see she hasn't the strength to manage everything herself.'

'It's not far,' pleaded Pete.

The officers looked at each other. 'All right,' said the first one. But I'll check things first and hand them to you.'

I began to breathe a little easier as they lightened my load and we managed to reach the next room. But I realised then that perhaps this was more than ordinary tiredness.

Each day started badly now. For some unknown reason, I was never allotted a space in the car park, so I often had to park some distance away from the prison and walk there, carrying everything I would need that day. It was probably never more than a quarter of a mile on the flat, but now it seemed like I was climbing Kilimanjaro, with my backpack in my arms.

I set aside an easier day in the office, so that I didn't have to rush around the prison so much, and I had a lot of paperwork to sort out as I was planning a bid for new funding based on extending our project into other prisons and the community. I was excited about this plan, but apprehensive about how I would manage it in my current state of health. That afternoon, Carl popped in to see me.

'I was in the IT workshop,' he said, so I asked if Bob could escort me over here to have a quick chat with you. He's waiting outside.'

I sat back and smiled. 'That's good timing,' I said. 'I hate all this paperwork!'

'I've come to cheer you up,' he grinned. 'I've been thinking about it, and I want to volunteer to take the project to another prison for you. It's about time we extended it.'

'Are you sure about this?' I asked him, excited by his offer, but sad at the thought of losing him. He had become my right hand man in the prison. 'You're such a great boon to this project here, and we'd all miss you if you went.'

'You mean you'd miss my happy, smiling face?' he teased.

'I'd kick you if I was allowed to!' I replied. 'Bur seriously, a large part of the success of our project is down to the great support you've given me, and all the lads.'

'Gee thanks!' He grinned. 'But I still have a long sentence to do, unless my appeal is successful. I hope it will be – it bloody well ought to be – my brief thinks the verdict was unsafe at my first trial.' He paused, looking serious, but then his grin returned. 'Do you remember that day when the solicitor was due to visit me, and I was really nervous about whether they'd allow me to appeal? He was going to tell me that day.'

'Yes, I remember. I brought in ...'

'... a white feather,' he finished my sentence. 'Because you said that whenever bad things are happening for you, there always seems to be a white feather that brings you luck.'

'That's right. But I don't think I told you what trouble I had to be allowed to bring that single white feather in for you that day.'

'No, really?'

293

'Yes, I think they thought I was smuggling drugs or something.'

'You wouldn't have got much in the spine of that feather,' he said. 'It was tiny!'

'Yes, it was rather small, but it worked didn't it? You won the right to appeal.'

'That was a huge relief.' He paused. 'But while I'm waiting for all that to happen, I'd really like to help you spread this project so that other guys can benefit, like we have here. I know it's all down to you really ...'

'Not just me,' I interrupted.

'Well mainly you,' Carl continued. 'And I want to help you get it into other prisons, so let's make a start. I like the idea of being a pioneer in a new prison.'

'Yes. That sounds good, doesn't it? Well, I think you should take some time to think about it and make sure it's what you want.'

'Too late for that,' he said. 'I've already put in my transfer application. And so have three of the others.'

'Really?' I was shocked, but very grateful for their generosity. 'Which three?'

'Wes, Tony and Pete. We've all applied.'

A few days later, with the support of the other prison who were keen to take our project on board, Carl and the others heard that their applications had been successful, so they could all be moved over there on the Friday, just three days away. We went into overdrive trying to get everything sorted out – all the course-notes, learning and assessment materials copied and ready for them to take, together with some new multi-sensory materials and other items. I managed to drive myself on, getting everything ready, promising myself a relaxing weekend to follow.

'Do you think there's anything we've forgotten?' I asked Carl before I went home on the Thursday evening.

'Probably,' he said. 'But you can always send it to me. You could even visit me and the lads and get permission to bring anything extra in with you.'

'That's true, if I can find the time. How will I know how you are getting on?' I asked. 'I don't want you have to use all your phone credits on me.'

'I'll write you a diary, if you like. That way you can see how things are developing. I can write letters too. Then maybe, when I've got it all set up with some new trained mentors over there, I could apply to come back here again.'

'That would be great. And, yes, I shall miss you, Carl. I'll miss all the teasing and the banter, of course, but I'll also miss all the hard work you do all the time, without my even telling you.'

Four volunteers from the local community had come forward to help us by supporting the mentors, so that evening I contacted them all and planned out a few training sessions for them about using the multi-sensory approach. As I couldn't get permission to do this in the prison, I had to train them in the evenings over the next week, in my own house. There was no funding for this, of course, but I did it anyway. These four all volunteered to help Carl and the others in their new prison, only a few miles away, so that was arranged and I wrote to tell Carl about them and what things I'd trained them to do.

A few days after my hospital tests, I received a letter to come in to see the consultant in two weeks time.

Now the day came around and I sat down in the chair opposite Mr Scott, a good-looking man with beautiful brown eyes, about ten years younger than me. I waited while he read my notes, then he looked up, with a sympathetic smile.

'Ah, Ms Hewitt-Main,' he began. 'I see that you've had a number of tests and check-ups over recent years.' He paused, turning to a report on coloured paper. 'Did you know that an x-ray you had soon after your pneumonia showed that you had something abnormal protruding into your chest?'

'Yes,' I nodded. 'That was years ago. I remember vaguely. I think my doctor told me about it, but I seemed fine and we assumed it was something to do with my thyroid problems. He said it was nothing to worry about.'

'Well, yes, it could be something to do with your thyroid, but it seems to have grown quite a lot since then, as your scan showed.'

'Oh,' I said, suddenly anxious that this might be bad news. I was so glad at that moment that I had asked Dawn Amey to come with me, and reached across to touch her arm for reassurance.

'Well, I'm a consultant surgeon, Ms Hewitt-Main, and I'd like to schedule you in for an operation to remove this growth before the end of the week.'

'You say it's a growth,' I began, tentatively. 'Do you mean it's ... cancer?'

Dawn took my hand as we both sat upright in fear.

'I can't say what it is at the moment, I'm afraid. We'll do a biopsy on the growth after the operation, but I think we should remove it anyway as it's almost certainly the cause of your fatigue and breathlessness.'

'Right,' I nodded, thinking of all the things I must do back at the prison, before I could afford to take time off for an operation. 'Will it take much time for me to recuperate afterwards?' I asked.

'I'm afraid you will need quite some time to recover,' he said. 'It might be a long operation and, because of your history of asthma, we shall need to take good care of you after the anaesthetic and keep you under observation for a while, just to make sure.'

As I drove home that evening, I felt numb. I don't remember anything of the journey. I could have driven through red lights or anything, the state I was in. I knew I would have to tell my son, Stuart when I got home, and I went blank trying to think what to say, so as not to worry him.

I can't remember what I did say to him when I got in, but Stuart was his usual practical self. I needn't have worried.

'Just be positive, Mum,' he said. 'It will be a good thing to have that lump removed. You'll be able to breathe much more easily and get back your old energy again. You'll be as mad as a box of frogs again in a few weeks' time.'

'I thought I already was!' I said. 'Mad, I mean. Whacky – that's what the men call me.'

We had a light-hearted chat about it, but I didn't find it easy to feel positive that Monday evening, with only four days to the operation.

On the Tuesday morning, I arrived as usual to work with 'the little professor', only to find he had gone.

'Where's Jackson?' I asked a friendly officer. 'Has he been moved to a different wing?'

'No, I'm afraid he's not here any more.'

'Why? Don't tell me he's been moved to another prison.'

'No. A new doctor came to see him yesterday. He spent twenty minutes with Jackson and had him transferred to a mental health unit.'

'No! That's terrible. He's not mentally ill at all. He has Asperger's Syndrome. Didn't anyone tell the doctor that?'

'I don't know, Jackie. I wasn't on duty at the time. I just know he was taken away first thing this morning. He said to thank you for helping him. He wanted to stay here, but he wasn't given a choice.'

I was appalled at this snap decision, after just twenty minutes, compared to all the hours I'd spent with him over the past few weeks. This is what used to infuriate me about the prison service. Prisoners don't seem to have any rights, not even regarding their own health and wellbeing. Twenty minutes, and a stranger jumps to the wrong conclusion, making a decision that can and probably will ruin a man's life.

The next couple of days passed by in a blur, until the Thursday, when I went over to the new prison, where Carl, Wes, Tony and Pete were now well into getting the project under way and keen for me to come and see what they were doing.

'It's been going really well,' said Wes, with his friendly grin. 'And the management have been very supportive.'

They showed me around a bit, but I found it difficult to walk far, so they came and sat with me and told me all about the progress they were already making.

'It's great to see the men opening up when they realise how different this approach is,' enthused Pete.

'We've assessed seventy prisoners already and we're working with most of them now,' explained Carl.

'And as well as the others, I'm working with a couple of self-harmers,' smiled Tony. I think I've already helped them quite a bit.'

'We started the Learning Workshops this week,' said Wes. 'Everyone wants to be in them!'

'I'm so proud of you four,' I congratulated them. 'You're obviously doing a wonderful job here. At this rate, I'll be redundant before long!' Then I told them about my operation the next day. 'So you see, I won't be able to visit you for a while.'

'Never mind, Jack,' said Carl. 'We'll send you some cards to cheer you up and help you get better quickly.'

'We'll keep you posted about the project over here, so you won't need to worry about us,' promised Pete.

'And I'll send you a white feather,' said Carl. That made me laugh, though it puzzled the others.

As I drove home that evening, with the operation looming only a few hours away, I felt really bad. My head was pounding, my skin was clammy and I felt as if I wasn't quite there. *'Please God, get me home safely,'* I prayed out loud. Somehow, I managed to get back without causing an accident, but I don't have any memory of what happened after that, till Stuart drove me into hospital early the next morning.

CHAPTER 18

WES, JAZZ and RORY

They put me in a side room to have my pre-med and I remember lying back in the hospital bed, early that morning, gazing at the row of white seagulls, sitting along the window sill outside, looking in at me. This wasn't just one white feather. Maybe I would need them all to give me enough luck for the operation. They tapped on the window with their beaks to reassure me, so I knew then that it wouldn't be cancer. I smiled back at them all to thank them. They seemed to bow their heads slightly, as if they knew how pleased I was to have their company.

At this moment, two porters came in to wheel my bed down to the operating theatre.

'How come you're smiling so much?' asked the taller one. 'People don't usually look this happy when they're about to have an operation.'

'It's the seagulls,' I explained. 'They came to wish me luck.'

'I think they've overdone the dose of your pre-med!' laughed the other porter.

The surgeon told me later that this was meant to be the first of three operations, none of them too major. But it didn't turn out as he had expected. He and all the operating theatre staff were astonished at the enormous size of the growth that stretched halfway down my chest and filling my throat so tightly that they had great difficulty getting a breathing tube in. They couldn't believe how obstructive the growth had become, or how I had been managing to drink, let alone eat. To be honest, I hadn't had much appetite for a while.

'The full extent of the obstruction didn't show up on any of the scans,' the surgeon told me when I was awake enough to understand, which wasn't for several days. 'It was such a major operation, we had to keep you sedated for a couple of days, to help your body recover.' He paused. 'How are you feeling?'

'Weird,' I smiled, or at least I think I did. 'I feel very woozy, as if I'm not really here, but up on a cloud.'

'That's the medication we're giving you for pain-control.'

'Well it's working!' I said. He wrote something down on the chart at the end of my bed. Meanwhile I was desperately trying to think what it was I should be asking him.

He came back to my side. 'We did a biopsy,' he said. 'And I'm sure you'll be glad to know that it's fine. You have nothing to worry about. We did have to remove the whole of your thyroid, but we've put you onto the substitute, thyroxin. That should get you back to normal again, while your wound is healing.'

That was it, the question I couldn't remember. Then I thought of another one. 'What about the other two operations after this?'

'No worries. We did all three in one,' he explained. 'So, that's the other good news. No more operations.'

'Thank you,' I said, feeling all emotional. The tears ran down my cheeks. 'Sorry.' I smiled. 'I don't know why I'm crying. I just want to thank you for doing such an excellent operation for me.'

'It's all part of the service,' his brown eyes twinkled when he smiled.

I lay back, elated with the relief of knowing it would all be all right now. Except that it wasn't. The thyroxin wasn't doing what it should and I lapsed in and out of consciousness for the next few weeks. My body seemed to react so badly to it that eventually they decided I must be allergic to thyroxin. This was a huge problem.

'I'm afraid thyroxin is the only real substitute for the thyroid, Ms Hewitt-Main,' said one of the nurses in one of my lucid moments.

I remember waking at odd times in the day and mostly the night, wondering about this statement. So why didn't they think of that before they removed my thyroid? Or didn't they have any choice? And what were they going to do about it now? Surely there's something they can give me that won't actually make me ill?

But mostly I just slept, or perhaps lay unconscious sometimes. I don't know. I was there for ages, in that hospital, unaware of time, of the prison, and even of my family. My Mum and my sister Lorraine came to see me a lot, and so did Stuart. Richard had further to come from university, but he came whenever he could. They were all a great support, but sometimes I didn't even know they were there.

The one good thing, when I was awake enough to be grateful for it, was that I could breathe much more easily and didn't have to chew everything to pulp when I ate. Over the weeks I improved enough to go back home again, though I was still very ill and needed a lot of looking after. My son Stuart gave me all the care he could, just as I had done for him all those years before when he'd had his brain injury. At least he didn't have to teach to me how to do everything, but he did look after me brilliantly and it helped me a lot to be home in my own surroundings again.

Somehow, several of the ex-offenders who had been mentors or learners in my project got to know about my illness and found ways to keep in contact with me. First, I had lots of cards, from Carl, Wes, Pete and Tony, delivering our project in the other prison.

'Do you remember the first time I met you?' I asked 32-year-old murderer Wes one day, during a lovely, long phone conversation after he'd been released early for good behaviour.

'Yeah. You said I looked like a red Indian!'

'Well, it was true. It was your hair. When you came into the room, you had this fantastic, brightly-coloured Mohican.'

'I still have,' he said.

'You were a great mentor. I hope you have kept those skills?'

'I'm looking to work as a mentor, or adult literacy teacher,' he said. 'Thanks to you, Jackie. You taught me how and gave me the confidence to do it.'

'Well, before you came into prison, you were a carer for all kinds of people weren't you? The elderly, youngsters, special needs, disabled, and didn't you work in a children's home too?'

'Yes. You've got a good memory.'

'So you knew how take time and to listen to people. That's such a great gift.'

'I like listening to people,' he said. 'Everyone has a story.'

'I remember that first time, when we met, and I explained what the project was about, you got it straight away,' I reminded him. 'You understood what I was trying to do.'

Several others from the project phoned me or texted me, and a few emailed or wrote letters. Jazz was one of those. He wrote letters and put them in his beautifully painted envelopes, which always made me smile when they arrived. His mother kept in touch with me too. She'd always been so grateful for how I'd supported her brain-damaged son and how helping with the project had changed his life, even when he was still inside.

'In some ways, Jazz was so like my son Stuart was after his head-injury.' I told her on the phone one day. 'I already knew how to help him, and he wanted to help other people too, so he changed his own life really.'

'But you were the one that made it possible,' said Jazz's mother, Wendy.

'And you've been a great support to him too,' I added.

'Well, he was such a lovely little boy. Always well-behaved and fun. He was cheeky of course, but in a nice way. That was before he had an accident and hit his head when he was eleven. That totally changed him. When I took him to the hospital, they said he had not done any damage and to

305

take him home and let him rest. I found out later that they hadn't even x-rayed him on that first visit.'

'Really?'

'When they did, finally x-ray him another time, they told me he had suffered a skull fracture. It totally changed his personality. He became a real problem child.'

'Yes, Jazz told me about how much trouble he caused you. He felt bad about that, but he said he never realised at the time. It was as if he was compelled to misbehave.'

'Yes, he'd always done well at school before, but after the head injury his schoolwork suffered and he started to get into trouble with the police.'

'That's like my son too. I was always going down there and apologising for him when I picked him up,' I said.

'I went down to talk to the police about Jazz's behaviour several times,' Wendy continued. 'They eventually got a psychologist to see him. He kept playing truant from school and we didn't realise. My husband and I were in the pub trade then. Most nights, after closing the pub, we were out across the fields looking for him. That's how we discovered he was sniffing glue. Later it was other drugs. He and his junkie mates even came and stole from the pub. They stole a huge takings one night. We nearly lost our tenancy of the pub over that. We were paying it back for years.'

'That must have been awful.'

'Yes, but the worst thing of all was the way he and his gang terrorised his younger sister when we were out. They were all stoned when they broke in. She had to lock herself in her bedroom, frightened to death, while they shouted threats at her and tried to break down her door.'

'He ended up in prison several times, didn't he?'

'Yes, usually for violence. He was in various prisons, more than forty times. But he's trying hard now, since he came out from the prison where he met you. He says you changed his life.

'He did it himself. When I persuaded him to be a mentor, he loved it. He was a natural with all the youngsters, who really respected him. I'm sure he helped a lot of them to think about changing their lives too.'

Another mother who kept in touch during my illness was Tony's mum. I think all these messages of support for me throughout the worst months, helped cheer me up and keep me going. One day Tony's mother phoned me in a bit of a state. She said she was worried about him and wondered whether I could go and talk with him.

'You're the only person he will talk to, Jackie. If you can't help him, nobody can.'

I couldn't refuse, but I knew I wasn't well and hadn't been out for months, so I called Jazz to see if he would come with me, knowing I'd feel safer if I had someone with me. Jazz and Tony always got on OK and it was a long way to drive on my own, still not feeling well, so I was relieved when he answered his phone and I explained the situation to him.

I had an appointment to go to the hospital for a blood test first. 'If you can get a bus to the hospital, Jazz, I'll meet you at the front entrance at three o'clock.'

'OK. See you there at three,' he said.

'It felt strange getting in the driving seat of the car again, but I didn't let myself get too worried about it, knowing it wasn't far to the hospital. I was early so, for the first time since my operation, I stopped at the supermarket to do a bit of shopping on the way.

When I got to the front entrance of the hospital after my blood test, at exactly three o'clock, there was no sign of Jazz. I sat on a bench and waited for ten minutes, then went and looked in the cafe in case he was there, but he wasn't. I tried calling him, but there was no answer. So I went back to the car park and drove the car down to wait a bit longer, till an officious little man moved me on. So I called Tony's mother and explained that I didn't feel well enough to drive all the way to Tony's place on my own.

'How about coming over here instead?' she asked. 'I'll put the kettle on and we could chat about how I should handle the Tony situation. I don't want to upset him, but I am worried and he hardly ever gets in touch.'

So I agreed. It was only about fifteen minutes to Tony's mum's house, and I knew the way, or I thought I did. But as I got closer, I kept missing turnings. I felt quite woozy and it just got worse. I did eventually get there all right, so we had our cup of tea and chatted together for about an hour.

'You're an angel,' Tony's mum kept saying to me. 'To do what you've done with my Tony, keeping up with him even when you were ill. Do you know what he told me?'

'No.'

'He said "She believed in me Mum. Why can't anyone else believe in me? Jackie is my angel." And he's quite right too.'

I felt better after the tea, and sitting down for a rest. But as I drove away from her house again, I felt weird – spaced out. I have no idea how I managed to get home without causing an accident. I don't know about me being an angel, but I definitely felt I must have had a guardian angel with me that afternoon as I drove home. I parked the car askew in our drive and almost fell as I got out. That was when things really started to go wrong.

I held on to the car and managed to get round to the boot to get my shopping bags out, but I couldn't lift them. They weren't very heavy, but I just couldn't seem to co-ordinate myself properly When I finally managed to haul them out, my legs went wobbly, I dropped the bags in the front garden and staggered to the door. As I finally got the key into the lock and pushed the door open, my home phone in the hallway started ringing. It was the doctor.

'Are you all right, Mrs. Hewitt-Main? I've been trying to contact you because the hospital emailed through the results of your blood test ...'

'But that was only a couple of hours ago,' I gasped. 'It usually takes a week.'

'Yes, I know, but they were concerned about you, so they processed your blood straight away. The results are so high that I was really worried about you when you didn't answer your phone the first time. The hospital tried to phone you too. Are you all right?' he repeated.

'Well, no, not really. My head's going funny.'

'Stay right there and I'll call an ambulance,' he said. 'Your blood results are far too high and we need to find out why. You'll have to go back in hospital for a day or two at least so that we can try and stabilise you.'

So back to hospital I went for a few days, but fortunately my levels did go down, so I was able to go home again after that.

My health continued to be unpredictable, but mostly poor over the best part of four years altogether, during which time it had become impossible for me to get back to my passion – my project. But it was great to know that the prison staff, led by Dawn Amey, together with some of the mentors, had kept the project going for several months after my collapse, until a new management regime took over and rigorously swept it all away. In the other prison too, it gradually petered out, after Carl and the others left.

True to his word, Carl had kept a diary for a while for me, but not at the first prison. It was when he was moved again, immediately prior to his appeal, that he started to write his diary. Because of the move, he had to start over again and wasn't allowed to work for his first few weeks there. He was so bored that he wrote in his diary every day, about the tedium, being banged up for 23 hours each day watching TV, and his frustration at not being allowed to work, when he had so much to offer.

'I need to get a job,' he wrote, *'as being in my cell all day will do my head in.'*

Finally, they let him become a listener again, working on the wings and in the prison hospital where, amongst others, he read and wrote letters for the notorious 'Great Train Robber', Ronnie Biggs, now an old man and recaptured after so many years on the loose in South America.

'I talk a lot with Ronnie Biggs,' he wrote. *'It's a shame how he is now. I hope my life doesn't end in here.'*

Another day in his diary, Carl described some of the other patients in the prison hospital:

'Busy at work today. One patient cut up, one set fire to his cell, and another flooded his cell out, but it keeps me busy. Read

Ronnie Biggs's letters today and also wrote a couple for him. It's nice to help the old boys ... All I do and see would be terrific reading! All about Ronnie Biggs, and at the moment the man charged with the murder of the five prostitutes from Ipswich ... there are quite a few naughty cons in the hospital that the public don't know much about as most of the serious cases don't get into the papers.'

Later, Carl makes a sad diary entry:

'Well, what a day today. I got to work (in the prison hospital) and was told one of the patients had hanged himself on the ward. It was a shock to the system as I've known him since I came here and also talked with and listened to him a number of times every day. I'm now feeling so sorry for his kids and family. I was very busy as there were five lads in the ward with him and it was them who found him hanging. They tried to cut him down. They are all feeling very low now, and I'm also feeling a bit drained as I've been listening with them all day. I hope they feel a bit better tomorrow. RIP Michael.'

Another entry shows a different facet of prison life. *'Work was hard today as we had a dirty protest and I have never seen or smelled a cell so, so bad. I had to seal it off as they have to get outside contractors to clean it as it was that bad ... the dirty protest lad is back in healthcare. He is totally off his head. Hopefully he will be better now, but by today's performance, I don't think so.'*

Carl wrote too about the preparation for his appeal and his hopes for early release, whichever way it went, with the new circumstances of the case. He sent me a copy of the report ordered by the High Court, with a scribbled note on it.

'Here is the report I said I'd send you. I think it is great for my appeal. It helps me a lot. I am hoping this expert will also come to the appeal to tell everyone his concerns.'

311

I read through the dense text of the report for Carl's appeal with some difficulty. It was a four-page report written by the Forensic Audio Consultant, an expert witness who had given evidence at Carl's first trial. Basically it seemed to say that he felt the recordings made by the police when Carl was first arrested were unreliable. He said that they could easily have been tampered with and that he had been misled about their authenticity when he had given his expert evidence the first time around. He was keen to express his current view that the evidence now suggested these recordings may have been manipulated by the police to make it seem as if Carl was guilty.

This expert actually wrote in the report that: *'I was now convinced that the evidence and software were anything but safe.'* Additionally, he said he had only just discovered an unusually high number of unrecorded calls, with the police logs not matching the phone records. He wondered whether these calls would have been significant in Carl's defence.

So it seemed there was good cause for optimism and, when the big day of his appeal finally came close, I sent Carl an envelope full of the white feathers that had fallen that morning onto my patio.

A few days later, at the end of his appeal, he rang me to tell me the news.

'I'm out!' he said. 'I wanted you to be the first to know. I won, thanks to that expert ... and your feathers! Now I'm on my way home to surprise my Mum.'

'Brilliant!' I exclaimed. 'That's wonderful news! But don't you think you ought to let her know you're coming? You don't want to give her a heart –attack.'

'Good point. I'll come and see you as soon as I can,' he added. 'I can't wait to tell you all about it.'

'Great. And if I'm well enough,' I said. 'I'll take you out for a meal to celebrate.'

It was like buses. These men wait for so long for their appeals to be heard, and then two come along together. Rory, another of the dyslexic men in my project had been writing short letters to me from prison. I remembered him as a young church-mouse character. He never argued or kicked off; just quietly mulled over his frustration at being in prison when everyone knew he was innocent. Of course, lots of the men used to say they were innocent, and perhaps some of them might have been, but Rory was different. Everyone knew he hadn't done the crime. He had got in with a drugs gang, yes, but he wasn't there when the murder was committed. Somehow, he'd allowed himself to be bullied and falsely grassed on by the gang-leader, who shopped him for shooting a man from a rival gang and the judge sentenced him to life for murder.

Rory's letters were sometimes hard for me to make out I could see one of his big problems was that the lawyer arranging his defence kept sending him copies of his court papers, but he couldn't read them properly, so of course he couldn't respond to them either. He didn't feel brave enough to tell the barrister. He wanted me to help, but I wasn't yet well enough to go and visit him in prison. I tried to persuade him to call his defence lawyer and explain that he had dyslexia. I think he did in the end.

Rory's was quite a notorious case when it came to the appeal court. It was in all the newspapers and across the internet. He later told me what everyone had said and how it all went.

'The real murderer was a lying shit, a grass for the police, a supergrass some call him, and he framed me for the shooting, to get himself off.'

'How did he get away with that?' I asked.

'They say he bribed the police. They made an arrangement with him that if he could find someone else to blame, they'd let him off the hook with a short sentence, then give him a new identity. So that's what they did when he shopped me. It wasn't fair. I wasn't even there that night. I didn't know anything about it till they came to my door.'

Rory, being so meek and mild, couldn't believe what hit him when the police called round and arrested him. He was stunned into silence, like a frightened rabbit.

At his first court case he barely even protested. An eye-witness gave evidence that the murderer had blue eyes, but Rory's eyes are brown. Nonetheless he was convicted with a maximum sentence. One of the newspapers called the trial *'a miscarriage of justice that will stagger the mind of anybody that reads about it ... I do not believe there has been a trial like this since Elizabeth Clarke was tried and convicted of being a witch in 1645.'*

In preparation for his appea, Rory was given a lie-detector test which he passed with ease, but sadly it seems this is not admissible evidence in court. I was astonished that Rory's appeal failed, despite all the mounting evidence to the contrary. Apparently there was an investigation at about this time into these particular policemen – into their lack of integrity and falsification of evidence, so this was unhelpful timing for him, as the police had obviously closed ranks to protect their own, at his expense.

I talked to Rory a lot in the following weeks, trying to give him hope and help him focus on planning some more vocational courses to equip him with skills for his eventual release. I hope one day he will get a new appeal and be released.

Nearly four years after my operation, still struggling to regain my health, I found the name of a private consultant in London who specialised in endocrinology and who had made a study of thyroid problems and ways to treat them. It was going to be expensive, but I was at the end of my tether, so I went to see him.

This appointment changed everything for me. He had asked me to have some blood tests done and they showed various imbalances. The most important of these were apparently something to do with T-numbers. I didn't really understand it all, but looked it up on the internet when I got home. He put me on some new medication and it wasn't long before I began to feel better than I had in many years.

Finally I began to regain my energy enough to be able to work again. So now I set to in earnest to get back to promoting the project. I wanted to get it going again, but this time across other prisons too, with better funding if I could get it organised.

While I had been ill, on my few good days, I had started to go through all the assessments and results of the men in my project, and now I put it all together in some tables. I was amazed at what this showed. A friend of mine, who is good at data, went through it all with me, explaining the project's outcomes.

'Look Jackie, this is astonishing!' she said. 'Look at these first seventeen project prisoners that were released. It's great that you've managed to keep in touch with them all, or their families, so that you know what happened after they left the prison.'

'Yes. There were one or two I couldn't contact, but fortunately some of the other ex-prisoners had heard from them, so I know what each of them is doing now. I know that only one of them has gone back inside, and that was for a breach of his probation, when he went out of county to get his daughter back.'

'Well,' she said. 'Over the four years since they were released, sixteen out of these seventeen men have not gone back inside. That is a re-offending rate of just 5.9%, compared to the national average of around 70%. That is amazing! Your project has given them their lives back.'

'Well, even better than that, most of them are now in work,' I explained. 'And some of them are now teaching in adult literacy or mentoring young offenders. One is even doing a university degree! And the three men who had each been in prison more than forty times – usually each sentence within weeks of the previous one – none of them has reoffended at all in the four years since.'

'That's wonderful. You ought to publish these findings.'

'Yes, I think I will.'

The final report of the project, *'Dyslexia Behind Bars: Four years on'* was now printed and we had two launch events

316

planned. The first was to be at Middle Temple in London, and the second in the Houses of Parliament. The arrangements were all under way.

I was just drying my hair one morning, when the phone went. I turned the dryer off and answered it. At the other end was a newspaper reporter who had done quite a few articles about me in the past, but I hadn't spoken to him for ages.

'Hi Jackie. What were the years you were working in the prison?'

I told him the three years. 'I started it in Autumn 2006,' I said. 'But mainly it was 2007-2008.'

'Wow!'

'What do you mean?'

'Well, the new ten-year report of assault-rates at individual prisons has just been released. I've got it here in my hands and it's spot on.'

'What do you mean?' I repeated.

'The assault rates by prisoners on staff, and prisoners on other prisoners in that prison dropped dramatically in those two years of your project, then shot straight up to the old levels a few months after you left. Isn't that further proof of how successful your project was?'

'Wow – yes, it's great. How much did it go down?

'The assault rates for the first year of your project went down to a third of what they had previously been, and stayed there for the second year, then rose again to even higher than their previous levels after your project ended. Isn't that remarkable?'

'Yes. It's amazing.'

'Let's do an article on it.'

317

One day, completely out of the blue, I received an invitation to be the key-speaker at an international conference in Holland, called *'Dyslexia in Detention'* This was right up my street, so I said yes straight away. Delegates were attending from several European countries, as well as the Dutch Minister for Justice and her team.

Airports are still a nightmare for me, with signs everywhere in different languages, so I took along a friend to help me on the journey. Just as well I did – when I spoke at the conference, the audience were all very enthusiastic about my project, and this poor friend had to organise and chat with the queue of delegates from Turkey, Italy and several other countries who wanted their turn to speak to me at the end of the day. I had requests for help from prisons across Europe. All I needed was the funding to make things happen.

As I was checking the final arrangements for the first launch event, I received an email from Laura, the teacher who joined me for two days in the prison for the *'Teachers TV'* programme, after which she had introduced many aspects of our project into her own school in Kent. It was quite a long email and my smile widened as I read it. She began by explaining all the things they'd done to change the curriculum and they way they taught throughout the school.

They had started by asking the students themselves what they felt and what would help them, just like I had done in our prison project. One of the things they'd done was to develop Literacy Pods, which were purpose-built suites of rooms, all newly decorated, furnished and equipped. She said they even had a dog.

Laura described their new approach with the students, including a lot of multi-sensory teaching, then ended her email with great news:

'Students are making outstanding progress and most behavioural issues with these students are now a thing of the past. ... The legacy of my visit to your project will hopefully be that many students will now be provided with the literacy skills they need to become successful in the near future and so avoid turning to crime.'

I was so thrilled I immediately emailed Laura back and invited her and a colleague to come and speak about this great success at our first launch event, along with some of the ex-prisoners themselves, plus a prison officer, a Lord and the leader of the *Lexion* dyslexia software team.

The two launch events went so well, even better than I had hoped, that this was the point when my project started to gain VIP interest and support from various quarters, including government agencies, Lords, Baronesses and MPs. We were mentioned again in Hansard and gained a following that started us off on the road to fulfilling my dearest wish – to extend the project across more prisons, with the prospect of secure long-term funding.

What happened next deserves a whole book to itself.

WHERE ARE THEY NOW?

FRED (Chapter 1) – **The armed robber who didn't know his ABC**

Fred was serving a long sentence when I worked with him. He made huge progress over the four years of the project and passed a number of computer courses. He kept in touch with me by phone throughout my illness and told me all the things he was doing in preparation for his life outside. After his release, he got a job cooking in an old people's home, which he loved. The last time I spoke to Fred, he was training to be a fork-lift truck driver.

'I'm having a great time,' he said. 'I love having all these choices I never had before, when I couldn't read or write. I'm making up for lost time!'

Despite now being in his seventies, he has a great sense of achievement and is in a more positive frame of mind about his future than he's ever been. Previously a lifelong criminal, **Fred has not reoffended since his release three years ago.**

ROCKY (Chapter 2) – **A violent young murderer with a stutter**

Sadly, I was not allowed to work with severely dyslexic Rocky because he was moved to another prison the day after I interviewed him. As far as I know, he is **still in prison, serving his life sentence**.

ALEX (Chapter 3) – **The bodybuilder who stabbed his sister's rapist**

In the middle of working with us, making excellent progress, Alex was transferred to another prison, so was not allowed to continue his learning to reach his goal of knowing how to spell 100 words. However we had given him a taste for learning and when, a few months later, he was transferred back to our prison he rejoined the project.

He had many family problems that affected his concentration, but he told all the inmates in his wing about me and how much I had helped him, with the result that they all wanted to come and join us, even if they didn't have any learning difficulties.

Alex gained confidence that he could read and write and learnt to fill in simple forms. He finally learnt to spell 100 words ... and more. A marked difference in him the second time around was the way he conquered his anger – he was happy with his progress and became much calmer, reaching a sufficiently literate level to gain his CSCS certificate to enable him to work on building sites. He told me he really wanted to help other lads not to go down the same path as him. **Sadly, I have not been able to track him down since his release five years ago.**

PERRY (Chapter 4) – **A businessman owing years of VAT who robbed a warehouse**

'It's been enlightening for me as I never knew I am not hard-working if something in me that not understand what's wrong,' wrote Perry on his evaluation sheet. His dyslexia makes him muddle the order of words when he is writing, but he explained that he meant he just didn't understand why he couldn't learn when he was a child, but our project has helped him to see what his difficulties are and has given him the coping strategies to deal with them, through multi-sensory learning and using the computer software. He worked very hard and improved his skills considerably. Sadly, Perry was another prisoner who was transferred mid-way through his course with us, and **I have not been able to track him down since**.

CARL (Chapter 5 onwards) – **The drugs importer who became head of mentors**

After his successful appeal, Carl was released in 2008 and has since been employed in construction work on building sites and doing some voluntary mentoring work alongside. He spoke eloquently at the first launch of our final project report at Middle Temple law courts in London and chatted with some of our VIPs. Carl will shortly be back working on the project again with me and others in another prison, this time as a free man.

He is now settled down, regularly spends time with his daughter, is engaged to be married and enjoying his new life. **Carl has not reoffended since his release on appeal five years ago.**

DON (Chapter 5 onwards) – **The thief who helped run a session for violent inmates**

When Don left the prison, he became very involved with his church, helping the elderly in his community, which he really enjoys. Some of this work is voluntary, but he is also employed on a part-time basis. **Don has not reoffended since he left the prison six years ago.**

322

TONY (Chapter 6 onwards) – **The self-harming drug-dealer**

Despite many ups and downs since his release, when he lived alone in a caravan for a while, Tony has managed to keep out of trouble. He is now living in a flat he shares with some friends, by the sea. He is unemployed and looking for work, but he sounded jolly and happy the last time I spoke to him, enjoying his life and no longer self-harming at all, which has been a huge step forward for him. After more than forty previous prison sentences, **Tony has <u>not</u> reoffended since his release six years ago.**

WOLFIE (Chapter 7) – **A wheelchair-bound weapons smuggler**

In 2008, Wolfie confounded the medics by getting out of his wheelchair and back on his feet again, using a special electronic device wired into his spine. This prevents nerve-signals reaching his brain when pain levels would otherwise be too uncomfortable. Wolfie is now working full-time for a charity, helping disabled people get back into work. He said to me recently: 'Having gone through it myself, it's great to be helping other people to find work.' **Wolfie has <u>not</u> reoffended since his release six years ago.**

SANDY (Chapter 7) – **The disabled thrill-chaser, caught in possession of weapons**

After eight months working with me as a mentor on the project, Sandy was suddenly given early release. At the time, I didn't think he was ready as he still needed help to maintain his confidence and develop realistic goals. As he left he gave me his sister's number so that I could stay in touch with him. A few weeks later, when I phoned her, she told me how desperately keen Sandy was to go straight this time. He'd gone to the probation service and signed up at the adult education college for a course. Everywhere he went and each person he spoke to, he showed them examples of work he had done on the mentoring course with me.

He enrolled on a computer course and was keen to help some of the younger lads, but it was all so different from my approach to learning. He found it very hard and felt the teachers didn't really understand the way I'd taught him to work, which frustrated him. What was even worse, his sister told me, was that whenever they didn't have anything better to do, the police would always come and sit in their cars outside the family home, where he was living, certain that they'd catch him doing something wrong again, as always happened in the past. He was disillusioned that his high hopes and expectations were being so miserably quashed.

Sure enough, a week or two later, Sandy came back into the prison after committing a minor burglary. This time he wouldn't resume his role as a mentor, no matter what I said to boost his confidence. 'I really tried my hardest,' he said, 'and it didn't work.'

I felt so indignant on his behalf that the system seemed to conspire against him like that. Although he wouldn't continue with his mentor work, he did seek me out to talk quite often and I tried to help him regain his self-esteem, build his resilience and develop more realistic goals for his next release.

It was this experience with Sandy that made me realise how important it would be for me to develop another stage of this programme, through opening transition centres for men (or women) when they first came out of prison, where they can have support and counselling. Such a centre would be a halfway house, residential for some, to help them adjust and find work, or provide them with continuing education to help them develop skills, fill in forms, apply for jobs and all the other important aspects of re-integration into society.

I have not been able to find out where Sandy is now or what he is doing.

NEV (Chapter 8) – The abused Christmas day murderer

Despite the fact that Nev was given a 99-year life sentence by the judge at his trial for murder, he has made such great progress that he is now waiting to go on day-release, which he has been told should be soon. At the time of writing, **Nev is still serving his life sentence in prison.**

BARRY (Chapter 9) – The electrocuted shoplifter with a high IQ

Despite his many physical handicaps, Barry's high intelligence (an IQ of 160) enabled him to understand what my project was about and in the short time he was there, he made excellent progress towards his literacy goals. However, he was transferred to another prison after two weeks. In some ways I was pleased for him as I hoped it was somewhere that could cater better for his physical needs, but I was sad that I was not able to continue working with him and **I have been unable to trace what happened to him after that.**

PADDY (Chapter 10) – **A drugs dealer who designed mind-maps**

Paddy was the first prisoner to alert me to the problem of only having only £46 to cover all his expenses for the first two weeks after release. It was this that had brought him back inside the first time. We worked together on finding ways to cope next time around and he put together a wonderful mind-map for the presentation ceremony in the prison, which he proudly explained to everyone.

He was released again nine months later, before the end of the project, and I hoped that this time I had given him enough skills and guidance to be ready to cope and put into action his mind-map showing what he would do and how he planned to achieve his goals when he left prison. **Sadly, because of my illness shortly after his release, I lost touch with Paddy and do not know how he has fared since.**

SHANE (Chapter 10) – **An abused drugs dealer who could have been a top athlete**

Shane started at a low level and attained literacy skills above those of an average 12-year-old, which demonstrates the excellent progress he made in the project. After this, he took the mentoring course and learnt some useful skills which he hoped to use on the outside. **Shane was released six years ago and did not reoffend in the first two years when I was still in touch with him.**

GILROY (Chapter11) – **An offender with birth defects that plagued his life**

By the time I fell ill and was forced to leave the project, Gilroy had gained much higher self-esteem and confidence, as well as high level computer skills. Along with the rise of his self-assurance, he had become less frustrated and more relaxed with other people, with the result that his speech impediment had improved enough to help everyone understand him. **Sadly, I do not know what happened to him after his release**, but I hope his new confidence and skills enabled him to realise his goal of going straight.

JOE (Chapter 12) – A traveller imprisoned for a murder he didn't commit

Joe, who took the rap for his brother without complaint, continued to make great progress and before I had to leave the project he was reading all the *'GI Joe'* books he could lay his hands on. He had raised his literacy levels from that of an average nine-year-old to age 12+, developed good computer skills and had learnt to write numbers up to a million. His confidence soared. 'I now know there's a future for me outside prison,' he told me. **Joe is now serving the last years of his long sentence at a prison near his home.**

ARNIE (Chapter 13) – The drugs dealer, dogged by his brothers' reputations

Arnie 's literacy and numeracy went up to age 12+ levels. He is now a self-employed mechanic, working in various garages, living by the sea. He says he understands himself better now. **Arnie has <u>not</u> reoffended since his release seven years ago.**

REGAN (Chapter 14) – **A young offender jailed for a gangland shooting**

Regan made great progress in the project and gained various qualifications. What was particularly pleasing too was that he had become calmer and more confident in himself, so was involved in far fewer arguments than when we first met. **I have not been able to trace what happened to Regan after his release**, or whether he ever got the book given to him by the film-crew and confiscated by the prison.

PETE (Chapter 15) – **The music-lover who stabbed his neighbour**

Pete developed a love of learning while on the project and took 35 short courses in his next three and a half years in prison. He gained some useful qualifications and is now living by the sea and working full-time as a manager, for a charity supporting the homeless. He is in charge of five hostels, housing fifty people and also provides outreach advice to branches in other areas. I recently noticed on *YouTube* that he has been rated an excellent interviewer.

His understanding of dyslexia and other hidden disabilities, gained in our project, helps him to have a better understanding of his clients' needs. In his leisure time he often plays games on Facebook with me, which we both enjoy. **Since his release four years ago, Pete has not reoffended.**

GREG (Chapter 15) – **A youngster who attacked a running man at the shout of 'rape'**

Now living in Devon with his partner and her child from her previous marriage, Greg is happily settled and is currently looking for a job in the adult teaching sector. Greg was the only prisoner of the first seventeen released who re-offended, though not from any criminal activity. He was released under licence, which meant that he had to obey the rules, including not to go out of his own county. However, soon after his release, when Greg was trying to renew contact with his young daughter, he discovered that her mother had put her up for adoption, without telling him, and this was going ahead in Cornwall. He went straight down there while the adoption court was in session to try and stop it happening. He was arrested and sent back to prison for breaking his licence.

Although Greg was unsuccessful in preventing the adoption from going ahead, when he was released from prison again a few months later he obtained permission from the family court to have access twice a year, which he does from his home in Devon. **Greg has not reoffended since his release from prison three years ago.**

DEAN (Chapter 16) – **The murderer who smeared himself with margarine**

Lifer Dean was the man spoiling for a fight, who I had been told was a 'waste of space' and whom nobody liked. Having changed his attitudes and developed a love of helping people while on the project, Dean was transferred to another prison and started up a dyslexic group there. While I was ill, he wrote to me and asked me to send him anything I could to help him. I put together a package of dyslexia assessment and learning materials, together with course notes and guidance materials, so that he could get things started there.

He told me once when he phoned me that he was so busy photocopying materials and printing new ones that he had fallen asleep in the print room. Once the prison officers saw how well he was doing, helping the dyslexic prisoners, they moved Dean to a large double cell, just for himself ... and all his folders and files. He needed an office, and now he has one. **He continues to serve his 99-year life-sentence.**

JACKSON (Chapter 17) – 'The little professor', in prison for assault

Jackson, who had undiagnosed Asperger's Syndrome, was transferred by a psychologist to a mental health institution to serve out the rest of his sentence there and **I have not been able to trace him since he was taken away from the project.** But I fear for him in those unsuitable circumstances.

WES (Chapter 18 and elsewhere) –The murderer with a Mohican haircut

When Wes left prison, he was employed on a temporary contract as a teacher of adult literacy, where he met his partner, who is also an ex-prisoner. They are happy and settled, having been together for three years now. Wes was the first person to have spotted his partner's dyslexia and has worked with her to improve her literacy skills. Thanks to him, she has recently gained her Advice and Guidance qualification. She is now working part-time for a charity and Wes himself is currently recovering from a second operation on his injured arm.

He now has feeling back in his arm and is looking for teaching work again. Meanwhile, he hopes to do his

Assessor's training and take on some charity work. They both hope to join me in my work when the project extends across more prisons, to help in the centres we plan to open for newly released prisoners. **Wes has not reoffended since he was released four years ago.**

RORY (Chapter 18) – The church-mouse 'murderer' who was framed

Despite a huge body of support for Rory, and a conclusive lie-detector test in his favour, his appeal failed. This caused considerable consternation in the press and online, where he has wide support.. Brendan O'Malley has written a book about Rory's case, called *'The Essex Boys'*. Everyone in the prison and in his local area believes he is innocent and his lawyer is currently attempting to secure another appeal hearing for him. Meanwhile, **Rory remains in prison to continue serving his life sentence.**

JAZZ (Chapter 18 and elsewhere) – An artistic, brain-damaged, persistent offender

Jazz is currently unemployed due to ill-health, but he is doing some part-time marshalling on a voluntary basis for his local football club. Meanwhile, he is co-operating with his doctor to balance his medication and therapy, which he was never motivated to do until recently.

Although unable previously to sustain a relationship of any kind, Jazz is now in a very stable relationship with his girlfriend of three years, living together not far from his parents. They recently had a beautiful baby girl. Jazz has also established a loving father-son bond with a previous child, who now comes to stay with them from time to time, enjoying their first family Christmas together in 2012.

Jazz is happier than he's ever been, and much calmer too. There are many family photos of Jazz at the heart of his extended family for the first time since he was a child. His loyal and long-suffering mother is delighted to have her son back in the fold. **Jazz, who had previously been in and out of prison more than forty times, has <u>not</u> reoffended since his release five years ago.**

TOBE (Various chapters) – a Ghanaian student enticed into gang crime

After his release, Tobe was accepted at a top UK university, where he is now in his fourth and last year, studying for an architecture degree. He rents his own flat and has recently begun a good relationship with his new girlfriend. He is proactive about looking for a job when he has completed his studies. Meanwhile he loves university and is mostly positive about his future, though a little worried about whether his record will affect his job-prospects. **Tobe has <u>not</u> reoffended since his release four years ago.**

MAX (Various chapters) – A film-director imprisoned for kidnapping

Max went straight back into his former job at the film studio, where he immediately set to work to change things for the better. Having learnt all about dyslexia, as a mentor in the prison, Max taught his staff all he knew and made sure they became a dyslexia-friendly company. In the past, before he met me on the project, he used to sack people or turn job-applicants away if they misspelt even one word, no matter how creative they might have been. Now he realises he probably missed taking on some of the brightest recruits around. These days he makes a point of employing creative people with dyslexia and works with them, mentoring them, to help them succeed. **Max has not reoffended since his release five years ago.**

NB Any prisoners mentioned in this book, but with whom I have lost contact since their release

At the time of the project each prisoner was allotted a number specific to that prison and sentence only, so they could not be traced across other prisons or through the probation service. (Now each prisoner is given a unique number that stays with them in any prison and after release, which would make it much easier to trace them.)

Further complicating matters, prisoners are only given £46 on their release as travel and living expenses for the first two weeks after prison. This does not allow for them to maintain a phone of any kind. Even when they were able to give me a contact number, they would run out of credit, or their phone might be stolen or lost.

However, the good news is that I haven't heard that any of them have gone back into prison, so hopefully that points at the positive outcomes I would expect them to have had following their release, but of course there is no guarantee. The only prisoner out of all those in this book known to have gone back inside after completing the project was Greg, and that was on a technicality, as you will have seen above. Since his re-release he has not reoffended.

The following prison personnel were instrumental in helping me to make the project a success.

The Deputy-Governor

The Deputy Governor was the key figure in enabling and supporting this project. She removed obstacles, solved problems and made things possible for us. About a year after I fell ill and had to finish the project, she left for Afghanistan, where she took on a senior role in the prison service.

Senior Officer Dawn Amey

Dawn, herself dyslexic, was very supportive during the life of the project and became a good friend at that time, which she has remained since. Shortly after I left, she had to retire from her arduous job on the grounds of ill health and retrained in clinical hypnotherapy. She is now part of my plans for the roll-out of our programme, in a new prison and other detention centres across the UK.

ACKNOWLEDGEMENTS

I would like to thank all the people who have touched my life:

- The Army for giving me a shoulder to cry on and helping me to settle into my new life
- Gingerbread for playing 'spot the mistake' and giving me confidence
- The customers who bought sandwiches from 'Jackie Catering' and put on a pound or two
- Dr Vogel and Jan De Vries for believing in me and building my library
- The Samaritans for having foresight and saving people
- Employees of a rival health food company for poking holes in my packets
- Jane Williams for comparing me to Anita Roddick and making me cool
- Southend College for diagnosing my dyslexia and kick-starting the change in my life
- My mentor, Tony Kimberley, for focussing me with story-telling and listening to mine
- For those who nominated Main Support Systems for our first business award, giving us the chance to meet George Krawiec, who helped us find funding, leading to our winning the Spirit of Ingenuity Award
- The training providers for giving me the whole country to work in
- To those connected with *Lexion* (you know who you are!)
- Ken Lewis OBE, Vince Hagedorn and Mentfor for funding the start of our prison journey

- The efforts of the Lords, Ladies and MPs fighting on our behalf
- The Deputy-Governor of the prison at that time, Senior Officer Dawn Amey and Sue Clayton, Head of Learning Skills, for enabling me to work my magic
- **And a special acknowledgement to the prisoners and their families for showing the world that my magic works.**